Whenever You're Ready

NORA POLLEY ON LIFE AS A
STRATFORD FESTIVAL STAGE MANAGER

— — — — — — — —

Shawn DeSouza-Coelho

Published in Canada by ECW Press
665 Gerrard Street East
Toronto, Ontario, Canada M4M 1Y2
416-694-3348 / info@ecwpress.com

Cover design: Tania Craan
Cover images: © Elyse Booth/www.shutter-fotos.ca

PRINTING: MARQUIS   5   4   3   2   1
PRINTED AND BOUND IN CANADA

**Get the
eBook free!***
*proof of purchase
required

Purchase the print edition
and receive the eBook free!
For details, go to ecwpress.com/eBook.

LIBRARY AND ARCHIVES CANADA
CATALOGUING IN PUBLICATION

DeSouza-Coelho, Shawn, author
Whenever you're ready : Nora Polley
on life as a Stratford Festival stage manager /
Shawn DeSouza-Coelho.

Includes bibliographical references and index.
Issued in print and electronic formats.
ISBN 978-1-77041-402-0 (softcover)
ALSO ISSUED AS: 978-1-77305-174-1 (PDF),
978-1-77305-173-4 (EPUB)

1. Polley, Nora. 2. Stage managers—Ontario—
Stratford—Biography. 3. Stratford Festival (Ont.)
—History. 4. Stage management. I. Title.

PN2308.P645D47 2018   792.02'3092
C2017-906182-8   C2017-906183-6

The publication of *Whenever You're Ready* has been generously supported by the Canada Council for the Arts
which last year invested $153 million to bring the arts to Canadians throughout the country, and by the Govern-
ment of Canada through the Canada Book Fund. *Nous remercions le Conseil des arts du Canada de son soutien.
L'an dernier, le Conseil a investi 153 millions de dollars pour mettre de l'art dans la vie des Canadiennes et des
Canadiens de tout le pays. Ce livre est financé en partie par le gouvernement du Canada.* We also acknowledge the
Ontario Arts Council (OAC), an agency of the Government of Ontario, and the contribution of the Government
of Ontario through the Ontario Book Publishing Tax Credit and the Ontario Media Development Corporation.

Ontario
Ontario Media Development
Corporation

ONTARIO ARTS COUNCIL
CONSEIL DES ARTS DE L'ONTARIO
an Ontario government agency
un organisme du gouvernement de l'Ontario

Canada Council
for the Arts

Conseil des Arts
du Canada

Canadä

RECYCLED
Paper made from
recycled material
FSC
www.fsc.org   FSC® C103567

To Jeannie,
For giving me July,
And to my parents,
For everything else.

All these stories have some basis in truth. Over time they may have acquired embellishments in the telling. If you are mentioned in one, please accept the compliment in the spirit in which it is offered.

1969

Prologue

"So, how've you been?"

His question wasn't very formal, but then neither was the interview. Jack Hutt was one of the first stage managers at the Stratford Shakespearean Festival of Canada, a festival that had begun only sixteen years prior in 1953. I was six then; now I was twenty-two.

"I've been good," I said, taking a sip of my coffee. "Things are a bit busy what with the end of term."

Jack had asked to meet at Murray's Restaurant in the Park Plaza Hotel, just a stone's throw from my residence at St. Hilda's College at Trinity College in Toronto. It was a chain of diners that served traditional Old English fare: chicken pot pies, baked macaroni, tea and crumpets. It was the kind of place with regulars the staff called by name. The restaurant was half-empty, and through the snow-speckled storefront window the afternoon sun laved the chestnut-brown seats, backlighting Jack and illuminating the blue haze of cigarette smoke drifting patiently above us like a thin cloud.

"Is this your last year?" Jack asked, lighting a cigarette of his own. Jack was the production manager at the Festival now. He was soft-spoken, efficient, and humble, taking care of business without the need for fanfare. Jack Hutt always took care of business.

"Yes it is."

Jack nodded and then flagged down a waitress.

We'd met before, he and I. Rather, I'd seen Jack around, in the green room or in the hallways, sometimes when I was visiting my dad, Victor, who was the Festival's administrative director at the time.

"More coffee, dear?" the waitress, a middle-aged woman with a beehive 'do, asked.

"Yes, please." The waitress nodded and hurried off.

"Any plans for after you finish school?" Jack then said to me.

Plans for afterwards . . .

I hadn't really planned to do a sociology degree to begin with. I never really had any ambition to do anything. I grew up three blocks from the Festival but never had any ambition to work there, either. I didn't think there was anything in the theatre I could do, though I did act some in my childhood and in high school. I didn't tell Jack any of that. Instead, I told him no, I had no plans, and that was when he asked me about my involvement in *The Memorandum*.

The Memorandum is a play by Václav Havel that was put on earlier in the school year by the Trinity College Dramatic Society. A play about conformity, the main character spends most of his time within a fictional bureaucracy, trying to translate a memorandum written in a fictional language. Eventually he hates the new language and opts for his mother tongue. Given the fact that Mr. Havel was in internal exile in Czechoslovakia at the time, the play garnered a bit of publicity.

I was the so-called producer of the production, selling and taking tickets on opening night. I was standing behind a small table in the foyer

SHAWN DESOUZA-COELHO

outside the auditorium at St. Hilda's College. It was still fifteen minutes before the house opened so earlycomers were milling around, chatting. A man in a grey suit walked in and approached the table, leaving his wife behind to gaze at the equally grey carpets near the door.

"Is this where the play is showing?" he whispered, as if in a library.

"It is," I replied.

He turned back to his wife, who was wearing a blue chintz dress and white gloves, and nodded. She smiled. Another man with a round, stern face entered. He was middle-aged, his hair the beginnings of a widow's peak. He wore black, thick-framed glasses. At the sight of him I almost gasped.

"Ah, good," the first man said, relieved. "This place was very hard to find."

"Yeah, the campus can be a bit of a maze. Do you have tickets set aside?" I pointed to the list of names on the table, while still keeping one eye on the second man. I suddenly felt anxious.

Why are you *here?*

"No, no," the first man replied. "We thought we'd just buy them now."

I nodded, giving him two tickets. I put his money in the safe deposit box and said, "The house will be open in about fifteen minutes. You can feel free to wait here or outside, if you'd like."

He thanked me and then rejoined his wife. That was when the second man approached the table.

"*The Memorandum*?" he asked, pointing casually to the brown auditorium doors.

"Yes," I said, still in awe.

It was *the* Nathan Cohen, and he was standing right in front of me. The drama critic from the *Toronto Telegram* was here to see our student play on opening night. Jesus Christ! It must be a dead night for Toronto theatre, I thought.

Mr. Cohen asked for a ticket and I was happy to oblige.

"The house will be open in about fifteen minutes," I said.

He thanked me, turned to leave, but then whipped back around. "Is there a place near here I can get a coffee?"

Shit. There isn't.

"Certainly," I smiled. "What do you take in it?"

"Cream, two sugars."

"Just one moment."

I walked down the corridor until I was certain I was out of sight and then sprinted up the stairs to a friend's room to boil some water in her kettle. As I caught my breath, I watched the water bubble, never once second-guessing my impulse. To make Mr. Cohen a coffee seemed natural, like aging: he needed some, the ingredients were upstairs, so that's where I ran. After I made his coffee to order, I bolted downstairs, and when he was in sight again, I strolled, as if I'd just popped in to an empty café across the street.

"Here you are," I said cheerfully, suppressing my laboured breathing.

He tested the brew and smiled approvingly. Relief streamed all the way out to my fingernails.

At Murray's, Jack took a sip of his coffee before saying, "Jean read Nathan's review."

"*Gascon?*" I blurted out. Jack chuckled and I couldn't help but do the same.

Jean Gascon was the flamboyant artistic director of the Festival. At the frequent parties my parents threw at our house, Jean and his company would carouse, sometimes in song. He was very French: everything was garlic and wine. Suffice it to say it startled me to hear the review of our tiny production had made it all the way to him.

"Jean asked your dad if you had anything to do with the show," Jack said. "And then he asked if you'd be interested in working at Stratford." I looked at Jack then as if he had just told me a strange riddle. I'd worked at Stratford plenty of times, but those were just high school summer jobs: available, close, and nepotistic. Coming from Jean, this meant something different. "So, would you be interested in working at Stratford?"

"Doing what?"

"The Canada Council has given us the means to hire two apprentice stage managers for the 1969 season, and I'd like to know if you'd be one of them."

I paused.

Stage management?

The truth was I had never given a thought to stage management. I had worked with stage managers backstage throughout university, so I knew what they did, or at the very least thought I knew. But the job itself didn't speak to me. Then again, nothing spoke to me.

As I ruminated, I found myself listening openly to a conversation between the beehive waitress and a big woman sitting alone at the counter, smoking. She had long, curly red hair and was a regular, it seemed from what the two of them were chatting about.

"How's your dad?" the waitress asked, taking the woman's plate.

"Not doing so well," she sighed, ashing her cigarette. "They thought he was in remission."

"He'll pull through. He still in London?"

"Yeah. Still there."

"The pay is $65 per week," Jack seasoned, and I turned back to him. "You would work shadowing an assistant stage manager to begin with." He took a drag of his cigarette before gently prodding, "Well?"

With little more than a featureless horizon before me, I said yes.

1969 was to be my first season in stage management with the Stratford Festival, and I would only ever miss two shows in my entire career.

1956

With a small black comb in hand, I stood at the landing just up the stairs at 75 Front Street, my home. There were three bedrooms on the second floor, two of which were for me and my four siblings. My brothers, Fred and David, shared one room, while I shared the other with my sisters, Susanne and Margaret. Dad was in my parents' room, to the left. As I pushed my thumb between the teeth of the comb, I glanced down the stairs, ears perked up like a rabbit's. Outside, a bell rang as a cyclist rode by. Inside, pots politely clanged. My mom, Elizabeth, or Lyb as she was called, was busy making dinner. I smoothed my short, sandy-blond hair and crept towards my parents' room.

Dad had gotten his tonsils out only a few days before. He was normally a sturdily built man, with an oval face and deep-set eyes. The surgery must've been painful because he'd spent the time since seemingly crumpled up in bed, enveloped in darkness. Every so often he'd groan and Mom would run to check on him. She had told us many times to leave him alone. But I thought I might cheer him up.

We weren't a hugging family by any stretch of the imagination, but we had our moments. For Dad and me, it was when he let me comb his rich, dark-brown hair. He valued appearances; we all had to be well dressed and well kempt. After all, he went to work every day in a tux. So, he'd lie on the couch, head on the armrest, and I'd first comb his hair in front of his face, and after he'd fought and squinted in submission, then I'd comb it how he liked: parted to the left. "Ah," he'd say, his voice frank and calm, as if his words were measured with a ruler. I'd smile. "Ah" was his pet name for me.

I put my ear against his bedroom door, listening for any signs of life. It was then that I jumped. Downstairs, the door to the kitchen had burst open and a man's bellowing voice vibrated the still house. Mom responded in whispers. Afraid that Dad might stir and Mom would come, I scampered into the bathroom opposite my parents' room. In the mirror, I told myself it was only Boyd, the milkman, making his rounds, coming into our kitchen with its green banquette and red linoleum floors and opening our fridge to see if we needed butter or something. Staring at the flocked wallpaper across the hall, I listened closely to the scene below, to the back door's creak and its eventual click. Mom must have told him that Dad wasn't feeling well. In the quiet that consumed the house again, I took a moment to collect myself and then made for Dad's room.

I had only just stepped across the bathroom threshold when a large form loomed over me and I screamed, smacking the back of my head into the doorframe as I jerked away.

Mom shushed me, her finger to her mouth. Quicker than ever possible, she had indeed come to check on Dad. As I winced and rubbed my head, she gave me a concerned look. Then concern gave way to disappointment as she saw the comb in my other hand.

SHAWN DESOUZA-COELHO

"Nora Catherine Polley," she scolded, "I told you to leave your father alone."

"But—"

She held out her hand. That was enough. I placed the comb in her palm and watched her set it down on the edge of the sink as if it were a delicate flower I'd carelessly uprooted. "Come here," she added in a much kinder voice, bending down. "Let me have a look at you." She had a round face, like mine, and her short, dark-blond hair was always done up. After inspecting my scalp, she rinsed a hand towel with some water. She knelt and touched it to my head. It was warm and soothing. Her hands were a mother's, a homemaker's, a hard worker's. She shopped, cooked, and cleaned for all six of us with style, and sometimes with a cigarette and a glass of whisky.

"Come on," Mom said, seeing that I was better. "Help me with dinner."

I nodded.

Leaving the cloth with me, Mom left for the kitchen. I lagged behind, stopping at the landing to gaze at my parents' room as a muffled groan escaped through the walls. I couldn't fathom why Dad would want to be left alone.

"Found you!"

"Shh!"

The voice came from the wings, and while I couldn't see her, Coral Brown was unmistakable. Equally so was six-year-old Dave's embarrassment. He let go of Marg, seven, who had been hiding behind a shelf backstage, and the two of them, along with Fred, ten, slumped to the dressing rooms to wait for their scenes.

Every year the city's Anglican churches put on a Christmas pageant play. The production started quite small, but with Coral running the show it grew, eventually moving to the Festival Theatre stage, which was no less a church for those involved in creating and caring for it. By now, everybody in town knew the story of Tom Patterson's religious zeal. Though Dad was always proud to say he didn't care much for the idea of the Festival when Tom pitched it to him at the Rotary Club over split pea soup. There were ten angels and a full choir. Mr. Sylvester, the town pharmacist, played King Herod. He was the nicest man in town, but he relished playing Evil. Dave was Herod's servant, responsible for bringing out Herod's chair. Fred was a page to the black magi. The town had run out of black kids either young enough or interested enough to play the part, so they painted Fred's face a very dark brown. Marg was an angel. I was an angel too when I was her age, as was Sue before me. It was how we all got our start. And, while there wasn't a real baby, there were real doves. But during every performance the doves sat perfectly still, as if to look as artificial as possible.

I gripped my empty water skin tightly, standing backstage just to the left of the upstage centre entrance, called *upstage* because at one point in history stages were raked, with the back of the playing area vertically higher than the front, called *downstage*. I was wearing a red floor-length gown with a large green scarf with white trim that I draped over my head. I shifted my weight from leg to leg anxiously. I was to go onstage, entering from under the balcony, and pass the skin around to the shepherds so they could have a drink. It wasn't the part I wanted.

A few weeks earlier, as the congregation was exiting at the end of Sunday service at St. James Anglican Church, the minister greeted each person by name. I waited to one side of the centre aisle, looking for an opening. While waiting, I nervously picked at the sides of my white skirt, not knowing how to phrase my request. I glanced back at our pew, near the front of the nave on the left, the same pew my family had sat in for as long as I could remember. There was a large placard on the wall beside it dedicated to a woman who once donated money to the church, a Margaret Jane Polley, who bore no relation to my sister, Margaret Jane Polley. Up near the altar, where Mom had once set up flowers, wine, and wafers as part of the altar guild, I watched Colonel Garrod pick a handkerchief off the ground and then shuffle down the far aisle in search of its owner. He was the kind old man who helped take care of the church and who once ran over Dave's foot with his car.

"Nora?"

I snapped around to find the minister standing in front of me. "Hi," I said, looking around him as if he were a very bright light. I was still unsure of my phrasing. I tried anyway. "For this year's pageant I don't want to be an angel."

"Oh?"

"I would like to be a shepherd."

He smiled, as if I'd told him a little joke. "But, Nora, there weren't any female shepherds."

I tried to think of a response, but nothing came. In the antechamber, my family was waiting for me with their coats on, nodding and waving to people passing by. The same column of morning light painted the floor over and over again as the red doors opened and closed.

"Well," I finally said, "I don't know why."

"It's just the way things have always been done. It's tradition." Seeing my confusion, he then added, "Here's what we can do, though. You'll enter the shepherd scene with a water skin and pass it around for them to drink. That way you're still with the shepherds."

As I put on my coat to leave, I wasn't sure whether I'd won or lost.

Coral waved me on. I took a short but deep breath, gripped the water skin tightly, and entered through the centre corridor. I took my place beside a balcony pillar, stage right, and handed the skin to the first shepherd. As I waited, I glanced around at the audience, lit faintly yellow with reflected light from the stage. I just barely made out my parents centre-right, sitting with nineteen-year-old Sue and Aunt Dorothy, my mom's older sister. When Sue was younger, she eventually got to play the Virgin Mary. She said she felt like a star while she did it.

I would never say I was comfortable onstage, but I certainly knew the building better than most, having visited Dad in his office upstairs many times. There, overlooking the Avon River, he would teach me how the theatre ran, how different-coloured map pins were used to plan the season's schedule. I always considered the dialogue a gift because Dad was an impatient father, at least for children too young to carry on a decent conversation.

I turned my attention to the stage once more, and the shepherd handed me the water skin. I took the skin from him and, for what reason I didn't know, I put it to my lips. I took a big glug and with gusto wiped my mouth with the back of my hand. All the shepherds onstage looked as if I had just slapped all of them at once, but it was the sound from the audience that brought me joy. Dad was nearly killing himself with laughter. Sue joined in, and maybe it was in response to the two of them, but so did some of the audience as well.

When the scene ended, and I exited, I felt strangely proud of my dramatic impulse. Then I saw Coral Brown shaking her head. As her disapproval mixed in with my satisfaction, I still wasn't sure whether I'd won or lost.

 When school ended, I sprinted to the Festival Theatre. A ceiling of thick clouds draped the whole town in a big grey tent. I took Ontario Street and then Waterloo until it reached Lakeside Drive, passing the bridge, the casino, and the arena, arriving at the stage door just in time for the tail end of the student matinee. This was my ritual this year. I just couldn't get enough of him. John Colicos, an actor with soft features, a wide nose, and a great smile. He was playing King Lear.

Panting, I waved to the doorman, who knew me as my father's daughter, and effortlessly climbed the stairs to the second floor. I wound through the offices to the stairwell just beyond the green room, and, on the landing, stood before the door leading to the lobby.

I took a moment to catch my breath. I was forced to take such an awkward route because the front lobby doors were shut after the performance began, and the management frowned upon people sneaking in, father's daughter or not.

I slid into the lobby calmly and just as I gripped the silver handle of the house door, a stern voice seized me.

"Excuse me!"

Shit.

I swung around to see a short, bald usher I didn't recognize. "What are you doing?" he said, eyeing my hand, the muffled sounds of the actors emanating through the wooden doors. "Can I see your ticket?"

Just play it cool.

"I'm afraid I don't have one," I said, casually.

"Then I can't let you in."

"Oh, but I'm Cordelia's understudy. I'm just coming to make sure nothing's changed in her blocking, you know? You know how things can change from night to night. Theatre is so emepheral, you know."

Emepheral? Is that the right word?

The usher stared, squinting as if I were very far away. I remained steadfast, never once releasing the handle. Finally determining I was legitimate, he let me in. I thanked him, and slipped through the door, creeping to the nearest aisle seat next to a boy with buzzed hair.

Edmund was lying onstage and around him were Albany, Edgar, and the Second Officer. I smiled. My favourite part hadn't come yet. Edmund began to speak, and even from the back row it sounded as if he were talking to me and only me.

EDM.   I pant for life; some good I mean to do
    Despite mine own nature. Quickly send —
    Be brief in it — to the castle, for my writ
    Is on the life of Lear and on Cordelia.
    Nay, send in time!

As the Second Officer left to save Cordelia and Lear, I glanced around the theatre at the sea of children. The boy beside me wiped his eyes, transfixed. I swelled with pride. It was Dad who started the school matinees with a single performance, to which a nun from the Loretto Academy in Toronto wanted to bring 1,200 girls. Thereafter, the Festival took up the initiative wholeheartedly.

ALB.   The gods defend her.

Sitting on the edge of my seat, I watched as Edmund was carried off stage. Then my John entered with Martha Henry's Cordelia in his arms, her head resting against his chest, a little bird with broken wings.

LEAR.   Howl, howl, howl, howl! O, you are men of stones!
                Had I your tongues and eyes I'd use them so
                That heaven's vault should crack. She's gone for ever.
                I know when one is dead and when one lives;
                She's dead as earth. Lend me a looking-glass;
                If that her breath will mist or stain the stone;
                Why then she lives.

His words were strained as he lay Cordelia down, but turned tender as he saw her alive once more, standing over her still body. And when the house lights finally rose, I was out of breath. Every performance the same thing. I never knew if I was holding it too tightly or if he was taking it so slowly, without me knowing. I could have watched him forever.

--

"Sue, would you like to say grace?" Dad asked while Sunday dinner tempted us in white dishware: fluffy potatoes, steamy vegetables, glistening roast beef, the works. We bowed our heads.

"Let us pray," Sue said. "Bless, O Father, thy gifts to our use and us to thy service, for Christ's sake. And bless this wonderful home and the family in it, who work hard for you. Amen."

Amen.

Knife in hand, Dad began carving the roast, a slice for each plate stacked beside him. He passed the first plate to a sullen Fred on his left and Fred passed it down the line to Mom, who had embarrassed him by calling the pool hall because he was late for dinner again. Seamlessly, Mom began to pile vegetables on it.

BRRING! BRRING!

Mom handed Sue the plate before mechanically leaving to answer the phone. We were static then as the question of Dad's presence once more thickened the air. As the company's day off, Sunday was one of the few days when Dad didn't have to rush home, switch suits, and return to the Festival in the evening to run, organize, or assist with something. It was our day, our chance to act like a normal family. In the backyard, a woodpecker began to attack a tree. Across from me, Dave clacked away at the keys of his first calculator.

"Hello?" Mom said, and after a slight pause, added, "One moment, please." She returned to the dining room. "It's John."

Dad set the knife down on the table and left as Mom returned to her seat.

"Yes?"

"David," Mom nagged, "put that thing away."

"I see."

I glanced at the stack of unused plates.

"Is Jack there? No, Jack Hutt."

A moment passed.

CLICK.

As Dad returned to his seat, he told us that something had happened at the arena, but Jack was there. He would take care of it. With that, the atmosphere lightened and Dad continued his carving, together with Mom making sure our plates were full. We began to eat. Dad was always happy to oblige the Festival whatever it needed, whenever it needed it. We all understood that. I just liked it more when his chair wasn't empty.

"Is Paul Newman at the arena too?" Mom quipped. "Or did you forget to mention that again?"

"Who's Paul Newman?" Marg inquired.

"Someone your mother will likely never see," Mom replied.

Dad nearly dropped his fork. "You'll never let me live that down, will you?"

"Whadihelolik?" Dave asked while chewing. Dave spoke too fast normally, but with food in his mouth he was completely unintelligible. We all turned to Fred, who could somehow translate. Fred perked up at the sudden attention.

"He wants to know what Paul Newman looked like."

"Your mother will never know," Mom said, drolly.

"Oh, boy," Dad guffawed.

As we ate, Dad told us what had happened. Apparently, Paul Newman had come to the Festival, and he was just wandering around the lobby after a performance, so Dad asked him if he wanted to go to dinner at the country club where he played golf. Paul said he would.

Mom stabbed a floret of broccoli.

"I asked you if you wanted to go to dinner at the club," Dad defended.

"But you didn't say Paul Newman would be there!"

I couldn't help but laugh. Neither could Sue or Neil, Sue's fiancé.

"I don't get it," Marg said.

"Margie," Dad stated, "if you don't understand it, I'm not going to explain it to you."

Marg's eyes fell back to her plate.

"What do you do at the Festival?" Dave asked through Fred. "They were talking about what their dads did at school and you came up and I didn't know what to say."

"Well," Dad explained, "you tell them that I'm in charge of the money at the Festival. The artistic director, Michael Langham, tells me what he wants to do and I find him the money to do it."

"Does that mean you're good with numbers?" Dave asked. Dad nodded. "Can you multiply big numbers?"

"Some."

"Do you think you're faster than my calculator?"

Dad chuckled. "Only one way to find out."

SHAWN DESOUZA-COELHO

We were all rapt by the proposition, an audience moments before the stage lights came on.

"I'll call out two numbers," Fred spurred, "and whoever can multiply them faster wins." They both nodded. "Ready? 67 times 39!"

Dave began smashing buttons, while Dad crashed numbers together beneath his eyelids.

"2,613." Dave stopped dead in his tracks, his eyes on Dad, who humbly added, "But you should check to make sure."

Dave did. 2,613. After a rapturous applause, we took turns throwing Dad harder combinations, but nothing fazed him. Then he explained, like a magician revealing his trick, that he constantly had to figure out how much money was gained or lost every night depending on audience attendance and ticket prices. Just two numbers, different each night, multiplied.

Huh.

When dinner was over I was left to clear the table. I stacked the plates and set the cutlery on top, not minding at all. It was better than doing the dishes. I hated doing the dishes. Besides, I kind of enjoyed the quiet of a room well used. It was as if the ghosts of what had passed still haunted it. I listened for a moment, thinking maybe something would speak to me. Only the gentle conversations of my family in the living room came through.

1967

"It's a long one, that's for sure."

"Longest, do you think?"

"No way, mate. *Hamlet* is definitely the longest by far. Hamlet's probably got more lines than Antony and Cleopatra combined."

"When does Plummer get here?"

"Couple o' days, I believe."

"I've got something planned for him. I hope he'll be okay with it."

"Probably. As long as you don't do it while singing about all of your favourite things."

They all laughed.

I didn't know all their names, but I loved to hear them talk. There was an Australian, a Brit, and a couple of Canadian men and women, all lit with the height of summer streaming through the huge windows at the back of the green room. The modest staff, all dressed in white, all wearing aprons, were busy making coffee and sandwiches for actors on break from *Antony and Cleopatra*. Idly, I toyed with the swan badge on my green jacket. I was on break as well, from another day working in the Festival box office.

I was one of three girls who worked in the lobby before any given show, all dressed in sleeveless white blouses, green skirts, and jackets. One took pre-ordered tickets, one sold tickets, and the other checked cameras. But once the show began there was nothing more to do, so we'd either go to the green room or hang out in the lobby. Today, the other two girls were with our house manager Bruce Swerdfager, a stout man with thinning sandy-blond hair. He was getting them to strike a pose and then snapping pictures with the checked cameras. We all found it amusing trying to imagine the looks on the unsuspecting patrons' faces when they developed the film.

I sipped my coffee. I should have been using the time to knit, but being around the actors was exciting. I felt like I was peeking behind the curtain of the great and powerful Oz. But the most exciting part was that even with what I did see, I still couldn't figure out how they did what they did, let alone how they made it look so effortless. It was unbelievable.

"Hey, Leo. Have a seat."

"Most noble sir, arise!" Leo Ciceri exclaimed as he entered. "The queen approaches." He was a handsome actor from Montreal, with kind eyes and short, dark hair. He sat next to an actress who was beside herself with laughter.

"You angling for my part?" chirped the actor with the plan for Plummer.

"Not on your life."

The actors around him settled down. Near the counter, another actor turned a sandwich over and over again in his hand, as if interrogating it for missing information.

Finally, Leo said, "How about this show, eh? Whaddya think? Sold out?"

"No doubt about it."

"Well, it's Plummer."

"What?" Leo scoffed. "You mean they aren't arriving by the wagonload for me?"

I chuckled behind my cup.

As their break ended, the actors trickled out of the room upstairs to the rehearsal hall. Through the windows, I could see strands of thin white clouds ambling, and my mind drifted to my knitting and Aunt Reta, my dad's younger sister. She sold tickets at the Avon Theatre, when it was still a movie theatre, and Dad would say, "She could knit you a vest during the movie, but it'd have to be a double-feature if you wanted long sleeves." Earlier in the year, Sue and Neil had their first child, having been married for going on two years now. They decided to name her Sonja. A pretty name. I took up knitting a sweater for her but completely misjudged the size of a newborn, so it'd be a few years before she grew into it. Mom said she'd quit smoking, just so she could be around for Sonja's wedding day.

1969

"Hold still."

With Jack Hutt's job offer, four years of university in Toronto, and an aimless sociology degree in tow, I patiently watched as Ann Skinner drew a curve through the centre of actor Powys Thomas's bare chest. Powys's eyes were closed and his aquiline nose twitched so that, from the doorway, it looked as if he was enjoying the feeling of wet marker being dragged across his skin. Or maybe it was his character, a con man named Subtle, enjoying it. Behind me, two stagehands were smoking, one reminding the other about a prop. A dresser darted by with a gown in hand. *The Alchemist* was on tonight, and backstage at the Festival Theatre was a blur of preparation. Ann, the spritely assistant stage manager (ASM) I'd been told to shadow, looked up from her handiwork and instructed me to finish up with the call sheets and then meet her back at the office.

"Sure thing," I said.

In my hands were the next day's call times for every actor in every production at the Festival Theatre. I was responsible for making sure these sheets were posted at the end of every day. Apprenticeship was never glamorous, but I didn't mind. I figured they gave me these tasks because I wasn't qualified for anything else, and my time with Dad had already taught me where everything in the building was. I headed up the stairs, passing by Dad's office on my way to Rehearsal Hall 1, which was large enough to house a full replica of the Festival Theatre's stage.

"Getting along, Nora?"

I turned to see Jack leaning out through his doorway.

"Learning a lot, Mr. Hutt," I said, flashing the papers in my arm.

"Atta girl."

Up another set of stairs, I strode past the armoury, which housed all of the Festival's weaponry. Through the glass, beyond the reflection of my long blond hair, shelved broad swords, fencing swords, axes, and muskets twinkled under yellow light. Their presence never ceased to amaze me.

I entered Rehearsal Hall 1. It was a sprawling room, with a high ceiling that conformed to the contours of the Festival Theatre's roof, moulded as it was to resemble a tent canopy. The floor was cement grey, upon which brown lines traced the edges of the stage, steps and all, so that directors could accurately block their productions and seamlessly transition to the real thing when the time came. There were windows all along the side of the room facing the Avon River. The creative team would sit at the tables in front of them. The stage manager and ASM sat there too. As I pinned the call sheet to the corkboard on the side wall near the door, everything was quiet. Rehearsals had broken for the day. For a moment, I closed my eyes and smiled, knowing Paddy could easily be there and I wouldn't even know.

It was the beginning of a rehearsal day for *Hamlet*, and while I wasn't part of the production's stage management team, I had been asked to help prepare the rehearsal hall. I was supposed to be graduating from university today, but instead I chose to go to work. I had just placed an ashtray down on a table, one of many items I was told should be present before the actors arrive, when I saw Paddy McEntee by the door where the chairs were stacked. Dressed in a plaid shirt and black jeans, he was a British stage manager who loved the theatre and loved to listen, understanding that nobody came to the stage manager with good news, and if he was going to help then he needed to hear every word. I set some sharpened pencils down, and when I looked up, Paddy was setting two chairs upstage. I did a double take, perplexed by the distance he'd covered in that fraction of time. I'd never seen anything so efficient and stealthy before. As I stared, his eyes caught mine and flashed me a curious look, as if to both say hello and ask why I wasn't working. I quickly placed the remaining ashtray down on another table.

A hum of chatter slowly filled the room as actors arrived, cigarettes and coffee in hand. When Paddy took his seat at one of the tables facing the stage, he said I was free to go. As I made for the door, Leo sauntered in and, seeing me, raised his eyebrows.

"So," he began gently, having met me near the exit, "I see that's all settled then."

I nodded, feeling as though I should apologize, but not really knowing why. Mom was being stubborn, not me, adamant I attend my graduation, while I maintained that it was pointless and dumb and that I'd rather go to rehearsal. Later on I found out from Sue, who had seen them together, that Mom had gone for a walk to cool down and met Leo along the way, walking his dog. The two of them chatted for a while, and when Mom came home neither of us brought up my graduation again.

"What did you two talk about?" I asked Leo.

"Oh," he shrugged. "This and that."

An energetic voice echoed from the hallway, signalling the start of rehearsal. Leo smiled and took a seat along the side wall.

"Okay, okay," director John Hirsch said in his rich Hungarian accent, rushing into the room, throwing down his bag, hiking up his pants, and adjusting his glasses. I stopped to listen briefly, just outside the doorway, on my way out. "Today, we are going to court." At this, the actors involved in the opening court scene walked to the centre of the room. "And I want you to play eet, Ken, like everybody ees laughink at you. Not badly, not so loud dat you can hear eet, but you can feel eet. You wear dare laughter on you like a second skin . . ."

When I had finished distributing the rest of the call sheets, I returned to the stage management office on the ground floor. It was a tiny room with brown desks, pale green chairs, a couple of typewriters, and walls lined with corkboard. Ann was on one of the phones, checking the time.

"What's next?" I asked.

In the corner, Keith Green, the British production stage manager (PSM), chuckled proudly. "You're learning." It wasn't so long ago I had come into the office having just finished a task and made the mistake of saying so. My mistake had been met with, "If you want a pat on the back, grow a longer arm": a stage management wisdom coined and oft doled out by the martinet PSM the season prior, Thomas Bohdanetzky.

"Follow me," Ann said, dimming the lights in the office. "Pre-show check."

The backstage area murmured as actors arrived, shuffling across the cement grey floor having just signed in with the stage doorman before heading to their dressing rooms. It was important that every actor signed in at the stage door so that stage management could account for their whereabouts. Before every performance we checked with the doorman to make sure the full company was present. The house didn't open until they were, because if company members were absent, then we could still rehearse things onstage with understudies.

I followed Ann past the ASM console, which consisted of a goose-neck microphone capable of speaking to different parts of the building and a black-and-white monitor displaying the stage. We were both dressed in our blacks — the dark clothing the production crew wore to blend into the darkness backstage during a performance — but it was the other similarities between us I couldn't help but notice then.

SHAWN DESOUZA-COELHO

She deftly checked the escape lights by the balcony and the left and right louvres, turned off unnecessary lights, and set full water pitchers on designated tables, but it was all just motions for her, a side effect of having drifted into stage management like I had. First, she had worked in props, not really knowing why she was there, then in wigs, and when that fell through, she became an ASM. She was still learning when I arrived. Maybe it was that mixture of floating and forging that made her the best teacher for me.

Ann checked the props in the underworld: the low-ceilinged pathways under the stage and auditorium that allowed actors to enter and exit from the trap door centre stage and the left and right vomitoria, which is the name for the tunnels below the house seats leading out to the stage. "Almost the fifteen," she said, checking her watch in the dim blue and soft yellow safety lighting.

Back at the ASM console, I snickered to myself. The actors looked as if they were caught between worlds, dressed in both 17th-century costumes and 20th. Ann tilted the mic towards her and in pitch-perfect neutrality said, "Ladies and gentlemen, this is your fifteen-minute call. Fifteen minutes." It sounded as if she were asking someone to wake up without wanting to startle them. Sure enough, without flinching, the actors picked up the pace, as if on cue. I thought the same thing every time.

How cool is that?

--

"Eee!"

I looked around the stage management office, my head a searching antenna. Tom Hooker, a short, blond, slightly bow-legged stage manager, had his head down at the typewriter. He didn't budge. Did he not hear that?

Maybe I'm hearing things.

I got back to work, stapling some sheets together. My next task was to sharpen the stack of pencils to my right, their flat ends like graphite eyes watching me and waiting.

"Eee!"

Okay, what is going on?

"Tom?" I said, turning to him. He lifted his head. "Did you hear that?"

Tom closed his eyes for a moment, taking in the whole building, and then shook his head. Finding his thought once more, he continued clacking away.

I wasn't hearing things. I was sure of it. Standing, I edged to the door. In the backstage area there were only a few earlycomers milling around prior to the evening's performance.

"Eee!"

"There!" I blurted out. "There! Do you hear that?"

Tom faced me, crossing his arms.

"Aww!" the voice bellowed again, deeper than before. The sound rattled around backstage like a marble in an empty can.

"Oh," Tom tittered. "That's Bill Hutt."

"Ooo!" the voice thundered, somehow even deeper.

"That's his warm-up," Tom said. "Has he been doing it long?" Seeing the wonder on my face, he pointed to his ear. "I can't hear some registers."

"No, not long."

"Kikiki!"

I faced the hallway and then Tom, expectantly.

He shook his head. He didn't hear a thing. As he faced the typewriter once more he chuckled, confiding, "I've never heard Martha Henry speak a word onstage."

--

Kenneth Welsh flashed me a little smile before transforming, all at once, into Barnardine in *Measure for Measure*. His cue light came on, adding red to the blues and yellows of the underworld, and it was as if, in that moment, Ken's dark-haired footballer's body evaporated to fill every last inch of Barnardine's thick beard, tattered rags, and round leather bottle. And I would have thought it magical were it not for the

SHAWN DESOUZA-COELHO

significance of my job then. Standing opposite him, to one side of a steep staircase leading up to the trap door of the stage, I was the most important person in the building.

I'd been given all sorts of little tasks throughout the run, like making sure there were no gaps in the chain gang that entered from the vom earlier in the show. "It's a living," one actor would moan, slipping into the shackles, and I'd slap his butt as if to tell him he was terrible. Though I was never prudish to begin with, believing that sex and love weren't necessarily mutually inclusive, at first I was shocked at what I'd done. But, with time, I grew to like the physical intimacy tacit in the Festival: bum pats, back rubs, hugs that sometimes looked as though people were melting into one another. For the most part, it was a salve that helped the actors continue to pour their guts out night after night.

The floorboards muffled the audience's laughter. I steeled myself, reciting the events to come in my head.

Soon Barnardine will ascend the staircase, drunk. Barnardine is Ken. Ken is also playing Hamlet. Protect Hamlet. Without Hamlet, there is chaos. Who goes on for Hamlet? Who goes on for that guy? And that guy? And that guy? And that guy? Hamlet is irreplaceable. Hamlet cannot break his neck. Better yours breaks instead.

Thud! Thud!

ABHO.   What, ho, Barnardine! Barnardine!

Barnardine craned his neck upward as Pompey swung open the trap, and a cool air rushed down carrying with it the unfiltered laughter of nearly two thousand people.

BARN.   A pox o' your throats! Who makes that
               noise there? What are you?

The cue light went off, and Barnardine stumbled upward. With each inebriated step I drew closer to him, my muscles tensing. I planted my feet as the scene continued, my slender arms outstretched, ready to embrace the falling weight of this grown man. And I didn't let up until Barnardine slammed the trap shut, once again sealing away the audience, and Ken descended sure-footedly. With a thankful wink he left for the dressing rooms and I breathed easy. I gazed up, through the boards and past the plodding actors, to the muffled audience laughing heartily. I smiled proudly. They'd never know that every performance, for a brief time, I was responsible for the entire Festival.

SHAWN DESOUZA-COELHO

 *Parchment. Check. Portraits: Sir Richard Ravelin, great-aunt Deborah, his mother's grand- father, William and Walter, the mayor of Norwich, the two al- dermen, assorted other paint- ings making up the rest of the family, and Sir Oliver. Check.*

"Nora," Chris Root called, stepping out from the wing of the stage. He was our stage manager, a tall Brit with short, dark hair. "Need you to call the five."

"Sure thing," I said from onstage, taking one last look around. Just below the stage curtain I could see the faint glow of the house lights and hear the wandering conversations of the few lingering people in the auditorium during the interval. I finished mentally checking off the items that needed to be pre-set for the beginning of the second act of *The School for Scandal*. Set in an attic, it begins with Charles auctioning off his family's heirlooms to cover his debts.

Muslin. Check. Furniture. Check.

Confident that everything was in place, I went backstage.

It was still hard work for me, having confidence. Having apparently proved myself as an apprentice, I was given the Jean A. Chalmers Apprenticeship Award and a handsome thousand-dollar cheque. Shortly after, I was invited to be an ASM on the Festival's tour to Ottawa and Champaign-Urbana, Illinois. The idea was to embrace the Festival's consistent growth by giving it a winter home elsewhere, playing to more audiences. So here I was, a small-town ASM on tour in the United States with the pride of Canadian theatre. I just wanted to get things right.

At each dressing room, I repeated the same phrase: "Ladies and gentlemen, five minutes. Five minutes."

"Thank you, five minutes," the actors replied in some variation to let me know they'd heard me.

In the time that passed between my warning and the beginning of the second act, I stood backstage, off to one side, and watched the four shadowed, veteran actors take their starting positions. They whispered playfully to one another, as if it were a comfort, until the audience settled. Then there was silence. An audience member coughed. The lights hummed to life, the curtain opened, and four characters strode on.

CHARLES.   Walk in, gentlemen, pray walk in; here they are, the family of the Surfaces, up to the Conquest.

SIR OLIVER.   And, in my opinion, a goodly collection.

With much of my responsibilities out of the way for the time being, I was able to watch the scenes and laugh quietly with the audience. Using a rolled-up family tree as an auctioneer's gavel, Charles sells his

SHAWN DESOUZA-COELHO

family's portraits to Mr. Premium, who is actually Charles's uncle, a disguised Sir Oliver, come to test Charles's character. And it's when Sir Oliver's portrait is on the auction block and Charles refuses to part with it for any sum that Sir Oliver decides Charles is a good man. In the next scene, Sir Oliver then plans to meet his other nephew in a different disguise. In the scene that follows—

"*Where's the chair?*"

I stared blankly at actor Gary Reineke's urgent lips. "Nora! Where's the chair?" he repeated, shouting in whispers. My eyes snapped around, finding two more actors, Powys and Mervyn "Butch" Blake, already in the wings, offstage.

No . . .

My body suddenly felt very light and my conscience very heavy. Onstage, underneath the muslin in the nearly-ending scene change, there was a gaping hole where once sat a library chair, needed for the following scene. It was then the chain of events slid around my neck like a noose, and I realized what I'd done. I ran faster than I ever had in my life, knowing exactly where the chair was because I had left it there. During my pre-show check, I saw Butch backstage — short, round, affable Butch — sitting on it, looking deep in thought. I didn't want to disturb him, because of hierarchy, inferiority: he was Butch Blake, a veteran playing Sir Oliver, and I was Nora Polley, a novice playing at ASM. I told myself I'd get it after I was done onstage.

When I found the chair, exactly where I'd last seen it, I heaved it under my arm and sprinted back to the wings. But, by the time I arrived, the next scene had already begun. I felt crushed.

We gathered in a huddle, a few of the actors, Chris, and myself, trying to solve the problem in hushed voices, though my self-condemnation drowned my ability to speak.

"It's not the end of the world," Butch said to everybody and me.

Maybe not your world.

"What if one of you just goes on and puts it down?" Chris asked.

"When?" Gary inquired.

We all played out the rest of the scene in our heads, slotting the chair in as we would a key in the dark.

"Where's the chair?" Jimmy Hurdle whispered, having just left the stage as the Servant.

I sighed inwardly, the chair just behind me, and wanted to crawl into a deep hole.

"We're trying to figure that out," Chris replied.

"Why don't I just take it on?"

"When?" Gary repeated.

Jimmy turned to the stage, saying ruefully, "One place is as good as any."

He took the chair from me, and the group dispersed. Standing by the edge of the stage, Jimmy listened for the right moment, like watching a skipping rope, and then entered.

> LADY TEAZLE.   I believe so for tho' she is certainly very pretty
> —yet she has no conversation in the world—and
> is so grave and reserved—that I declare I think
> she'd have made an excellent wife for Sir Peter.—

Joseph Surface threw his servant a dismissive glance. Lady Teazle tried her best to ignore him.

> SURFACE.   So she would.

Jimmy calmly arrived offstage, and the scene continued.

> LADY TEAZLE.   Then—one never hears her speak ill of anybody
> —which you know is mighty dull—

> SURFACE.   Yet she doesn't want understanding—

I smiled as relief swelled in me like a balloon.

> LADY TEAZLE.   No more she does—yet . . . yet . . .

SHAWN DESOUZA-COELHO

"Line!"

Did she just . . . ?

The word echoed around the auditorium and inside my head, sinking my heart far below my stomach.

She's dried. Helen Carey has dried. I'm fired.

From the opposite wing, Chris prompted, "one is always disappointed when one hears." Every word was a hammer to my skull. Helen continued on.

There was enough strength left in me to wait until the show ended, but when it finally, mercifully did, the tears came in floods. I sat behind a table backstage, hidden, waiting to be hanged while mentally replaying my crime over and over again.

Of course she dried! Something happened onstage she wasn't expecting. Jimmy shows up with a chair in the middle of a scene, unrehearsed, completely unrehearsed . . . Of course she lost her words!

"Hey," Butch said, sitting down beside me. I sniffled in response, thankful my hair was a long enough shield. "You know, I was doing this show one time, and the gal in the scene with me had to fall backward. She was swooning and I had to catch her. It was a trust fall, really. Well, we get into the scene and one night, for whatever reason, I get really worked up on my line and I walk away from her." He chuckled, tapping my knee. "And the sound of her hitting the floor . . . Christ, it was loud." He was laughing now. "I thought I'd never live it down. I thought, well, my career is over. I've killed the leading lady. I mean, thankfully she was young. She survived. Could you imagine if she had been an older gal? I'd have felt like I'd murdered the poor thing." He tapped my knee again, smiling, as if to make sure his words weren't clinging to the side of the glass. I smiled back, thankful.

One after another the actors came to me, crying altar that I was, and confessed their sins, the moments they thought their careers were over. And with each story I felt just a little bit better, a little less alone.

"I forgot the letter so she just read thin air . . ."

"Somebody replaced the knife with a real one and I actually cut his throat . . ."

"I was too into it, completely forgot the choreography, and ended up strangling him. He passed out and woke up in the hospital . . ."

"All you can do is ask forgiveness and forgive yourself . . ."

With that, I apologized to Helen, to everybody, and I vowed then to do better next time, to learn my lesson and move on.

--

TESMAN.   Have you just arrived in town? Eh?

As covertly as possible, I circled the incorrect words of the line in my binder. Still, Gordon Jackson noticed I had marked them as soon as he'd said them, squinting for a moment and then returning to the scene. It was impossible for him not to notice. The acoustics of the Festival Theatre were that good, and Peter Gill, the director of *Hedda Gabler*, was that insane. From the front row, where Peter had asked me to be ASM on book, I was practically scratching the pencil in Gordon's ear.

The stage management team had many responsibilities during rehearsals. Among those responsibilities, the stage manager documented in his or her prompt book every aspect of the performance from the blocking of the actors to the cues for the lights and the orchestra. The prompt book, I came to learn, was sometimes called the bible because it was the written account of how the production was supposed to be performed every night. The ASM on props kept track of stage properties, while the ASM on book prompted and made sure actors were saying their lines correctly. Typically, this was done at a merciful distance for both actors and ASM, but as I watched Gordon's scene play out ten feet away, mercy felt in short supply.

MRS. ELVSTED.   I arrived yesterday, about midday. Oh, I was quite in despair when I heard that you were not at home.

HEDDA.   In despair! How so?

TESMAN.   Why, my dear Mrs. Rysing . . .

"What," Gordon called out, the word a dart landing inches from my
head. Rehearsals were so stop-and-go in the early stages, it didn't take
long for me to learn what each actor called out when needing a prompt.
For some, it was "Line." For others, "What is it?" For Gordon, it was
a terse "What."

"I mean Mrs. Elvsted," I called in reply.

Gordon huffed and started over.

TESMAN.   Why, dear Mrs. Rysing—I mean Mrs. Elvsted—

The line had more bite to it this time and, unfortunately for both
of us, it was wrong. He forgot "my." I bracketed it, touching the tip
of the pencil to the paper so lightly that I could have been imagining
writing. Still, Gordon noticed. I cast my eyes downward.

Why in God's name am I right here?

Far off to my side, I spotted Leo and searched him. He shrugged,
seemingly sharing my wonder at my position. I wished he could also
share in my embarrassment and frustration.

HEDDA.   I hope that you are not in any trouble?

MRS. ELVSTED.   Yes, I am. And I don't know another living
                     creature here that I can turn to.

HEDDA.   Come—let us sit here on the sofa—

MRS. ELVSTED.   Oh, I am too restless to sit down.

HEDDA.   Oh no, you're not. Come here.

Hedda sat Mrs. Elvsted down on the couch, and the latter got comfortable. And then again she got comfortable. And then, again, she got
comfortable. It was Gordon's line next.

"Well? What is it—" I prompted.

Gordon's eyes widened. "Mark that as a pause," he instructed disapprovingly. Inwardly, I rolled my eyes.

Okay. I will. An awfully long one, but I will.

TESMAN.　　　Well? What is it, Mrs. Elvsted—?

HEDDA.　　　Has anything particular happened to you at home?

MRS. ELVSTED.　　Yes—and no. Oh—I am so anxious you should not misunderstand me—

HEDDA.　　　Then your best plan is to tell us the whole story, Mrs. Elvsted.

TESMAN.　　　I suppose that's what you have come for—eh?

MRS. ELVSTED.　　Yes, yes—of course it is. Well then, I must tell you—if you don't already know—that Eilert Lövborg is in town, too.

HEDDA.　　　Lövborg—!

TESMAN.　　　What—

"Has Eilert Lövborg come back?" I called out.

"I was saying the line!" Gordon spat. My face felt very hot then, filled with equal parts shame and loathing at the whole scene. I dug the pencil into the page.

"By the end of it," I said to Tom later in the day, "I couldn't say anything. He missed a whole section of text and I didn't have it in me to say a word." We were in the stage management office, and even there I felt very small. Paddy was facing his desk. "He just kept going until he realized he'd missed a vital piece of information and then didn't know who to blame."

"You're to blame," said Tom, as simply as if he were telling me the time.

"What!" I cried, looking to Paddy for help.

"You're to blame," Paddy confirmed, barely looking at us.

"Actors get mad," Tom continued, "and they'll yell at you, but they're yelling at you because they can't yell at themselves. They'd look crazy yelling at themselves. So they yell at you. It's not because you did something wrong. Though you did eventually, but it's got more to do with the fact that actors need to blame somebody. They'd blame their dying mothers if they could."

"I'm sure some have," added Paddy.

"But you have to understand that what it all comes down to for them is that they're afraid of losing their memory. What is an actor without his lines?" I opened my mouth to say something, to protest, but nothing came. I still felt tense, like a current was running through me. Tom crossed his arms. "Next time, just take the blame. The faster you do that, the faster everyone, including you, can move on. When an actor dries, it's the prompter's fault."

"When an actor dries," I mumbled, "it's the prompter's fault."

"And," Paddy added, having turned to us at last, "if they've broken character, you've missed it."

"Missed what?"

"The moment to prompt. I wouldn't worry about it. It takes practice, but a good prompter should be able to get in there when he's needed, the moment he's needed, give as much as the actor needs, and then just fade away."

Tom wiggled his fingers back and forth, as if Paddy were telling a ghost story.

"I was in the front row!"

"Doesn't matter. It has nothing to do with that. Remember what Thomas Bohdanetzky said?" I stared blankly. "'If anybody notices you are doing your job, it's because you've just made a mistake.' You could be on the moon and they'd still notice if you'd screwed up. But *good* stage management is invisible. Even in the front row. Don't worry. You'll get it. Just takes time."

I looked from Tom to Paddy and then to the floor, suddenly feeling like I'd imposed on them. These weren't their problems. They were mine. I should deal with them. I should learn the lesson and move on.

"Just be happy you weren't prompting from the God mic," Tom joked, putting things into perspective. "*That's* never good."

Located in the Festival Theatre stage management booth, which was a high and lonely fifty-eight-foot beeline from the stage, the God microphone allowed the stage manager to prompt an actor who had dried in the middle of a performance. It would be bad enough to dry on that stage, thrust into the audience as an actor was. But to then hear a voice shatter the auditorium, a voice every audience member could hear clearly through a speaker behind the balcony's centre pillar?

"Yeah," I resigned. "It could always be worse."

--

"I need you to come in," Tom said, his voice wavering. "Leo's been in an accident."

I nearly dropped the phone. "Is he alright?"

"We need to put his understudy on. You'll have to come in."

"Okay."

On my way to the theatre, I tried to not play out all the possible ways in which Leo could have been hurt, to not focus on the infinite fragility of the human body. I focused on the theatre instead and its solid canopied roof, the Canadian flag at its centre lifeless in the still air. Somehow this assured me that things would be okay.

In the stage management office, Tom was alone, on the phone.

"I'm sorry to say that Leo has died . . . No . . . When I have more I'll give you a ring . . . Take care."

CLICK.

Tom stared at the phone for a moment and then looked up at me. His eyes were very red. "They're in Rehearsal Hall 1," he said, before turning back to the phone. I couldn't move.

"W-What happened?"

"We don't know yet."

I nodded. Tom picked up the phone once more.

"Do you need any help?"

"No. It's my job. It's my responsibility."

I nodded again, though he didn't see it. He was busy dialling another number to tell another person that Leo had died. Seeing the list in front of him, I realized he was calling every member of the company to tell them personally. I felt such respect for Tom then, as a person, and a stage manager.

When I grow up, I'll be lucky to be half as good as you.

--

I stood backstage with Malcolm Armstrong, Leo's understudy, and I waited for the final scene of *Cymbeline*. His eyebrows gathered, as if in deep concern. The final scene is a long one, each character coming forward and telling the others exactly what the audience already knows, so I thought I understood what was going through Malcolm's mind: with a part as big as Iachimo's, he just didn't have enough time to prepare. Instead, with eyes never leaving the direction of the stage, he asked, "Does the audience know it's me?"

"Yes. All the program slips are in place." We were required to inform the audience of any changes to the cast performing on a given night. Usually, this was with a slip of paper in the house program.

"But they don't know why Leo isn't here?"

"No, they don't."

Malcolm sighed, relieved. He knew he wasn't ready to go on. Understudies rarely ever were, never being allowed the time to do the task justice. But that wasn't it. Malcolm just didn't want the audience to know that the reason he was there in the first place was because the person who was supposed to be playing the part was dead.

When it came time, Malcolm entered and did his best. He had to be prompted a couple of times from the God mic, but somehow it didn't seem to matter, not to him, not to anybody. We all just did what we had to do.

--

Dad stood to carve the Thanksgiving turkey with military precision, while Mom waited to spoon vegetables onto our plates as we passed them from one end of the table to the next. He looked tired, but at fifty-four he wasn't exactly young anymore. At fifty-two, neither was Mom.

"I wan' carrots," a three-year-old Sonja demanded, pointing to Neil's plate. She was wearing a cute pink-and-white wool sweater, the one I had knit for her three years ago. It was only now she was big enough for it.

"What do we say?" Neil asked, as if teaching. Confused, Sonja looked around the room and then down at her plate. "Please," he prompted.

"Please, I wan' carrots!" Sonja belted giddily.

Mom spooned some onto her plate, saying brightly, "There you go, dear."

"What's wrong?"

What?

Sue was looking right at me. It suddenly felt like everybody was. I didn't know why, but I noticed then how long and blond my hair was compared to hers, short and brunette. I noticed Dave, sixteen years old and looking more like Dad every day. I noticed Fred and Marg, eyeing Dad's handiwork. Fred was twenty, the tallest of us all next to Dad, and Marg was seventeen, with bangs down to her eyebrows. Behind them, Fred's dog Macduff was eyeing the bird as well, patiently sitting on his hind legs. Sue was spoonfeeding her second daughter, Jannine.

"Nothing," I said, casting my eyes down at my plate.

"She's so big," Dave said of Jannine, shovelling potatoes into his own mouth. "How old is she now?" His elocution classes had paid off because we all understood him, even through the food.

"Almost a year now," Neil replied.

"Has it been that long," Dad chimed. "Gol-ly."

BRRING! BRRING!

"Let it ring," Dad said dismissively, stopping Mom as she rose to get it.

SHAWN DESOUZA-COELHO

We ate quietly as the phone rang out.

"They'll just keep calling," Mom said.

"Who will?" Marg asked.

"The Festival," Dad answered.

I tried to think what the Festival might have wanted at this hour, but having been a part of it for two years, I knew it could be anything and everything. It struck me as odd, though, that my dad would ignore the call.

"Malcolm ready for the tour?" Dad asked me.

"Yeah," I said, reaching for the gravy. "He's had plenty of practice by now."

"A shame about Leo," Mom said, taking a drink and, after considering something, taking another.

"What happened?" Fred asked, flicking a morsel of turkey backward to Macduff. The dog caught the treat before it hit the ground. Fred had taught him well.

I told Fred about the crash. Late one night, Leo was returning to Stratford from Toronto Airport with his dog and a passenger, a Catholic priest. He lost control of the car and it smashed through the guardrail, rolling down an embankment nearly two hundred feet high. Both Leo and his dog were thrown from the wreckage. Only the priest survived, completely unscathed.

We all sat for a moment, unsettled by the image of Leo's crumpled car. Fred was looking at Macduff.

"Turkey!" Sonja yelled obliviously. All we could do was laugh.

"We leave in a couple of days," I added. "First to Champaign-Urbana, then to Ottawa, same as before."

"That must have been terrifying for Malcolm," Mom remarked.

"He did fine," I assured the table.

As dinner went on, my thoughts strayed back to *Hedda Gabler*, and Leo. His character is only in the first part of the play, but because Leo had to stick around for curtain call, to pass the time he started hooking a rug in the likeness of a famous Matisse painting of a black figure on a blue background. *Icarus* was the name, he told me. He didn't get a chance to finish it.

"Barry!" I panted, startling him. "Have you . . . seen . . . the boys? I think they . . . ran this way."

Barry MacGregor, a handsome British actor with lush black hair, looked up and down the white cement hallway of the National Arts Centre in Ottawa. Behind me a stagehand lugged a lighting instrument into a dark room. "No," Barry said, "I don't believe I have. My apologies."

"You're it!" one of the boys screamed as he ran down a hallway perpendicular to ours.

I bolted off in chase. "Don't worry about it!" I yelled back to Barry. I would not let these kids get away from me again. As ASM, I was responsible for them.

The Festival had gone on a pre-season tour to the NAC, and it had taken me with it. The building was strange. Everything from the rooms to the elevators was hexagonal in shape, the building so complex that they had to paint different-coloured lines on the walls to ensure nobody would lose their way. It had three playing spaces: one for opera, another for theatre, and a studio space for smaller productions. But all three shared a common green room, so occasionally the cast of *Hair* would mingle with us. There were also two boys, local to each city we toured, that the Festival hired to play the Duchess's children in *The Duchess of Malfi*; two errant boys who had decided it would be fun to play tag in this labyrinth instead of getting into their costumes.

As I turned another corner, following their faint, boyish yelps, it suddenly struck me exactly how Coral Brown must have felt all those years with all those children during all those Christmas pageants. I had only tailed these kids for ten minutes now, but still the irritation sunk deep.

I turned left down another hallway, bracing myself against the wall. The sweat had begun to soak through my shirt. That was when I spotted the boys not far off, mindlessly tagging one another in a circle.

"All right!" I commanded. "That's enough." The boys were frozen. "We've got to get you changed for the show. Come on." They took my hands limply. "If anything happens to you it's my fault. Did you know that? We're going back to the dressing rooms." I looked to the lines on the wall.

Now, where the hell are the dressing rooms?

I had only just taken a step when a dozen nearly naked actors and actresses arrived from the corridor I'd just travelled. The cast of *Hair*. I glanced at their pale bare asses as they jogged past carrying their clothes, and then down at the children.

I can't be responsible for them seeing that.

Once the kids were back in their dressing room, with their dresser, I hustled around to check props. Luckily, it was late enough in the pre-show that the actors paid me very little attention as we all went about our preparations.

Tok! Tok!

Later that evening, near the top of the show, I arrived at Barry's dressing room to check that his personal props were set. "Ah, Nora," Barry said quietly, sitting on a chair. I was a bit taken aback. While everybody else was preparing for *Much Ado About Nothing*, Barry was still in his robe. "Put your head on my chest."

"Pfft. No," I replied, startled by his request. The theatre was a physical place, but even then this sounded inappropriate.

"Nora, please," he said earnestly. Something in his voice told me he wasn't fooling around. He opened his robe and I put my ear to his chest.

"Barry!" I let slip at the sound of his erratic heartbeat. "I think you should go to the hospital."

"Yes," Barry chuckled, "I thought so too." He turned to his mirror. "After the show."

"No, actually, Barry, I think you should go now. We can put Don on."

"It's quite alright, Nora."

"Barry."

He turned back to me, detecting a similar something in my voice. After a moment, he nodded.

A week later I visited Barry in the hospital to check on him. I didn't have much experience with hospitals or death, so everything was doubly present, vividly draped in a layer of itself. Barry told me he'd had a slight arrhythmia, but was doing fine now. I told him to rest up, and that we'd make it work for as long as he needed. I told him I'd heard how bored he was without even a radio to listen to, so I'd brought Scrabble with me. He promptly destroyed me.

--

A few nights later, head down in thought, I entered the elevator at the NAC. I was going over that evening's performance of *Duchess*, troubleshooting a costume change that, for some reason, kept running too long. I pressed the button for the ground floor but, as the doors closed, a woman I didn't recognize rushed in. She made for the same button but realized I'd already pressed it. The doors shut, and the elevator whirred to life.

What if we just use one dresser for the previous change and that way the extra dresser could help—

"I'm sorry to hear about your father," the woman said, angling towards me.

"Excuse me?"

"Your dad. Victor Polley, right?"

Who are you and why are you talking about my dad?

"What about him?"

"You're joking, right?" the woman laughed anxiously. I was silent, my question still standing. "He was let go from the Festival."

What the hell?

The woman was perplexed. "You didn't know?"

DING!

"Sorry to be the one to tell you," she added, getting off. I had to get off too, but instead the doors shut and I rode the elevator three or four times from top to bottom.

Let go? Why?

Back at the hotel, I gripped the receiver tightly, trying very hard not to yell.

"I had to find out from some stranger in the elevator? At the National Arts Centre?"

"Ah, come on," Dad said calmly. "I didn't make it a point to start calling everybody up as soon as it happened."

"When did you know?"

"Ah."

"When?"

"Since October."

"October!"

"Well, since '67 if I'm being frank. Right around the time they hired Bill Wylie. He wanted to expand the Festival with tours to Ottawa and America and movies and whatnot. I didn't feel comfortable with that kind of expansion. They even offered me the position of general manager, but I turned it down. I thought Stratford was reaching too far too fast." He chuckled. "Well, the Festival could only go one direction."

I couldn't help but glance around my hotel room: at the foot of the bed, the nightstand, the lamp, the ceiling, the very tour I was on. I suddenly felt like an accomplice, as if the two years of growth I'd experienced at the Festival were rooted in the grave of my dad's career. I sighed, curling the phone cord in my other hand.

"It wasn't the Festival calling all the time before I left, was it?"

"Reporters wanting a comment."

"And you didn't give them any?"

"The last thing the Festival needs is bad publicity. I would never say a disparaging word about it. It would do more harm to the town than the Festival. Besides, plenty of other people have said more than enough."

"What do you mean?" I asked, leaning against the headboard. My whole body was tense.

"Letters to the editor," Dad explained. "People complaining about the Festival's decision. It was *my* decision. I made it long before this. It just took them this long to realize it couldn't work with Bill and me running things. It was just inefficient."

We spent a moment in silence as I continued twirling the phone cord. Finally, I asked, "What did they say?"

"The Festival?"

"No, the people in the paper."

"Nice things about me. Mean things about the Festival. It was a bit like reading your obituary before you've died."

"How's Mom taking it?"

"Oh, like you."

"*You didn't tell her, either?*" Now I was yelling. But Dad wouldn't be baited into an argument about it. Instead, I fumed mutely, and he waited. "What will you do?" I asked.

"Go golfing, I suppose."

"Dad . . ."

"I don't want to work in theatre again. That's for certain. I also don't want to leave Stratford."

"The Festival *is* Stratford."

"That's why I'm going golfing, Ah. Can't really solve that problem in one day, now can I?"

When we hung up, I sat and stared at the wall for a while. I lit a cigarette and then caught my faint reflection in the window next to the bed. Inside me swirled a cocktail of emotions I'd never felt towards the Festival before: resentment, revulsion, frustration, impotence. The Festival was the town, and the town was Victor Polley. He grew up there. He worked at the knitting mill for seventeen years before it closed and he became the bookkeeper at the Festival, working his way up to administrative director, which I thought he did well. When Governor General Vincent Massey visited the Festival, it was Dad who welcomed him to the theatre. When the vice-regal party wanted a backstage tour of the Festival, it was Dad who led it. At the civic reception that followed, it was Dad the alderman who welcomed Massey to the city. And when Massey visited the armoury, where Dad was a senior officer, and saw Dad for the third time that day, he joked, "I suppose if the fire bell rings, you'll have to leave."

This is the man they left behind.

I took a long drag, the gravity of it all weighing on me.

If it'll leave him behind, it'll sure as hell leave me behind just as fast, if not faster. It'll gladly throw me overboard just to keep itself afloat.

It was then I realized I couldn't expect anything from the Stratford Festival. At all times, I was only a season away from unemployment. In the quiet of the hotel room, I told myself I would never expect anything from them again. There was just no certainty there.

--

NANDOR.   I know, I know. You don't love me either. Say it, my darling, you haven't said it today. Tell me that you don't love me anymore. Keep telling me; let me get used to hearing it. I knew quite well that your love doesn't last very long, but to be honest I thought the

end was due round about the first or second week of
September — and we're only in May!

The audience laughed lingeringly. On my stool backstage, just off
to the side of the set's upstage French doors, I didn't take my eyes off
my script. It was all I could do to hide my stirring ambivalence.

ILONA.   The month of May.

BELA.   Beautiful spring! Beautiful May!

ILONA.   Beautiful May.

NANDOR.   Why are you crying?

Out at Theatre Calgary, we were capping off a winter season with
The Guardsman, a play about two newlywed actors, wherein the husband, Nandor, believes his wife, Ilona, to be unfaithful and so dresses
up as a guardsman to seduce her. Eric Donkin, a talented, funny man
with a great singing voice and wavy blond hair, played Nandor. We'd
grown close over the rehearsal period, Eric and I. It was in him I con-
fided about the letter Tom Hooker sent me asking me to come back to
the Festival, to be a full stage manager next season.

ILONA.   I'm not crying.

I traced my finger down the edge of the page, clocking the words
as the actors spoke them.
I should write back to him tonight.

NANDOR.   Why are you pretending to cry?

What to say?

ILONA.   I can't help it; sometimes it just comes over me.

There's still so much I don't know.

NANDOR.　　　I know why you're crying. You're crying over your lost freedom. You remind me of a melancholy little cat, cowering in her corner all day long, without moving . . . almost inert. And I'm permitted to watch, to watch and wait . . . for the inevitable. Yes, I'm afraid I know what to expect . . .

I'm barely a stage manager as it is.

ILONA.　　　If you know, why do you ask?

NANDOR.

Wait. That's not right.

I tilted my head slightly, and waited. It was Eric's line, but the pause was unrehearsed. My eyes were still on the page, but my ears followed the silence and the muffled footsteps perforating it. Certain they were Eric's and that he was trying to stay in character while waiting for his line to float to the surface, I told myself not to prompt, to give him time. But when Nandor stepped through the French doors and onto the balcony only a few feet from me, I knew Eric had dried completely.

Staring off into the night, Nandor sighed wistfully. I wanted to applaud Eric's brilliance right then and there. Instead, I simply whispered his line. Never dropping character for a moment, Eric took the line in. Nandor took a breath of fresh air, strolled back through the French doors, and the scene continued on.

After the show, I went downstairs to check on Eric. He'd dried twice more before the show had finished, which I would have imagined was a nightmare. In his dressing room, though, he grinned at the sight of me and I had to laugh.

"I take it you're okay?" I asked.

Wiping his forehead with a towel, he said, "Oh, just fine. It's definitely not the first time, and it probably won't be the last." He sighed loudly as he sat, as if suddenly he were fifty pounds lighter. I leaned against the doorframe and crossed my arms. In the hallway, actors and dressers trickled past, saying "good show" to one another.

"Good show," I told Eric.

He shook his head back and forth as if to say, "Not my best." He turned to the mirror and began removing his makeup.

"I thought it was good that you had the sense to come out on the balcony. I'm always there."

"Exactly. I had told myself beforehand you were there if I needed some help. I figured I might. These lines aren't sticking. It happens, though. I've seen and heard worse, much worse." He shuddered, as if hearing whatever worse was. "You know, a couple of years ago Olivier himself told an actor not to look him the eyes because Olivier was afraid he'd blank out?"

"Wow."

"Can you imagine? And can you imagine being those other actors, knowing they've got the fate of *Sir Laurence Olivier* in their hands?"

"Well, I know I wouldn't have had the sense to do what you did."

"But you were smart enough to know I'd figure it out."

"I guess."

Eric stopped wiping his face. He turned to me. I felt the air change. "You know, if you don't think you're experienced enough," he said, "then you shouldn't go back, regardless of what Tom says." I looked at the floor, feeling as if I'd been caught. Maybe I'd come to him for this very reason: to talk about my indecision. Eric went on. "It's not his career you have to think about. It's yours. And if you think that experience is the issue, wait a while and get some more. You've seen what it's like at the Festival. Would you rather go there unprepared and mess it all up or go there knowing you're ready to do the job?"

I didn't answer him. There were so many things I wanted to say, about the Festival railroading Dad, about feeling unprepared for the task of stage managing the big house, about how stupidly enticing that job sounded in spite of my frustrations and insecurities, but all of it mixed together in my mouth like cement. I watched Eric remove his makeup for a little while longer, and then left, no more certain of my future at Stratford.

Back at my apartment, I smoked on the bed and stared at Tom's letter. I'd just opened it. It was four pages of handwritten words on grid paper. The sight of it made me feel important. A letter like this took time. Through my window, downtown Calgary was dead and the crescent moon bright. I took a drag and reflected on the events leading me here, to this moment and this letter.

After I returned from Ottawa and the tour, Sue and Mom caught me up on what had happened. In late November, the Festival held an annual general meeting, normally attended by tens of people. This time, there were over three hundred. Tom Patterson himself decried the direction the Festival was going in, accused it of losing touch with the town, with its foundations, and demanded the resignation of the president of the Board. Dad didn't even go. He just stoically went about looking for another job, eventually finding one as the theatre manager at the St. Lawrence Centre for the Arts in Toronto, a job that meant he'd both work in theatre *and* leave Stratford. He said he didn't mind. He understood that he was old, that nobody was hiring. My parents sold 75 Front St., moved to Don Mills in Toronto, and took Dave and Marg, and I rented an apartment on Elizabeth St., giving myself the summer to decide if I'd return. Not being qualified for much else, I took a job in the wardrobe department at the Festival and spent the season doing legwork, stuffing underwear into bins. In the fall, I was invited to Theatre Calgary, and I leapt at the chance to be anywhere but Stratford. I was still undecided when Tom sent his first letter, asking if I'd return. I replied with my fears and inadequacies. Squeezing Tom's pages tightly in my other hand, I started reading his retort.

In his letter, Tom told me he was waiting for me to leave Stratford and mature someplace else, that going to Calgary was the right thing for me to do. It was the same with Ann, who left a few months earlier to pursue a career in voice teaching. I found myself putting out my cigarette just to hold on with two hands as he told me I was special, and he was building a strong team, a real backbone that would take years to develop, his legacy. He cited the loneliness I'd feel being stuck in the booth, away from the actors and the action, and then added I'd only be stuck there for one show. He quoted my dismay at the neglect of understudies at the Festival, telling me I could work directly with them to help them prepare. He said that Bill Hutt and Jean Gascon wanted me. He said that for all of Eric's wisdom, he didn't see me the way a PSM did. He said that with Theatre Calgary under my belt, the time was right to return to Stratford.

I set the pages down, staring at them but nothing more. I knew the words wouldn't change no matter how many times I read them. I shook my head. It wasn't that he was right. It was that *he* was right. *Tom* was right. I wanted to be half the stage manager he was, and he wanted to make it possible for me to be more.

With some loose paper from my binder and a pen, I started my reply.

1972

"Only one hour and forty-seven minutes left to win the Special Guthrie."

I squinted at the tinny voice in my headset. They had been taking turns, the crewmembers, counting down since the top of the show. Now, nearly halfway through, I still had no idea what they were talking about. I asked Alan Scarfe if he knew, but he just shrugged, his eyes never leaving Bill Hutt.

"I didn't know he did that there," Alan muttered, his head on his hands beside me. He was the heavy and handsome British actor understudying Bill's King Lear. As this was the last performance of the run, he'd asked to come up to the booth to finally see Bill do it. He said he didn't want

REGAN. What need one?

LEAR. O! reason not the need; our basest beggars
Are in the poorest thing superfluous:
Allow not nature more than nature needs,
Man's life is cheap as beast's. Thou art a lady;
If only to go warm were gorgeous,
Why, nature needs not what thou gorgeous wear'st,
Which scarcely keeps thee warm. But, for true need, —
You Heavens, give me that patience, patience I need! —
You see me here, you Gods, a poor old man,

to risk being influenced by Bill's performance. I didn't think there was any risk of that. He was twenty-six and Bill was fifty-two. He was also married when our relationship began.

"**Warning Lights 243 to 315,**" I intoned over the headset, hiding the rigidity of my poised muscles. While I was away, the Festival had purchased computerized lighting and sound equipment, so the designers decided to use every bell and whistle to create a storm so full of flash and roar that the audience would reach for an umbrella. The only problem was I couldn't call it alone. It wasn't that I was inexperienced. That was certainly true. But there was just so much going on that it was physically impossible for anybody to call it alone. There were only so many words a stage manager could cram into the span of a second. "**Lights 243,**" I said. "*Go.*"

I reached up to the grey, metal cue light box above me and **flicked** the left tunnel switch up. Powys's cue light was now on. I kept my finger there, primed, while peering down at the stage through a pane of glass, as if the actors were in a zoo. In spite of the distance, though, their voices came in clearly through the Tannoy speaker on a shelf above me on the right, our monitor for the show in performance. I prayed it never cut out, else I'd be flying blind, and now in a storm no less.

As full of grief as age; wretched in both!
If it be you that stirs these daughters' hearts
Against their father, fool me not so much
To bear it **tamely**; touch me with noble anger,
And let not women's weapons, water-drops,
Stain my man's cheeks! No, you unnatural hags,
I will have such revenges on you both
That all the world shall — I will do such things,
What they are, yet I know not, but they shall be
The terrors of the earth. You think I'll weep;
No, I'll not weep;
I have full cause of weeping, but this heart
Shall break into a hundred thousand flaws
Or ere I'll *weep.* O Fool! I shall go mad.

Exeunt Lear, Gloucester, Gentleman, and Fool.

CORN.   Let us withdraw, 'twill be a storm.
REGAN.   This house is little: the old man and 's people
Cannot be well bestow'd.
GON.   'Tis his own blame; hath put himself from rest,
And must needs taste his folly.

Alan rubbed my other arm softly in the dim light of the booth, surrounded by a small desk, my script, a little lamp, the Tannoy, and the God mic, as if to assure me he was still there.

I **flicked** the switch down and, taking my hand away, leaned slightly over my desk. Onstage, the conspiring Goneril, Regan, and Cornwall were joined by Powys's Gloucester, entering from the left tunnel, right on cue.

Getting the actors onstage at the right moment was my responsibility. I was also supposed to call the lights, but at this point in the show there were so many cues so densely packed together that the lighting operator simply hit the 'Go' button on his machine and kept me up to date as the scenes went on. When, during rehearsal, we discovered this was the best way to tackle it, I was instantly nostalgic for only a year or two ago, for lights up and lights down with white or blue colour for day and night. To complicate matters more, the sound system was nowhere near as automated as the lighting, so those cues were enormous. On lights, I called the cue number and then said go. Simple. For every sound cue, Paddy had to tell the sound operator the cue number, the sound level, and what speaker it came out of in the auditorium.

REGAN.   For his particular, I'll receive him gladly,
But not one follower.
GON.   So am I purpos'd.
Where is my Lord of Gloucester? **X**
CORN.   Follow'd the old man forth. He is return'd.

Re-enter Gloucester.

GLOU.   The King is in high rage.
CORN.   Whither is he going?
GLOU.   He calls to horse; but will I know not whither.
CORN.   'Tis best to give him way; he leads himself.
GON.   My Lord, entreat him by no means to stay.
GLOU.   Alack! the night comes on, and the bleak winds
Do sorely ruffle; for many miles about
There's scarce a bush.
REGAN.   O! Sir, to wilful men,
The injuries that they themselves procure
Must be their schoolmasters. Shut up your doors;
He is attended with a desperate train,
And what they may incense him to, being apt
To have his ear abus'd, wisdom bids fear.

I reached up to the cue light box, Tom Hooker's creation. **"Warning Lights 244,"** I said while **flipping** the switches for the upstage centre entrance and the right tunnel.

I waited, and took a deep breath.

"Lights 244," I said as I **flipped** the switches. *"Go."* Alan's hand had settled on my other arm as the sounds of the storm began to tremble in the background. I sat up straight and adjusted my headset, making sure one earmuff was fixed firmly behind my ear. With both on I couldn't hear the Tannoy.

Here we go.

"Flash D and E," I warned, my voice low and pointed, knowing that on the other channel, Paddy's was the same. There was just more of it. *"Go."* And even as we coordinated lights and sound blind of one another, there was a trust between us. **"Flash A . . .** *Go." We* knew we'd get it right.

"Flash C twice," I said.

"Go."

Alan took his hand away, gazing intently at the stage.

Alan began muttering to himself again, probably about Bill's blocking.

"Only one hour and forty minutes to win the Special

CORN. **Shut up** your doors, my Lord; 'tis a wild night:
My Regan counsels well: come out o' th' storm.

Exeunt. X
Enter Kent and a Gentleman.

KENT. Who's there, besides foul weather?
GENT. One minded like the weather, most unquietly.
KENT. I know you. Where's the King?
GENT. Contending with the fretful elements;
Bids the wind blow the earth **into** the sea,
Or swell the curléd waters 'bove the main,
That *things* might change or cease;
Strives in his little world of man to out-storm
The to-**and**-fro-conflicting *wind* and rain.
KENT. But who is with him? X
GENT. None but the Fool, who labours to out-jest
His heart-*strook* injuries.
KENT. Sir, I do know you;
And dare, upon the warrant of my note,
Commend a dear thing to you.

"Guthrie," yet another tinny voice informed me over the headset. It was an actor this time.

"These guys are ridiculous," I mumbled, adjusting my earmuff a little further back on my head.

"Again?" Alan asked.

I nodded as I found the switch for the upstage centre entrance and **flicked** it up. "You sure you don't know anything about it?"

Alan shook his head. We were both in the dark, it seemed. I thought back to before the show started. This was probably why I saw people tittering with one another when I was telling the actors the house attendance percentage.

"**Flash C and D . . . Go.**"

I took another breath, my finger still charged on the upstage centre switch. I **flicked** it down, signalling Bill and Ed's entrance. I watched for the 1st Knight's cross to the edge of the stage.

"**Flash Black Go.**"

There it is.

"**Flash Black and Red Go.**"

Alan sat bolt upright. He'd never before seen Bill do any of this iconic speech in performance.

{59}

Now to you:
If on my credit you dare build so far
To make your speed to Dover, you shall find
Some that will thank you, making just report
Of how unnatural and bemadding sorrow
The King hath cause to plain.
I will talk further with **you.**

GENT. No, do not.

KENT. For confirmation that I am much more
Than my out-wall, open this purse, and take
What it contains. If you shall see Cordelia,—
As fear not but you shall—show her this ring,
And she will tell you who that *fellow* is
That yet you do not know. Fie on this storm!
I will go seek the **King.**

GENT. Give me your hand.

Exeunt severally. X
1st Knight to edge of main level
in Black as **thunder** dies. X
Enter Lear and Fool.

LEAR.
Blow, winds, and crack your cheeks! *rage!* blow!
You cataracts and hurricanoes, spout
Till you have drench'd our *steeples,* drown'd the cocks!
You sulph'rous and thought-executing fires,
Vaunt-couriers of oak-cleaving thunderbolts,
Singe **my** white head! And *thou,* all-shaking thunder,
Strike flat the thick rotundity o' th' world! **X**
Crack Nature's moulds, all germens spill at once
That makes ingrateful man!

FOOL.
O Nuncle, court holy-water in a dry house is
better than this rain-water out o' **door.** Good
Nuncle, in, ask thy daughters' *blessing:* here's a
Night pities **neither** wise men nor Fools. *X*

LEAR.
Rumble thy *bellyfull!* **X** Spit, *fire!* spout, rain!
Nor rain, wind, thunder, fire, are my daughters:
I tax you not, you elements, with unkindness;
I never gave you kingdom, call'd you children,
You owe me no subscription: then let fall
Your horrible pleasure; here I stand, your slave,
A poor, infirm, weak, and despis'd old man.
But yet I call you servile ministers,
That will with two pernicious daughters join

"Flash Black . . . *Go.*"
Bill was late on that entrance.
"Flash Black . . . *Go.*"
Last show. Doesn't matter anymore.

"Flash C," I warned, sitting at the edge of my seat, eyes glued to my script. "*Go.* Flash Red, Black, Red *Go.*"

"Flash C and A," I said, as the earmuff suddenly fell forward over my ear. "*Go.*" I rammed it back. *Stupid thing.*

"Cue 286," the lighting op said over the headset.

"Flash Red and Black," I said, knowing he was going too fast. "*Go.*" I couldn't fault him. This scene shot out like confetti. "**Cue 288** . . . *Go.*" I then added, "**Flash Black** *Go.* **Flash B** *Go.*"

Following the cues as I'd written them in my script, I could tell instantly that the lighting operator was back on track. Paddy's sound was also synched with my lighting. This had gotten easier over the course of the run, but it had never gotten less daunting. As lightning and thunder besieged the stage, I took a moment to catch my breath.

"Think Bill will stop the show again?" Alan whispered playfully.

I chuckled, but shushed him all the same.

"Flash Black," I said, reaching up. "*Go.*" Finding the right tunnel switch, I **flicked** it up.

In one student matinee, some high school students were being disrespectful to Bill, audibly mocking his "howl, howl, howl, howl." Finally fed up, he stopped the show entirely. He simply put Cordelia down and walked offstage. I **flicked** the switch down.

In another student matinee, he stopped the show to announce the score of a hockey game. I'd never heard such a sound. It was like a rock concert. There I was, dazed, amidst nearly two thousand screaming fans.

"**Flash Black and Red . . .** *Go.*"

It definitely wasn't what I had expected when I'd returned to the Festival. I glanced at Alan out of the corner of my eye, while cueing, "**Flash D and E.**" He crossed his arms, and I smiled. This year was full of surprises. "*Go.*"

"Cue 314," the lighting op said.

"Good," I replied. We were through the worst of it. In the respite, I moved to mark Bill's late entrance on a notepad, but stopped, reminding myself again that it didn't matter. I

Your high-engender'd battles 'gainst a head
So old and white as this. X O, ho! 'tis foul.

FOOL.   **He** that has a house to put's head in has a good
head-piece.

Enter Kent.

LEAR.   No, I **will** be the pattern of all patience;
I will say nothing.

KENT.   Alas! Sir, are you here? things that love night
Love not such nights as these; the wrathful skies
Gallow the very wanderers of the dark,
And **make** them keep their *caves.* Since I was man
Such sheets of fire, such bursts of horrid thunder,
Such groans of roaring wind and rain, I never
Remember to have heard; man's nature cannot carry
Th' affliction nor the *fear.*

LEAR.   Let the great Gods,
That keep this dreadful pudder o'er our heads,
Find out their enemies now. Tremble, thou wretch,
That hast within thee undivulged crimes,

Unwhipp'd of Justice; hide thee, thou bloody hand,
Thou perjur'd, and **thou** simular of virtue
That art incestuous; caitiff, to pieces shake,
That under covert and convenient seeming
Has practis'd on man's life; close pent-up guilts,
Rive your concealing continents, and cry
These dreadful summoners grace. I am a man
More sinn'd against than sinning.

KENT.
Gracious my Lord, hard by here is a hovel;
Some friendship will it lend you 'gainst the tempest;
Repose you **there** while I to this hard house,—
return and force

LEAR.
Their scanted *courtesy*.
My **wits** begin to turn.
Come on, my boy. How dost, my boy? Art cold?
I am cold myself. Where is this straw, my fellow?
The art of our necessities is strange,
And can make vile things precious. Come, your hovel.
Poor Fool and knave, I have one part in my heart
That's sorry yet for thee.

FOOL.
This is a brave night to cool a courtezan.

sat up straight, stunned by the routine that had possessed my movements. "**Warning Lights 316 and 317**," I added.

Right after we'd opened, Alan had come to me for help. As Bill's understudy, he had a lot to learn. So, we convened in the rehearsal hall after hours and went through his scenes. He played Lear and I played everybody else. At first I was seated, responding to him while he was onstage, but, after the futility of that dawned on us, I went up with him and skipped around from location to location, character to character. By the end of this process I had an exceptional grasp of everybody's lines.

"**Flash Black**," I warned, redoubling my focus on the page in front of me. It was hard not to think about the tour of Europe, and our plans, though. "*Go*." Blindly, I reached for the right door switch and **flipped** it up. Not long after we'd started, he'd asked me on a date, which I thought was bizarre considering his wife was in the company. But I went. We were being bad, but it felt good. Then the Festival announced a European tour to Denmark, Netherlands, Poland, and Russia, and what was developing between us became all the more thrilling and romantic. My head swarmed with images of us behind the Iron Curtain, standing on quaint bridges.

LEAR. **True**, boy. Come bring us to this *hovel*.

Exeunt Lear and Kent.
Enter Gloucester and Ed*mund*.

GLOU. Alack, alack! Edmund, I like not this unnatural dealing. When I desir'd their leave that I might pity the King, they took from me the use of mine own house; charg'd me, on pain of perpetual displeasure, neither to speak of him, entreat for him, or any way sustain him.

EDM. Most savage and unnatural!

GLOU. Go to; say you nothing. There is division between the Dukes, and a worse matter than that. I have receiv'd a letter this night; 'tis dangerous to be spoken; I have lock'd the letter in my closet. These injuries the King now bears will be revenged home; there is part of a power already footed; we must incline to the King. I **will** look for him and privily relieve **him**; go you and maintain talk with the Duke,

---

"**Lights 316**," I said, my one finger readied. "*Go.*" As Lear and his Fool left the stage, the storm rollicked overhead, and I **cued** Powys and Barry to enter. This done, I called, "**Lights 317**, *Go.*" Alan squeezed my shoulder. I smiled, relieved. He certainly wasn't what I meant or expected when I said I wanted to work more closely with understudies.

Sometimes, during work hours, I'd give Alan a backrub. It was just something we did, the theatre being rife with that kind of thing. It was playful, for the most part. Earlier in the season I'd watched a stagehand tape an ASM to a chair and roll her into the elevator. She was laughing as the doors closed, but something told me she didn't enjoy it very much. The boundaries were sometimes hard to discern.

"One hour and thirty-five minutes to win the Special Guthrie," another voice said.

I rubbed my temple, trying to dam up my patience for this nonsense.

"*Again?*" Alan asked.

I nodded, asking, "You sure you don't know?" Over the headset, I said, "**Warning Lights 318 and 319**," while reaching for the left tunnel switch and **setting** it up.

EDM. This courtesy, forbid thee, shall the Duke
Instantly know; and of that letter too:
This seems a fair deserving, and must draw me
That which my father loses; **no** less than all:
The younger rises when the old doth *fall*.

Edmund exits.
Enter Lear, Kent, and Fool.

KENT. Here is the place, my Lord; good my Lord, enter:
The tyranny of the open night's too rough
For nature to endure.

LEAR. Let me alone.

---

that my charity be not of him perceiv'd. If
he ask for me, I am ill and gone to bed. If I
die for it, as no less is threatened me, the King,
my old master, must be reliev'd. There is
strange things toward, Edmund; pray you,
be careful.

Gloucester exits.

"Positive," Alan replied, and then chuckled. "So Bill
actually told them the score, did he?"

"Oh yeah," I mouthed.

"What did David say?" Alan asked, referring to our
no-nonsense British director, David William.

"He was livid. After the show ended I got a telegram
from him. 'Confirm or deny: hockey score.'"

Alan clasped his mouth to stifle his laugh. "No. You
didn't."

"Oh yeah," I mouthed again.
"Tell me everything."

"In a minute." I followed the words to the last cues of the
storm proper. "**Lights 318,**" I said while **flicking** the left
tunnel switch down. "*Go.*"

One more and we're out of the woods.

"**Lights 319** *Go.*"
I watched as Edmund left the stage, and Lear, Kent, and
his Fool entered. I breathed deeply for the umpteenth time,
and my body instantly felt lighter, as if gravity itself had at last
relented. That was the last time I'd have to navigate that crazy
scene. I wanted to scream in joy tinged with agony, but instead
switched on all channels on my headset and said, "Great stuff."

KENT. Good my Lord, enter here.

LEAR. Wilt break my heart?

KENT. I had rather break mine own. Good my Lord, enter.

LEAR. Thou think'st 'tis much that this contentious storm
Invades us to the skin: so 'tis to thee;
But where the greater malady is fix'd,
The lesser is scarce felt. Thou 'ldst shun a bear;
But if thy flight lay toward the roaring sea,
Thou 'ldst meet the bear i' th' mouth.
When the mind's free
The body's delicate; this tempest in my mind
Doth from my senses take all feeling else
Save what beats there—filial ingratitude!
Is it not as this mouth should tear this hand
For lifting food to 't? But I will punish home;
No, I will weep no more. In such a night
To shut me out? Pour on; I will endure.
In such a night as this? O Regan, Goneril!
Your old kind father, who frank heart gave all,—
O! that way madness lies; let me shun that;
No more of that.

The ASMs and the operators replied back warmly, congratulating me. It almost felt like the show was over, but thumbing the side of the stack of pages left unturned in front of me, I knew we were still far from it.

While Alan and I watched Lear ramble on with Kent, I told Alan the full hockey story.

"The final game of the Summit Series hockey championships: Team Canada facing off against Soviet Russia. And the play began maybe halfway through, which meant none of the students were paying attention to anything that was happening onstage. Some of the students even brought radios in the house and were trying to listen on low volumes. Everybody knew, but nobody cared. Even the stagehands were tuned in backstage. We all were, in one way or another. Anyway, Bill had just finished the storm sequence and was exiting, but before he got down the right tunnel he stopped, onstage, and with a glint in his eye said, 'Henderson scored. Canada won 6 to 5!' The way the students cheered, I was floored. Of course, then I wondered what the hell am I supposed to do, you know? Bill left me alone in a room with twenty-two hundred screaming adolescents. What the hell am I supposed to do with that? So, I just cued on Powys and

Barry, and the students fell completely silent. They must've gotten it all out of their system. David was so pissed."

"Oh, David William's always pissed," Alan quipped.

"Only one hour and thirty minutes to win the Special Guthrie."

Oh, for the love of—

KENT. Good my Lord, enter here.
LEAR. Prithee, go in thyself; seek thine own ease:
This tempest will not give me leave to ponder
On things would hurt me more. But I'll go in.
In, boy; go first. You houseless poverty,
Nay, get thee in. I'll pray, and then I'll sleep.

"This has to be it," Joe said to us, stopping in front of a set of wooden doors with cast-iron hinges. I shivered, my fur coat only doing so much to dissuade the biting cold of the Warsaw night. The building looked like a church, and the name out front was a collection of Polish markings none of us understood, but the reptilian image above its doors was unmistakable: The Alligator. Cheers rang up softly between the five of us. We'd been searching for the bar for some time, and the casual pointing of strangers only got us so far. Joe opened the door. "After you."

Joseph Totaro was an American actor with dark, shaggy hair and a moustache. He was playing the Herald in *King Lear*, for which I was the stage manager, and the ass-end of a horse in *The Taming of the*

Shrew, for which I was the ASM. By now, only one of these had been worth the trip.

Peter, Pat, and Roy dove in first. I thanked Joe and followed closely behind.

Inside the bar, Pat Galloway was standing by the door, tussling her straight pageboy hair. She was a slender woman, and a fierce actress. Standing beside her was Peter Roberts, our bearded head of sound, brought to Europe to ensure that as little as possible was left to chance while we toured to different theatres, each run in a language not our own. Together with Roy Brown, our wide-smiling head of props, who stood behind, the two of them were searching for a table.

The bar itself was dimly lit, not too full, with wooden furniture and a thin layer of smoke ambling overhead. It made me want a cigarette, but I reminded myself that I had quit. It wasn't for health reasons. The doctors on TV recommended Camels. There was just no way I was paying a dollar for a pack of cigarettes. Too expensive. Around me whorled a white noise of languages foreign to me. To my left, a group of burly men was shouting in French, while on my right, just a few tables down, two young women were speaking in Polish, and beside me a man was asking where his wallet was in what sounded like Italian. Whenever I heard the odd English word I turned to it as if it had grabbed me by the shoulders.

Joe nudged me, pointing to the other three, who had already decided on a table near the bar and were taking off their coats.

"So what'll it be?" Peter asked as Joe and I arrived.

"Oh, anything," I said, hanging my coat on the back of the chair.

"I'm sure that's what they'll end up giving us," Pat joked.

We laughed and then watched the bartender flash five fingers inquisitively at Peter, and then, upon receiving confirmation, begin to point to beverages as if to say, "Tell me when to stop."

When our drinks finally arrived, Peter handed me a pint of something pale and amber. It certainly looked great. But I was untravelled, so almost everything did.

Roy raised his glass. "Cheers."

"No, no," Peter said, stopping him. "What is it?"

SHAWN DESOUZA-COELHO

"*Na zdrowie*," I prompted, and then chortled, shaking my head at myself.

"Thank you, stage manager."

"Naz droh vee ya!" we all said in one form or another, clinking glasses. The two Polish women to our right giggled. Roy held up his glass to them as well.

"Naz droh vee ya!" he called.

"*Na zdrowie*," they echoed, raising their glasses.

As the night went on, and The Alligator's jaws filled with more and more people, Peter and Roy had taken to chatting with the two Polish women, both tall and slender. Because neither of them could speak English, and neither Peter nor Roy spoke Polish, their compromise was to eke out a conversation in French. Everybody was laughing and enjoying themselves with it. I realized I had spent an inordinate amount of time staring at them because suddenly one of the women pointed at me curiously. I whipped my head back to the table, my beer, and Joe.

"You've got fans," he snickered.

"Please," I scoffed, covering up my poor manners. "A stage manager?"

He chuckled.

"No, no, it's like this," Bill Hutt told Pat at the table just behind Joe. English words aside, I recognized Bill's baritone voice anywhere. Mom would call it "The Voice" whenever he called our house to speak to Dad. Bill had arrived shortly after we did. He was portly, sporting a devilish salt-and-pepper goatee. He and Pat were embroiled in a debate about how to swear in Polish.

I took a sip of beer and winced. My pale amber pint had been replaced first with a fruity concoction that tasted of honey, and now with something dark brown. It was heavy, with an aftertaste that reminded me of the scent of tires.

"Not a good *piwo*?" Joe asked, emphasizing the word the bartender had taught us to make our lives and his easier.

I shook my head. "I don't really drink beer."

"What do you drink?"

"Dubonnet, mostly."

Joe took in this information with a sip of his lager. "Why were you staring at those women?"

"Admiring, really. They can just get dolled up and go to a bar."

"So?"

"Oh, that's right!" I said, slapping the table. "You're American. I wonder if it was different there. But in Ontario, not too long ago, I wouldn't have been allowed to go into bars by myself. I would have needed a male chaperone."

"Huh," Joe said, as if he'd learned something new.

I nodded. "Draconian."

"No kidding. If I had known Ontario was so dry, I would have brought something with me from the States."

"I don't think anybody would have minded. My dad always said that nobody partied like theatre people."

"Oh, I know," Joe winked.

"You know the Festival used to have a *press club* on the second floor of the arena? It's true. It was really an after-hours bar, completely illegal. It would get raided and they'd phone my dad to go settle things with the cops."

"No!"

"Yeah! And once, when the cops were confiscating the liquor, they told my dad, 'You know, you keep this beer too cold.'" Joe was splitting his sides with laughter. I winced another sip of my beer. "Awful," I muttered.

"How's your dad doing? I didn't get to know him very well before he left. Too high up on the totem pole."

"He's fine. Working at the St. Lawrence Centre in Toronto."

"Doing?"

"He's their theatre manager. He's like the landlord for the spaces there, I guess. He's replaced all of the ushers there with female models."

Joe raised his glass slightly. "Clever."

"I don't doubt it."

We spent a moment in silence then. I glanced back to Peter, Roy, and the two Polish women. I tried to listen for the odd word, but the bar was pretty noisy. I turned back to Joe with a question in mind, but it was he who asked first.

"How are you handling *Shrew*?"

"Oh, please."

It was the simplest way to say it given how hurt I still was. While we were rehearsing for the tour, in spite of all our plans for Europe, Alan broke it off with me, forcing me to spend two of the coldest months of the year alone and away from home. If it wasn't for *Shrew* I would have avoided him altogether, but his final costume change wasn't working because the local dressers couldn't speak English, so I was asked to do it. It was bizarre torture, having to undress him, night after night. Once I forgot his comb and he asked me not to forget it next time. Next time, I forgot it on purpose.

"And no," I smirked. "I didn't win the Special Guthrie."

Joe laughed. "We had no idea what any of it meant!"

"Neither did we!"

"The ASMs just handed us a piece of paper and told us to read it."

I shook my head playfully, painfully. The Tyrone Guthrie Awards were an annual awards ceremony recognizing the achievements of members of all departments at the Festival. The "Special Guthrie" was created that very night, a surreptitious gag gift to reward the stage manager for supposedly being able to have sex in the booth without missing a single cue.

Slyly, Joe asked, "So, how many cues did you miss?"

"Ha, ha," I mocked, changing the subject. "So how did you come to Stratford, anyway?"

"That . . . is a long story," Joe cautioned.

"Well, our train leaves tomorrow night, and we've got no show tomorrow so technically we've got all night and all day."

"Okay, not *that* long. It was by fluke, actually."

"Fluke?"

He took a drink, and sat up as if readying himself for a long journey. "Complete and utter luck. I was scheduled for an audition in November of '69. I'd just finished my graduate work at Columbia in

June, and then did three shows back to back to back by Labour Day. I was completely spent, so I decided to take a trip to Stratford. I'd never been to Canada, so I said, 'What the hell,' and went.

"When I got there, there wasn't really much to do, so on a whim I went to the Festival stage door and asked if I could take a tour of the backstage. The stage doorman called up to the artistic director's office and a black woman came down to get me."

"Barbara," I said.

"Barbara," Joe confirmed. "She comes down and looks at me, and says, 'You're Joe Totaro.' 'Yeah, how do you know that?' She asks me what I'm doing there and I tell her I had some time off and I wanted to check the place out since I'd never been.

"So she takes me up to Gascon's office and I'm sitting there, and she asks me if I want a cup of tea. I tell her, 'No, thanks.' Then she tells me I should audition while I'm there."

I set my glass down. "What?"

"Yeah. So I say, 'No, no, no. I'll come back in November. I haven't even thought about what I'm going to do.' And then she says, 'What, are you that rich, you're going to come back up? You really should audition now.' I tell her no again. Then she leans in across her desk and says — I swear to God — 'You. Should. Audition. Now. While. You're. Here.' I took the hint, but I didn't have anything prepared. So I say, 'All right. I need at least a day.' She says that's fine and tells me, 'Tomorrow morning at ten o'clock.' So I say, 'Okay,' and then I spent the rest of the day just walking by the river brushing up on monologues.

"The next day I arrive early and Tom comes down and asks if I'd like a room to warm up in, and that's when he shows me to the Festival dressing room. Now, I was used to auditioning in closets and hallways for people, so I had no idea what was happening. At ten Tom got me, telling me they're ready. 'Are *you* ready?' he asks me, and I say, 'Yes. Where are we going?' Tom looks at me like I'm nuts. 'You're going out on the stage.' So now I'm shaking in my boots, I mean, *the* Festival stage, but as I step onto the boards, with the stage lights on, the house lights dull, and people sitting out there in the house—"

"Who was out there?"

"John Hayes, Tom, and Gascon. Yeah . . . I don't know . . . I got out there and I was overwhelmed, but in a warm and welcoming way, you know? I immediately understood the architecture of that stage. And I did the audition for them and, afterwards, John comes down and says, 'Mr. Hooker will take you up to the green room. Have a cup of tea and I'll be up to see you in ten minutes.'

"So I went, had tea, and then ten minutes later, John comes into the green room, sits down, and says, 'Jean would like you to join the company.' 'What?' 'Jean would like you to join the company.' 'When?' 'Now.' The first thing out of my mouth was — this is so embarrassing — 'I'm only here for the weekend. I didn't bring any clothes with me.' As if that was the most of my worries! But then John says, 'Don't worry about that, Joseph. If you want to work for the company, we'll take care of shipping things for you. Now, do you want to join this company or not?'"

My hand was to my mouth in awe at the complete serendipity of it.

"It was only later on I learned," Joe added, "that the reason I was hired was because one of the actors had been so drunk at one of those end-of-season parties, he jumped into a swimming pool that didn't have any water in it and injured himself. And so—"

"Everybody had to move up to fill the gap . . ." I interjected, knowing the routine.

". . . leaving a spot at the very bottom. Barb said, 'I took one look at you and thought, he can do that.' I was cast because I could fill a costume!"

"Doesn't matter how you're cast," Pat commented. By then everybody was back at our table. The two Polish women had left, and the bar was beginning to thin out.

"I lived in a town close by," Peter said triumphantly.

"I interviewed with Jack Hutt," Roy stated.

"Me too," I said, adding, "with a healthy dose of nepotism," since everybody was already thinking it.

"I threatened to leave," Pat said.

We all turned to Bill.

"I built that town," he said, completely stone-faced.

We laughed and spent the next few minutes taking turns admiring his humility.

--

As the train churned into Brest station, the first things we noticed were the machine guns. They were slung around the shoulders of the Russian guards stationed at the Belarusian border between Poland and Russia. There were a half-dozen of them that we could see, all uniformed in black fur hats and dull blue overcoats with deep-green pants. Who knew how many more there were inside the station itself, a large building with a looming colonnade adorning its facade. The morning sky was pale grey, and we could see the guards' breath plume in the air as we crept to a stop.

"Some fanfare," Jeanette Aster said, her hand fogging the glass. She was a thin, dark-haired ASM on the European tour and my compartment mate on the train.

We watched, she and I, as the car doors opened and an official and two guards filed on. They went from compartment to compartment collecting the company's passports. Jeanette and I had ours ready. The last thing I wanted was to cause any trouble.

When our compartment door opened, my heart murmured. I knew their rifles would be bigger up close, but I didn't expect them to be *that* big. They looked unstoppable, as if no living thing could ever impede them.

"Паспорт," the official said gruffly, his comrades standing to either side.

Neither of us could speak Russian, but when he held out his hand we assumed he had said "passport," and so I handed them over. I couldn't stop my hand from trembling. The guards were simply watching the corridor. Neither of them smiled. The official then slid our compartment door shut and the three of them continued on. I turned to Jeanette, collapsed as she was on her seat, and knew she too felt like she'd just passed some horrible test.

Then nothing happened for a long time. I wanted to check what

SHAWN DESOUZA-COELHO

was going on but my imagination petrified me. I saw myself being dragged off the train by my ankles into the guards' station and then never seeing my family or friends again, telling myself that kind of thing happened all the time here in Soviet Russia.

"Nora!" Jeanette gasped, peering through the window. I jumped.

"What is it?" I asked, joining her. I gasped too. Powys was being led into the station, a guard on either side of him.

What the hell is going on?

"Wait here," I told Jeanette.

She nodded, eyes fixed on Powys.

In the hallway, I scampered left to Powys's compartment to find Barry MacGregor and Max Helpmann arguing.

"What happened?" I urged. "What do they want with Powys?"

Max, a tall Australian actor, threw up his hands as if emptying them. "Ah, nothin' to do with me, mate."

"You're the bloody company manager, for God's sake!" Barry yelled softly.

"What would you have me do?"

"Go speak with them. Say something."

"And when they reply in Russian?"

This went back and forth for a minute or so, all of us, in our own ways, dealing with the fact that we had no idea what to do, with the fact that we were just nervous. We all tried to peek inside the station. It was the most we could have done, none of us wanting to move an inch. Eventually though, after enough time had passed without incident, I made my way back to my compartment.

I found Jeanette as I'd left her, peering through the glass at the unchanging scene. "What happened?" she asked, but before I could answer, a voice from behind me made my heart skip a beat.

"Пойдите со мной, пожалуйста."

I turned to see the official staring right at me. Two full beats. I glanced back at Jeanette, suddenly noticing how small we both were compared to him, how insignificant. In the presence of this man, this official, we were little more than paper to be folded or crumpled or crushed or left alone. Or asked to follow. I pointed to myself, as if to be sure. He nodded.

On the long walk down the corridor, I felt oddly calm. This was the first moment I didn't question anything. I didn't question why they wanted me, the *stage manager* of all people. I wasn't curious about where we were going. He couldn't answer me even if I asked. My heart was now a jackhammer, but my mind was oddly, serenely blank. As I marched by each compartment, company members stared at me. I wondered briefly what they were thinking. If they saw Powys and now me, then maybe they were thinking they were next.

Nearing the end of the corridor, the official stopped in front of a compartment on his right. Inside was a woman I'd never seen before, dressed in blue jeans and a black top. She was speaking in Russian with the two guards, one of whom looked to be holding all our passports. Beside them, our white-haired wardrobe mistress, Eleanor Nickless, looked on patiently. I flashed Eleanor a furtive glance, as if to ask what was going on, but she didn't see. The official joined his comrades and then pointed at me.

Okay, now I'm terrified.

How long they had been talking, or how much time had passed as I stood there, I didn't know, but eventually somebody tapped me on the shoulder and I jumped again, startled.

"Sorry!" Jeanette whispered. "You were gone for so long. What's happening?"

"I have no idea," I replied, never fully turning away from the guards. They didn't seem to mind that Jeanette had showed up uninvited. "I haven't heard any English yet."

As if on cue, the woman then spoke directly to me in a throaty Russian accent. "Ze gentle man does not know English. Could you return zese passports to who zey belong to?"

The official handed me the stack.

"Sure," I said, wanting nothing more than to leave. "I can do that."

When Jeanette and I were out of earshot she whispered, "What the hell was that about?"

I looked down at the passports in my hand. "I have no idea."

Heading back to our compartment, which wasn't so great a distance on the return, neither of us could figure out why the guards had

SHAWN DESOUZA-COELHO

asked me. The nearest we could figure was that everybody else was listed as actor or actress or designer or carpenter or whatever on some manifest they'd gotten a hold of, and something about me being listed as stage *manager* meant I was in charge. It was flimsy, but we weren't about to go and ask them to clarify.

I handed Jeanette her passport and she returned to our compartment, a spring in her step compared to moments before. I paused at the door in admiration of her bravery and wondered if I would have come to check on her had she been asked to follow. Telling myself yes, certainly, I then left to return the other passports. Alan seemed vaguely interested in what had happened. Vengefully, I imagined myself dying that day and him having to live the rest of his life with the guilt of us being on bad terms. I arrived at Barry and Max's compartment.

"Powys!" I yelled.

"Keep your voice down!" Barry cautioned.

I ducked slightly on instinct. "Sorry!" I whispered.

Powys, having returned safely, was grinning from ear to ear.

"You're in the company of royalty," Barry added.

Picking up on my incredulity, Max explained, "Turns out Powys's father is a national treasure. He had been invited by Stalin to come to Russia in . . . when was it, Powys?"

"1931," Powys remarked.

"1931. Well, it seems the Soviet Union never forgets. Our man Powys here came out o' that station like a star, shaking hands with the guards. They were even applaudin' him!" He chortled and slapped Powys on the shoulder.

"I don't believe it," I said softly.

"It's unbelievable," Barry agreed. "But what did they want with you?"

I handed them each their passports in reply.

"Why you?" Powys asked.

"Your guess is as good as mine."

"Welcome to Russia," Max quipped.

 I tapped my pencil on the postcard, in no particular way, at no particular speed. Staring out the window at the bright Sydney cityscape, it seemed like I had all the time in the world, and none. Robin Phillips, we knew, was going to be the artistic director of the Festival next season. And here I was, in the April before this year's season was to begin, in my cream-coloured hotel room halfway around the world, writing to him to remind him, on one of his many evaluative visits to the Festival as artistic director designate, that some of the company was away, but that we were coming back.

I looked down at the postcard and my faint mistakes, still glaring at me in relief, and then back through the window. A breeze grappled with the curtains. I stared aimlessly until my vision blurred on a point in space and I no longer saw the city at all, but the past and everything that had come before. I saw Dad's new home in Toronto, and the stomach parasites we contracted in Russia from garbage disguised as cuisine. I saw Paddy McEntee and me standing before John Hayes, the Festival's producer, after we'd returned, putting our names in for this Australian tour. I tapped my pencil some more, then saw myself in the elevator at the NAC and wondered, through it all, why I had been so angry. I thought I knew, and then suddenly I didn't.

My anxiety at Jean Gascon's departure as artistic director was veiled behind an understanding that it was time. The Festival had become a cultural machine where plays were put in one end and productions were ground out at the other. But when Gascon had taken over from Michael Langham, people fell by the wayside and were never seen again at the Festival. Now with Gascon leaving, I couldn't help but wonder if I'd be discarded in the fallout.

I'm not ready to leave yet.

Where from I didn't know, but the thought came with a kind of certainty I'd rarely felt in my otherwise meandering life. I chortled at it before it vanished, leaving only its meaning behind to sit with me like sediment. It meant that while I once questioned whether or not I could deal with the impermanence of the job and the politics governing it, I now accepted both with benign resignation. My time would inevitably be up. But, sitting in my hotel room across the world, the curtains rustling gently, I felt there was more for me before that time came, and I wanted to know what it was. And, it was with that subtle yearning in mind that I set my pencil to the postcard before me, a postcard to remind Robin that all of us abroad wanted a place in his and the Festival's future.

1975

His was the big, white house on Douglas Street. The Festival owned it, and used it to house its artistic directors. I took a deep breath as I walked up its long laneway, squeezing my copy of the *Measure for Measure* script tightly to my chest. In the quiet of the warm spring evening, I reassured myself that Robin had asked for me. Not just this evening, when we were to discuss scene changes at his home, an appointment I found petrifying and somewhat unprofessional given that he was the director and I was only the stage manager, but also this season. When I came back from Australia there was a note waiting for me that said, simply, "I will have Nora for *Measure*." I'd yet to figure out why.

TOK! TOK! TOK!

The door whipped open, and I gave a little start. Robin stood in the doorway, wearing a white sweater atop a white dress shirt and jeans. He was clean-shaven, and his brown eyes were vibrant, as if barely able to contain his boundless energy. His black hair was short and needed no work at all, just a bit of a comb. In that moment I wondered if I'd ever seen him dressed down and realized that these could very well be his pyjamas.

"Nora!" he said, clapping his hands together. "Come in, come in. May I take your coat?"

"Thank you," I said, giving it to him. For want of something else to say, and having taken nothing in, I then added, "Lovely place."

"A work in progress. Like all things. I'm making some tea. Would you like some?"

"Yes, I would," I said, not wanting to seem rude, while knowing I was so nervous I probably couldn't stomach anything.

We sat in his living room with our tea, surrounded by piles of unpacked boxes, and without much preamble Robin then began to discuss the scene changes. It quickly became clear to me that he wanted to discuss nothing more than the most efficient way to get things on and off stage. I felt my muscles uncurl in relief. We began with the pre-show work leading into the first scene.

"Don has some of them exiting through the tunnels, yes?" Robin asked, flipping between pages in his script.

"Uh . . ." I hesitated, kicking myself for not marking it down. Hoping my memory didn't fail me, I said, "Yes. He does."

The pre-show was Robin's philosophy in a nutshell. On the first day of rehearsal he walked in and told Don Shipley, the assistant director, that he, Don, was going to direct the pre-show. Don didn't give it away, but I could tell he felt as if somebody had pulled his chair out from under him. We all quickly learned that that was Robin's way of working. He threw us into the deep end and then expected us to swim. Oddly, it never felt like he'd let us drown.

Don did a great job with it, too. There was no text for the pre-show, so out of thin air he fabricated a small story involving servants and maids cleaning the Duke's office. The idea was that the office was being roused earlier in the day than anybody had expected. In the middle of the clamour a footman sat at the Duke's table, put his feet up on it, and flirted with all the maids. After they finished, they all left the stage through the closest exit, like mice scurrying away in light.

"There's something wonderful about the symmetry and progression of these scenes," Robin began, looking up at me from lines much later in the play. "The Duke is with the pregnant Juliet in prison, probing. We are reassured that the love between Juliet and Claudio is consensual. Then the very next scene we have Angelo's proposition, to which Isabella does not consent at all, you see? Then we're back to the prison, with the Duke and Claudio." He paused a moment, then grinned. "It's as if Shakespeare, again, cleaves them in two." I felt hypnotized by his mind at work.

Snapping to, I said, almost flippantly, "It'd be much easier if they were back to back."

Robin perked up. "What do you mean?"

Nora, what the hell?

"Oh . . . Well, it's just that . . . you have the Duke coming into the prison with Juliet, and then from the prison we have to go to Angelo's office, but then after that we're back to the prison. I just thought it would be easier if the prison scenes were back to back. It'd save us the trip, lugging the desks and chairs and all that stuff off only to bring them on moments later."

"Aha! Yes! Excellent. That's what we'll do."

"Oh, no, I—"

"Because then there is the possibility of them just missing one another!" And then Robin added, as if to himself, "Seeing Juliet and Claudio almost reunite but not doing so is in many ways more important than seeing them apart. Great. Good. Mark that change."

"Okay . . ."

I didn't know what else to say. I was dumbfounded. My comment was meant as an observation, not a revision, but now that he had taken it as one, I didn't know what to make of it. It was obvious to me how much simpler things could be, but I felt like I should have kept my mouth shut. It wasn't normally my place, but for some reason, with

SHAWN DESOUZA-COELHO

Robin, it was. Thankfully, however, for my heart's sake, I didn't have any other bright ideas for the rest of the evening.

--

It was only Robin, Martha Henry, Brian Bedford, and myself in Rehearsal Hall 1 when Robin placed a full pitcher of water on the table centre stage and then quickly took his seat. Just off to the side, lit by a pale afternoon, Martha shared my wonder, looking at the pitcher as if it were an oddly shaped tree. I saw her question as plainly as I did her: what was Robin thinking? Then the confident and handsome Brian, already onstage, became the bastardly Angelo, and the scene began again.

ANG.   O heavens!
                    Why does my blood thus muster to my heart,
                    fair maid?

Martha's Isabella entered the scene, slowly.

ISA.   I am come to know your pleasure.

ANG.   That you might know it, would much better please me
                    Than to demand what 'tis. Your brother cannot live.

ISA.   Even so. Heaven keep your honour!

ANG.   Yet may he live awhile; and, it may be,
                    As long as you or I, yet he must die.

ISA.   Under your sentence?

ANG.   Yea.

I found myself clinging to their every word, the two of them harmonizing so perfectly with one another. Robin, sitting to my left in his blue dress shirt, tie, and white suit pants, was completely engrossed as well. He was on the edge of his seat, bent forward, mouthing every word Isabella and Angelo were saying, as if he knew the whole scene by heart. It looked as if he felt it too. When Angelo presented Isabella with the choice to sleep with him in order to save Claudio's life, *Robin* was propositioning her. When the suggestion repulsed Isabella, I could see the grimace on Robin's face. He did nothing to interrupt the scene, but inside he was a firecracker waiting to explode, and I sensed what for. The scene continued to play out, but still neither Isabella nor Angelo had made use of the pitcher of water.

ANG.
Fit thy consent to my sharp appetite;
Lay by all nicety and prolixious blushes,
That banish what they sue for; redeem thy brother
By yielding up thy body to my will;
Or else he must not only die the death,
But thy unkindness shall his death draw out
To lingering sufferance. Answer me to-morrow,
Or, by the affection that now guides me most,
I'll prove a tyrant to him. As for you,
Say what you can, my false o'erweighs your true.

Angelo exited, leaving Isabella onstage. It was her line next. She was motionless, staring in the direction Angelo had left, but her eyes weren't looking at the exit at all. They seemed lost in thought. But I could tell, I didn't know how, the thoughts weren't Martha's; they were Isabella's. Robin looked on, as did Brian, and nothing moved. Then, slowly, Isabella took out a handkerchief and plunged it into the water, up to her wrist. Taking it out, she began to scrub her face and neck. I felt like I was watching the Milky Way turning. She was dirty. Angelo had made her feel dirty to the point where she needed to clean herself off, but no matter how much she scrubbed, his words wouldn't wash. Then she spoke.

When the scene ended, Robin didn't say anything about what Martha had done. Maybe he was used to these things happening

SHAWN DESOUZA-COELHO

under his watch. I still felt light, though, like I had suddenly acquired a new organ and my body was still trying to figure out its purpose. I wanted to yell, but Robin had directed a question to Brian about the word "prolixious" and they had decided it needed some clarification. Robin did this often: asked for the derivations of words, or their usage in Shakespeare's time in order to help the actors get a better understanding of the text. It was the kind of work we weren't used to.

Sifting through the massive Oxford English Dictionary in front of me and finally landing on the word, I said, "Prolixious: time-wasting, tedious, protracted."

"Yes," Robin said to Brian. "There's something to that, isn't there?" Brian nodded. "He's not mincing words anymore. He's not fucking around. This is business." He paused, as if to let that sink in. "Let's try it again."

"Where would you like to start from?" I asked.

"From Isabella's entrance, please."

"From 'Must needs appear offence,' please," I called out. Brian paused, as if rewinding a tape in his mind, and then took to the stage. Martha stood by her entrance. "Whenever you're ready."

They ran the scene again, and this time Robin stopped and started them, over and over, bolting up from his chair to join them onstage, to give notes on something as small as their inflection on a particular word. He would then sit down, and they'd continue.

When Angelo had left, and Isabella was alone in his office once more, Robin stopped the scene. He went onstage and knelt beside Martha, speaking to her in a voice so low that only she could hear it. We started again, and Isabella scrubbed herself once more. It was just as remarkable, if not more so for the simple fact that Martha was able to repeat it.

I was a compass needle then, gripped by the magnetism of everything I'd just witnessed. If there was any part of me that was still unsure of the direction my life was headed, it vanished the moment Isabella dipped her handkerchief in that pitcher of water. And as Robin spoke with Martha and Brian onstage, the three of them poring zealously over the text, I swore to myself that I was here to stay, if only to be the first one to witness those moments.

--

Every word from every character was a pinprick to my ears. This evening, I sat high above the Festival Theatre stage calling a preview performance of *Twelfth Night* for the show's actual stage manager, Colleen Stephenson, who was incredibly ill. Sebastian was onstage, waxing poetic before his marriage to Olivia. It was nearly the end of the show, and in spite of my success so far, it still felt as if I was wearing Colleen's clothes.

SEB.   His counsel now might do me golden service;
         For though my soul disputes well with my sense,
         That this may be some error, but no madness,
         Yet doth this accident and flood of fortune
         So far exceed all instance, all discourse,
         That I am ready to distrust mine eyes
         And wrangle with my reason that persuades me
         To any other trust but that I am mad
         Or else the lady's mad; yet, if 'twere so,

I touched my hand to the up-centre entrance switch on the cue light box and flicked it up.

         She could not sway her house, command her followers,
         Take and give back affairs and their dispatch
         With such a smooth, discreet and stable bearing

I flicked the switch down. Olivia and the Priest entered, right on cue.

         As I perceive she does: there's something in't
         That is deceiveable. But here the lady comes.

It was strange, following the rhythm of a show that wasn't mine. I had faintly noticed it before, but now, faced with motions I hadn't practised and actors I hadn't watched and words I hadn't prompted and a set I hadn't seen prior, it became patently clear that every production had a rhythm. And, in this instance, Colleen was its keeper.

When I found Colleen earlier that morning, she looked awful. Her brown, wavy hair was knotted at the ends, and there were heavy bags under her eyes. She had a wastebasket beside her bed, which didn't look to be used but seemed primed for the using.

"Nora," she said, sitting up as I entered, her script in my hands. "I'm so sorry for this."

"Don't worry about it," I said, trying to assuage her guilt. "I brought your book."

"I would call the show if I could."

"I know. How are you feeling?"

"Like somebody is — jabbing me in the sides." She then winced and clutched herself, as if to demonstrate the point. "The show is pretty straightforward though."

"That's comforting."

"I'll take you through—" she began, before lurching over the side of her bed and dry-heaving into the basket. I rubbed her back with both altruistic concern and selfish urgency. Neither of us knew how long it would take to get through this process because there was no formal procedure for it. It was rare that stage managers ever understudied one another. We were just expected to call the show regardless of loss of life or limb. "Sorry," Colleen mumbled. "Feels like something wants to come up, but nothing does."

"It's okay. So, *Twelfth Night*."

"Yes."

Flipping the blue cover open, we went through the production page by page. Thankfully, Colleen's script looked much better than she did. Everything was neatly laid out in pencil, legible to anybody who might need to read it. Unfortunately, there were certain moments that couldn't be translated to the page.

"In this section," I said, pointing to Olivia's text, "just before Viola enters, you've written 'anticipate on Maria veil.' What am I anticipating?"

"Yes, Olivia asks for a veil, and Maria gives her one. You need to anticipate when Olivia will be done veiling herself and call the cue before then."

"Right. As opposed to Olivia being done, and there being a pause and then Viola entering."

"Exactly."

"Got it."

Just then Colleen scooped up the wastebasket. I waited patiently, impatiently, until she was finished, and we continued on to the end of the play. When I left I was certain I was less nervous but still didn't know whether or not that meant anything.

"Warning Lights 153 auto-follow 154, Sound 24, Music 24," I said over the headset. Nearing the final scene of the play, I felt like an air traffic controller signalling an empty runway to a landing plane.

> OLIV.   That my most jealous and too doubtful soul
>   May live at peace. He shall conceal it
>   Whiles you are willing it shall come to note,
>   What time we will our celebration keep
>   According to my birth. What do you say?

I flipped the left door, left tunnel, and orchestra cue light switches up.

> SEB.   I'll follow this good man, and go with you;
>   And, having sworn truth, ever will be true.

> OLIV.   Then lead the way, good father; and heavens so shine,
>   That they may fairly note this act of mine!

"Lights 153 and Sound 24, go," I said, as I flipped the orchestra switch down. Seeing Olivia, Sebastian, and the Priest reach the right door, I turned the page. Suddenly my pulse quickened. Nothing was happening. With one finger still on the left tunnel switch, I leaned

SHAWN DESOUZA-COELHO

over the desk and peered down at the stage. It was completely empty. Music was playing, but the stage was completely empty.

This can't be right.

I shook the page in front of me, as if answers would somehow fall out of it.

What am I missing? What am I missing? Did Colleen say something about this section? Shit. I can't remember. Shit. No time. Uh. Go. Go!

I flicked the left tunnel switch down, and watched in confusion as Feste entered from the left door and Fabian entered from the left tunnel. I simmered in that state until the show was over and I found myself in the stage management office combing over Colleen's book with bewildered eyes. Where I had stumbled and where I swore I'd seen nothing but a blank space, the letters "LD" glared back at me. It was then I realized I didn't cue the left door. Tom Kneebone's Feste was waiting for a cue that never came.

How did I miss that?

Leaning back in my chair, I sort of laughed to myself. Colleen wouldn't have needed the letters at all. She would have felt them in her bones and known their place in time.

--

"Take it again," Robin called from the auditorium, and the air continued to stiffen. On the oaken thrust of the Third Stage, which was converted from the old casino on Lakeside Drive to its current form by Gascon in '71, the actors diligently saddled up. *The Importance of Being Earnest* was the sixth show Robin had directed this season, and this morning's rehearsal had been tough. Richard Monette had faced the brunt of it as he tried to cobble together a refined English accent, which was no easy task for a Quebecer. But now, in the afternoon, it was clear Robin had moved on.

"From Lady Bracknell's entrance, please," I told Bill Hutt. He nodded and left the stage. Kathleen steeled herself and followed. "Whenever you're ready."

Lady Bracknell and Gwendolyn entered.

LADY BRACKNELL.   Good afternoon, dear Algernon, I hope you are
behaving very well.

ALGERNON.   I'm feeling very well, Aunt Augusta.

LADY BRACKNELL.   That's not quite the same thing. In fact the two
things rarely go together.

Lady Bracknell bowed to Jack. Algernon turned to Gwendolyn.

ALGERNON.   Dear me, you are smart!

GWENDOLYN.   I am always smart! Am I not, Mr. Worthing?

"Stop," Robin called, and Kathleen whipped her character,
Gwendolyn, off as if it were a nasty bug. She shook her head and
beneath her dark curly hair and petite frame, I could tell that her
patience was riffled, that there was only so much more of this she
could take. "Let's do it again."
   I didn't say where to take it from and neither Bill nor Kathleen
asked. They just left the stage and, after a moment, entered.

LADY BRACKNELL.   Good afternoon, dear Algernon, I hope you are
behaving very well.

ALGERNON.   I'm feeling very well, Aunt Augusta.

LADY BRACKNELL.   That's not quite the same thing. In fact the two
things rarely go together.

Lady Bracknell bowed to Jack. Algernon turned to Gwendolyn.

ALGERNON.   Dear me, you are smart!

SHAWN DESOUZA-COELHO

GWENDOLYN. I am always smart! Am I not, Mr. Worthing?

"That's enough," Robin called yet again. All at once the actors faced him. "Kathleen," he continued. "I want you to play the scene as if you were a frightened bat."

Kathleen looked as if she were about to say something, but instead she said, simply, "Okay."

"Take it again from the entrance."

The actors returned to their places and the pair entered. For the first time, in the moments between their entrance and Robin's next intervention, I questioned my purpose in this room.

ALGERNON. Dear me, you are smart!

GWENDOLYN. I am always smart! Am I not, Mr. Worthing?

"A frightened bat, Kathleen!" Robin yelled.

"I don't know what you want from me!" Kathleen erupted. "I don't know what that is. A frightened bat? What am I supposed to do with that? What is it you want me to do?"

"Let's have a break, shall we?" Robin said, turning to me, his voice suppressing something else altogether.

"Fifteen minutes, please," I called. "Fifteen minutes."

Kathleen stormed offstage, to the surprise of no one. I left to follow, feeling as though it were my responsibility to console her, if for nothing else than to ensure her return. I went to the green room, but she wasn't there. Neither was she in the lobby, nor outside the building. Kathleen was gone.

Great.

I looked up and felt the heat of the sun on my face.

Should I have said something?

I sighed.

Now what do I do?

"Are we back, Nora?" Robin asked, glancing at his watch. I had just returned to the auditorium.

"Yes, but . . ."

"But?"

"Kathleen has left."

"What do you mean she's left?"

"I can't find her. She must have gone home."

Robin considered this for a moment and then, as simply as if he were turning a page, he said, "Let's break for the day."

The next rehearsal, Robin welcomed Pat Galloway into the cast. She would be playing the part of Gwendolyn. It was that quick. Strangely, as I watched Robin acquaint Pat with the stage, I wasn't surprised. Before the season began, Paddy McEntee had been summarily dismissed from the Festival after years of loyal service, over a homophobic remark he made at the bar after one too many drinks. I defended him, citing that we've all said and done things that don't define us, and I knew Tom would have too had he not already left to work at the NAC. But from that defence it became unclear whether or not I'd be part of the '75 season. Eventually, I was told I would be, but I wouldn't be working on any of Robin's shows. Then Robin's enigmatic note crossed the desk of PSM Jack Merigold and made its way to me. "I will have Nora for *Measure*."

"Let's take it from the top," Robin said as he strode up the aisle to his seat in the house.

"Beginners, standing by, please," I called to the actors. I still didn't know what to make of any of it, still wondered what my role was in these politics I cared nothing for.

7:00 a.m.

I open my eyes and the first thing I notice is the sweat on my forehead. I've had the nightmare again, the one where I rush to a performance I'm late for, only to throw open the stage management booth door and realize I'm in the wrong theatre. I take a deep breath and, through still-blurry vision, check the time.

Six hours of sleep. Not bad.

I swing out of bed and get dressed. I go over the day, as if it were more strategy than schedule.

Tech week for Antony and Cleopatra, *rehearsing* Measure for Measure — *no, that's not today, thank God — and PSM duties. Tech week: the crucible of theatre wherein all technical elements for which stage management will ultimately be responsible in performance, from lights to costumes, are painstakingly added to rehearsal. It'll be a ten out of twelve for the actors, so they'll work ten hours over a twelve-hour workday. Of course, that doesn't apply to stage management. Why would it? As long as we get eight hours away from the theatre, we're free to be fed to an insatiable sixteen-hour day and everybody's ass is covered.*

Downstairs my kitchen glows with the morning's light. I see the empty bowl on the floor by the counter and I search for the cat food. My memory these days has no patience for the little things. I also just bought the house not long ago, so I haven't settled on where everything should be. Boxes, open and otherwise, line every wall. As I search, a part of me soars at the idea that these walls are mine, that I own this house. Yellow brick with blue shutters, tall ceilings, and an awkward layout: the foyer for some reason leads straight to the dining room. I wanted it the moment I saw it.

Finally finding the cat food tucked deep in the back of a corner cupboard, I put some in a bowl, and set it on the floor with some water. I check the time. 7:45 a.m. I grab my coat from the foyer bench and run out the door.

8:00 a.m.

At the Festival Theatre, the stage management office is empty. I hang up my coat, pick up my script and my hunter-green tackle box containing all variety of marker, pen, pencil, thread, needle, and anything else that a stage manager might need in the line of duty, and take them into the auditorium.

As I make my way onto the stage, I pass through the bolts of draped greyish-purple fabric filling the hole upstage centre where Robin had done the inconceivable and made the iconic Festival Theatre balcony removable. Surprisingly, it took only two men and a hydraulic lift to push it anywhere, though it was too big to go down any of the backstage corridors, so it was just masked backstage by a black V-shaped flat.

From the deck, I spot Gil Wechsler standing in one of the aisles. A lighting designer at the Festival for many years, he's a thickly bearded man with big curly hair and a short fuse. "Good morning," I say.

"Is it?" Gil replies, before whispering something into his headset. He and the head electrician are checking lamps. High above me, lighting instruments flash on and off. If one doesn't work, it's swapped out for another and Gil probably twitches.

I place my script in front of the cue light box on the table in the auditorium, next to the gooseneck microphone that allows me to make announcements backstage, and rest my tackle box by my feet. Sitting, I throw on my headset.

"Hello, hello," I say plainly as I flip through the channels.

"Hello," is the response I get from all of them.

As much a prayer as an assertion, I tell myself this will be a good day.

8:30 a.m.

Michael Benoit arrives onstage and flashes me a smile. I can't help but blush. He's a new addition to stage management this year. He's my age, short, with a slight beard and short brown hair. When I had him over for wine a little while ago, we listened to Johnny Mathis vinyls and talked about ourselves and our cats — his being back in Montreal with his wife — until he left tipsy and I fought the urge to kiss him.

"Downstage centre, please," Gil calls to him. Michael moves accordingly. Gil whispers into his headset, and then Michael is lit in warm yellow. He squints to see into the auditorium. "Thank you."

Michael intentionally signed up to be a light walker this morning, his day off, which means that his sole responsibility is to stand wherever Gil wants him to, whenever Gil wants him to, while Gil sets lighting levels. I had told him how much of a hothead Gil could be sometimes, how in Russia two lighting operators weren't writing down a word

Gil was saying, so he flew off the handle and yelled, "Call me a cab, I'm leaving!" I had yelled back, "You're a Jew in Russia! Sit down!" So, Michael thought that if he gave Gil something pretty to look at, Gil would be a bit more docile.

I glance up at Gil. He hasn't screamed yet, so I would say it's working. I look back down at Michael. It's certainly working on me.

9:30 a.m.

Everybody else is on a coffee break, so I head back to the stage management office with Michael. In the hallway, he tells me he'll grab me one, pats my bum, and heads to the green room.

Inside, I find our production assistant, Heather Kitchen, already hunched over my desk. Colleen is at the other end of the room working.

"Good morning, Nora," Heather says.

"Morning."

"Sorry I couldn't drive you this morning. My car is still in the shop."

"It's fine. It's definitely not your responsibility." What I don't say is, "Of course, nobody knows exactly what a PA's responsibilities are."

Most mornings Heather drives Colleen, Vince Berns, and myself to work. One morning, Colleen got in and said, "You know, Nora, that house you love is up for sale." Heather drove by it so I could see for myself. That was a Tuesday. On the Wednesday and Thursday, Heather helped me put together a financial plan. I bought the house on the Friday. I'm still trying to figure out a way to thank her.

"We missed a double-call," Heather says.

"Oh?"

"A fitting and a voice class. The actor came in just before you did."

I'm just happy it was caught in time. "Let's fix it."

What ensues between Heather and me is a whirlwind of, "If we move this to here . . . No, that will conflict with this . . . But she's got time here . . . Yes, but here might work better . . . Give her a call and see . . . What is it? . . . She says she's double-booked too . . . You're kidding," all as we untangle the inevitable knots in the complex weave that is the Stratford Festival daily schedule. In my first season in stage management, not so long ago, I carried a stack of these around in my arms at the end of each day. That's Heather's job now. I'm in charge of creating them. But I'm too busy to feel even pride. Down the left-hand side we have every company member, and across the top we have blocks of time throughout the day. All rehearsals, costume and wig fittings, voice lessons, acting classes, scheduled interviews, and any number of other things are represented with different coloured pencils. Each theatre is responsible for its own daily schedule, but all of this information is culled, by hand, from the weekly schedule, created right here in the Festival Theatre stage management office by the PSM.

The weekly schedule, too, is a large grid. It shows each weekday versus each rehearsal hall and stage in all three theatres. This information is culled from the master schedule, created prior to the season's start. This schedule, too, is a large grid showing the primary, secondary, and tertiary rehearsals as well as the show dates for every production in the season. There are ten productions this season and there were fourteen last season, each one getting over a hundred hours of rehearsal and a combined total of hundreds upon hundreds of performances. Thankfully, it's the production manager's job to make all of those puzzle pieces fit. My job is to keep any number of them floating around in my head on a daily basis, and any change to the schedule, like rectifying double-booking an actor, means other appointments need to be shifted, only slightly on a good day.

As Heather and I work, Michael arrives with hot coffee. He hands it to me and I can feel the eyes of the whole building on me. I'm his boss. But even that's not the reason. It's because he's married, and as a woman I should respect that. To this I wonder, *shouldn't he?* I chug half of the coffee, as if the only place in the world it belonged was inside me. It burns slightly on the way down, and I'm thankful for the extra spur in my side. Satisfied, Michael heads back to the stage, leaving me to squeeze every last minute out of the break. I set the half-empty cup on my desk.

When I leave for the auditorium the schedule isn't nearly complete. But I remind myself we have until 3:00 p.m. to get a draft in. Afterwards, we'll correct any double-calls we see.

<h2 style="text-align:center">9:45 a.m.</h2>

Back in the auditorium, Gil continues setting levels with the head electrician. Michael and the other light walkers shift their positions when asked, standing around otherwise. It's impolite and distracting for them to even chat among themselves.

Meanwhile, I'm taking notes for the sound cues over my headset on a different channel and recording any changes in the script. I use the phone on my desk to keep up to date with stage management on any occurrences around the Festival. It's my job to know where every person is at all times, which is impossible. But if somebody goes missing, I'm to blame. And even if I'm not, I'll take it just so we can move on.

<h2 style="text-align:center">11:00 a.m.</h2>

The light walkers leave and Michael winks goodbye at me, knowing we probably won't see one another for the rest of the day. The actors of *Antony and Cleopatra* have all filed in for the beginning of rehearsal and fight warm-up. Before Robin's tenure, we had eight-hour rehearsals from Monday to Saturday, and Sundays off. Now, we have seven-hour rehearsals with an optional one-hour warm-up that Robin sometimes doesn't attend. Everybody treats it as mandatory, though, because sometimes Robin does attend. We also have Monday off instead of Sunday, which makes way more sense because no dentist is open on a Sunday.

Maggie Smith takes her position to warm up for the scene in which Cleopatra assaults the Messenger who has just brought news that Antony has gone back to Rome and married Octavia. The fight director, Patrick Crean, enters through the purple-grey fabric, greeting

SHAWN DESOUZA-COELHO

everybody. He's a tall British man with a thin moustache and receding hair. He was here from the very beginning of the Festival. He knows that he's leading this call. As the fight director, he has already written out all of the moves in any given stage fight, so my role as stage manager in fight calls is to document only where the fighters begin and end up. In other words, to simply keep tabs on everybody.

Maggie is a thin woman, with large eyes and equally large sense of humour. She's funny in that dry British way. In many respects she's the crown jewel of Robin's company this year. She's anything but a diva, though — she's always approachable if not herself approaching. Still, the other actors can't help but tiptoe around her.

Early one rehearsal, a couple of weeks ago in Rehearsal Hall 1, we watched the same scene play out. Maggie's Cleopatra was onstage with Jan Kudelka's Charmian, Patricia Idlette's Iras, and Gregory Wanless's Alexas. Maggie had just struck Nick Mancuso's Messenger as Paddy Crean looked on.

MESS.   Good madam, patience.

CLEO.   What say you? Hence,

Cleopatra struck him again and Charmian, Iras, and Alexas attempted to restrain her.

> Horrible villain! or I'll spurn thine eyes
> Like balls before me; my nails shall plough thy—

She jerked towards the Messenger and then, suddenly, Maggie dropped her character. She turned to her scene partners, who were no longer holding her. "You have to really stop me," Maggie urged. The room tittered. Jan, Patricia, and Greg all looked at one another, a bit embarrassed.

"Be a little more rough with her," Paddy said to them. "Run it again from after the first hit."

"From 'Good madam, patience,' please," I said to Maggie before offering her the scene. The actors reset.

MESS.   Good madam, patience.

CLEO.   What say you? Hence,

Cleopatra struck the Messenger again. The other characters gripped her shoulders tightly.

> Horrible villain! or I'll spurn thine eyes
> Like balls before me; my nails shall plough thy flesh.

She lunged forward, struggling with great might until finally Maggie dropped her character again. She turned to her captors and said, "And now you have to let me go!" The entire room fell apart laughing and the three culprits flushed red.

"Be a little less rough with her," Paddy chimed. "Let's take it again."

On the Festival stage, the fight goes as planned and Cleopatra beats the Messenger for the appropriate amount of time. Robin doesn't show. Paddy spends the remainder of the warm-up working through some other fighting bits before the actors break for lunch.

12:00 p.m.

On this day, out of necessity, I forgo lunch and hustle back to the office to continue crafting the daily schedule.

"I think I found a solution," Heather says, showing me what she has done with the schedule in my absence. "We move the voice class to the day after, and the fitting to a time when the actor has a secondary rehearsal that he isn't called for, and the designer is free."

"Is the voice coach free that day?" Heather hesitates. "I'll check."

SHAWN DESOUZA-COELHO

I'm on the phone with the voice coach when Clayton Shields walks in. He's the head of the wigs department at the Festival, a tall, soft, balding man in his mid-thirties.

"Cookie?" he says, stopping short when I hold a finger up. He loves giving everybody nicknames. Mine is Cookie. I'm not really sure why.

I continue talking to the voice coach, finding a time that works for her, and periodically checking the schedule until we finally agree on one. I hang up and turn to Clayton.

"What can I do for you?" I ask, remembering the half-empty coffee nearby.

"Just wanted to say that the eyelashes came in this morning."

"Great to hear. She'll be pleased."

I take a sip of coffee, flinch, and take another. It's cold, but it's also right there, and I'm aware that life is an endless compromise.

Clayton slaps the door frame twice and leaves. I turn to find Heather looking at me curiously, as if to ask, "Eyelashes?"

"Maggie only wears custom-made sable fur false eyelashes. Clayton offered her other kinds, but she refused. So we had to hunt down her supplier in England, mostly by calling around from one place to the next based on recommendations from Maggie and other actors. Once we found the supplier, we had to call them and have them ship some over."

Heather's eyes go wide, and I have to admit that even Maggie has her diva moments. "What did the voice coach say?" she then asks.

Uh . . .

"I'll call her back," Heather smiled. "You eat."

"Eat?"

It's only then I notice the sandwich on my desk, turkey breast with lettuce and tomato. I look curiously at Colleen.

She smirks and says, "Michael." I feel embraced.

1:00 p.m.

Having inhaled half the sandwich, I return to the auditorium and call places for the top of *Antony and Cleopatra*. All at once I hear a rush of thudding feet, the noise only barely muffled by the fabric draped where the balcony once was. This is a problem not even Robin foresaw. The house can hear everything going on backstage and vice versa. Our only solution is to just be quiet, which is what everybody backstage should be doing anyway.

When the actors are set and Robin is perched behind me with the designers, I call the top of the show. In the darkness that lingers briefly between the house lights being out and the stage lights coming on, my head starts to throb. I'm surprised it took so long. Yesterday it started much earlier. Through it, I focus on my cues. "Lights 299," I say over headset. "Go." Philo enters, and the show begins.

As the show progresses, Robin and the designers scribble furiously. Some things aren't working. What those things are, I don't exactly know, but I'll hear about them this evening when notes are given to all departments. Occasionally, I'm told to stop the show — by Robin, by Gil, by whomever — so something can be checked. This makes sense, of course, since we only have two hours allotted before the next coffee break and that isn't nearly enough time to do a full run-through of the show. That's what tonight's five-hour block is for.

Where the cues are off, I, too, scribble. Actors are late for their entrance and I have to troubleshoot why. It could be that I was late on the cue light or that they weren't paying attention or that something messed up in a costume change backstage or they were injured or dead. The first of these is the easiest to fix, so I always hope it's the case. It's usually not, though.

"Thank you, everybody," I say into the microphone. "Fifteen minutes." My voice bounces around backstage and Robin shakes his head, knowing he might have shot himself in the foot.

3:00 p.m.

Back in the office, I take two Aspirin with what's left of my cold coffee. I finalize the daily schedule with Heather, correcting all of the double-calls that we know of. There will be more, of course. There

SHAWN DESOUZA-COELHO

always are. Nobody can possibly get this right every time. Though it's expected that we do.

3:20 p.m.

In the auditorium, we try to pick up where we left off before the break, but one of the actors is late in returning. I put out a call throughout the building for him to come to the stage. After six minutes pass, he rushes on. I know the exact amount of time he's wasted because that's six minutes we no longer have to rehearse the production. I don't tell him this because the tremor in his apology tells me he knows. Besides, I'm not the person he's got to worry about disappointing — *that* guy is sitting behind me, a few rows up.

As we rehearse, I find myself going on autopilot, the circuits in me slowly breaking from the load. I miss a cue, and it throws the whole scene off to the point where we have to go back and start it over again. I apologize the moment it happens, not giving them reasons. Nobody wants those. They want solutions, answers. They want to move on. The Aspirin aren't working very well, and my head continues to throb as the play stutters along. My whole body feels anchored down and I feel myself sinking lower. It's days like these that make me question why I ever bothered to become a PSM in the first place. I thought I was ready for it, but the truth was I didn't really know what *it* was. Sure, I'd seen others ride the bike before, watched where they put their hands and how they moved their feet. But riding it myself isn't the same at all. Right now, I'm not even riding. I'm falling. I take a deep breath, grit my teeth, and regain my composure.

5:00 p.m.

"How's your headache?" Heather asks once I've returned to the office where she alone sits.

"It's not worse," I say glibly. "So that's something."

As we scan through the completed schedule for the next day, there are indeed double-calls that need correcting. One actor has been booked in two rehearsals, one for a show he's not even a part of, which was careless on my part. A director has an interview when he's supposed to be in rehearsal, so that's not going to fly either. It isn't Robin. In some ways we're lucky Robin is directing seven out of the ten productions this season. He can't be in two places at once, and that's six fewer directors to schedule. None of us knows where he gets the energy, but it certainly makes things easier for us. It would have to be a very off day to double-book him.

As we correct the schedule, I hear grumbling. I hold my hand to my stomach, almost shocked at how loud it is.

"Eat the rest of your sandwich," Heather says, pointing to it on my desk. I had completely forgotten I had it. I had certainly barely touched it: there's still a whole half. I take a bite. The bread is soggy from the lettuce and tomato, but I don't care. This is supposed to be the dinner break, and this soggy sandwich is food and it is good if only for its rarity. "Nora?" Heather is speaking to me. "Nora?" I can hear her voice, but it suddenly seems so far away, like she's speaking to me from the bottom of a well. "Nora." She shakes me, and I snap to. "Are you okay?" I nod. I look down at my empty hands. I had completely eaten my sandwich and didn't even realize it. I had gone on autopilot again.

"I'm fine," I say, looking up at her.

When did I sit down?

"I'll go distribute these," she says, holding in her arms a stack of completed daily schedules for the next day. I nod.

When did we finish?

Heather leaves, and I check the clock. I have five minutes to spare before rehearsal continues, but I can't afford to get used to relaxing. I get up and head back to the auditorium.

6:00 p.m.

We pick up from where we left off, entering the scene where Octavius Caesar is telling his two generals, Maecenas and Agrippa, that Antony has made Cleopatra Queen of Egypt.

OCT.   Contemning Rome, he has done all this, and more—

"Thank you!" I call, stopping the actors onstage. They drop their characters and stand around silently while we work out an issue with the cue. As we work, I can hear a growing hum. I can't figure out if it's coming from the headset, so I take it off and listen. It's still there. I look around and realize other people hear it too. I'm almost relieved that I haven't lost my mind.

"Do something about that," Robin says to me, pointing dismissively to the stage. It's then I realize what the humming is: actors talking backstage.

I put on my headset and switch to the ASM channel. "Tell the actors to be quiet backstage, please."

"Quiet backstage," I hear one of the ASMs call out, and the humming promptly ceases. In its place are apologetic murmurs and then stone silence. It's that simple — everybody gets it. Technical rehearsals are tests of stamina, and this can get to people in different ways. Gil gives himself an aneurysm, while Robin is mostly stoic, and the actors, forced to hang around the backstage area waiting for some cue or instrument or speaker to work properly so they can enter and do their job, become chatty. Mostly, this is fine, because nobody in the auditorium can hear it. But with the balcony gone, we can hear everything. I'm still waiting for the moment when Robin realizes it's a mistake, but it hasn't come. Even as Shakespeare's poetry evaporates into the backstage area, as opposed to bouncing off the balcony and back into the house, Robin is immovable.

We run the scene again, and Domini Blythe's Octavia is off her mark when she enters. I can't tell if she's at fault, or whether the blocking had changed in rehearsal and I had just neglected to document it. I write down my question so I can bring it up during the notes session following rehearsal.

11:00 p.m.

Rehearsal ends, and while we haven't gone through the show start to finish even once, we're right on schedule. Actors file onto the deck and sit, looking as if they've just dropped anchor. They know it has been a long day, but it'll be over soon.

"Good," Robin says, addressing the cast from the house. "Really good." He flips back to the beginning of his notepad, to the start of the show. "Let's see. Ah, yes, Mags . . ."

"The top of block seventeen," I say when it's time for my notes. "Octavia's entrance into Caesar's house—"

"My fault," Domini confesses, her long brown hair quivering as she shakes her head. "I was hung up on the old blocking."

"Do you need me to remind you of the new blocking?"

"No, no. I've got it. I'm not sure what happened. I've got it."

"Okay."

Selfishly, I'm relieved that the mistake isn't mine.

We solve what else we can then and there, and any problems that can't be solved we table until the next rehearsal. At 11:55 p.m., I break rehearsal. The company thanks me. It's a formality, but as I watch them lumber backstage I think they really do feel grateful to go home. I know I do.

12:00 a.m.

The moon is bright when I come out through the stage door. It looks as if the town is dipped in blue. An actor offers me a ride home, but I decline. I'm suddenly wide awake and know I need the walk to work off the day.

SHAWN DESOUZA-COELHO

I start down Queen Street and turn right once I reach Ontario. Orangey-yellow lamplight pools along Ontario Street and rarely does a car pass by. Reaching Nile Street, I turn left. It's dark, and as I stroll by a playground my mind wanders. I think about the enormous hill outside of Falstaff School on William Street that I'd have to climb to get to the front entrance when I was a kid, and I wonder if it's just as big now. I think about Fred, getting married to his fiancée, Janice, and the ceremony I'll miss because I'm stage managing a performance. I wonder how much more I'll miss due to scheduling decisions beyond my control. I wonder if I'll ever do this long enough that I won't be bothered by it.

When I reach Douro Street, I turn right and spy a raccoon walking away from a turned-over garbage can across the road. I stop and stare at it for a while as my thoughts drift to my new home, and the anxiety brought by being a single woman working in the theatre. I was afraid I wouldn't get a mortgage, and I was surprised when I did. Just two weeks after I moved in, I applied for an American Express credit card and was declined without any explanation. I work in a risky business, sure, but there are any number of men in my department who have an American Express. Yet, they aren't university educated like I am. They aren't department managers like I am. They don't own their own homes or even make as much money as I do. They haven't even been employed with the Festival as long as I have. The only reason I can think of is that I'm a woman, the truly sad part being that this is a natural thought for a woman to have. When I was declined, I vowed never to patronize them; my victory in defeat.

Finally home, I throw my coat on the kitchen counter, and stroke my cat half-heartedly. Upstairs, I undress and crawl into bed. I let out a huge sigh as my head hits the pillow, feeling suddenly eighty years older. It's 12:30 a.m. and by the time I fall asleep it'll be even later. Tomorrow is another ten out of twelve. I stare up at the ceiling and begin my nightly ritual of reciting the full text of *King Lear*, from the start, until I fall asleep; a holdover from all my time spent working with Alan when he understudied Bill.

NORA.   It did always seem so to us: but now, in the division
          of the kingdom, it appears not which of the dukes he
          values most; for equalities are so weighed, that curi-
          osity in neither can make choice of either's moiety.

NORA.   Is not this your son, my lord?

NORA.   His breeding, sir, hath been at my charge . . .

SHAWN DESOUZA-COELHO

 In our makeshift rehearsal hall, I noticed a cobweb had grown large in one corner. We were performing *King Lear* at the Neptune Theatre, a little jewel on the corner of a sloping street in downtown Halifax, too small to contain even its own administrative offices or rehearsal space. Afternoon light poured wanly through the arched windows of the abandoned church we were using instead. A derelict cross hung sadly on the wall to one side. It seemed I was looking everywhere but at the scene unfolding before me. A tremor ran down my leg and I put my hand to my stomach. I needed to pee again.

John Wood leaned back on the stage management table and took a cigarette from my pack as he eyed his actors mired in their work onstage. John was my first director as a professional stage manager back at Theatre Calgary, and he was just as prickly now as he was then. Middle-aged, dressed in a black turtleneck and blue jeans, with long shaggy hair and a moustache, he lit up. He wasn't a smoker, unless it was other people's cigarettes. This meant I had started smoking again. I didn't mind. If it kept John level then I'd suffer the financial burden gladly. Richard Blackburn, a tall, handsome actor, set himself downstage right for his entrance into the woods as Edgar. I felt my stomach tighten.

"Whenever you're ready," I said to him. Richard steeled himself and then entered.

EDG.   I heard myself proclaim'd;
                 And by the happy hollow of a tree
                 Escaped the hunt. No port is free; no place,
                 That guard, and most unusual vigilance,
                 Does not attend my taking. Whiles I may 'scape,
                 I will preserve myself: and am bethought
                 To take the basest and most poorest shape
                 That ever penury, in contempt of man,
                 Brought near to beast—

"What are you doing?" John called out.
"I . . . uh," Richard tried, before John cut him off.
"Start over."
Richard took his place, and began again.

EDG.   I heard myself proclaim'd;
                 And by the happy hollow of a tree
                 Escaped the hunt. No port is free; no place,
                 That guard, and most unusual—

"What are you doing now?" John repeated, and then before Richard could answer added, "Start again." He took a drag and I felt a twinge in my side. I was shaking my leg under the table now.

SHAWN DESOUZA-COELHO

Richard set himself, and began again.

EDG.   I heard myself proclaim'd;
                And by the happy hollow of a tree
                Escaped the hunt. No port is free; no place,
                That guard, and most unusual—

"What is that?" John asked, pointedly. Richard just stared. Around him the other actors looked as if they were watching some other tragedy. I wanted then to reach out to Richard, to assure him none of us was okay with this. But I didn't. "Take it again," John said.

Richard began again, a child too afraid to do anything for fear even the right move would somehow be wrong.

EDG.   I heard myself proclaim'd;
                And by the happy hollow of a tree
                Escaped the hunt. No port is free; no place—

"Say the text!" John screamed. "Nora, give him a chair."

I leapt up, and as I set a chair beside Richard, I was consumed with feelings of insurrection, confusion, and that same familiar impotence. I couldn't look anybody in the eye.

"Sit!" John said to Richard. "Nora, tie his hands together behind the chair."

Not knowing what else to do, I got some rope from the heap in the corner where we'd piled props and began tying Richard to the chair. In any other situation I would have said, "Not on your life, John," but here in rehearsal it felt like my duty. If Richard had told me to stop I would have, but instead he acquiesced. Maybe he also felt like he had no choice. I had to pee more than ever, suddenly understanding why. I just wanted to be anywhere but in this room, bound to responsibilities I still didn't fully understand.

I had recently tried to read Lawrence Stern's book, *Stage Management*, only because, after almost ten years, I felt like I should be reading something about this profession. I couldn't get through it.

It was very American, touching on producing and getting money for commercial theatres. It also tackled some of the daily responsibilities of a stage manager. There was nothing in it about buying cigarettes because it helped calm the director. There was nothing in it about tying actors to chairs.

"Now, *tell* me the story!" John demanded, after I had finished knotting the rope. "It's words, not hands."

With that, Richard began again. Sure enough, John interrupted him, the whole scene now resembling an interrogation more than a rehearsal. Few people watched. I felt I had to.

After I broke rehearsal, Richard was thinly stoic. Eric Donkin and some of the other actors offered to take him out for a drink, and I was glad they did. All that mattered to me now was Richard finding it in himself to come back tomorrow. If he did that looking through the bottom of an empty pint glass, then so be it.

Once they'd all left, and with a still-nagging bladder, I turned to John, who was packing his bag.

"That was too much," I said, partly because, with John, I knew I could.

"You think so?" he asked. He sounded as if I'd told him the weather.

"If you had asked what sex he was, he wouldn't have known because everything he'd tried, you rejected."

As if ignoring my comment, John stated, "He's better now than this morning. He'll be better tomorrow than today." He then took another cigarette from me, lit it, finished packing his bag, and left.

I didn't know what else to say to John's belief that Richard's growth as an actor justified what went on. Who was I to disagree? I was neither director nor actor. I was the stage manager, and instinct told me it wasn't my place to say or do anything, to take sides. Instinct told me to just make sure Richard came back tomorrow. But, as I packed my pencils away in the solitude of the abandoned church, glancing at the door through which Richard had left in the care of his concerned colleagues, I briefly wondered whose job it was to make sure I did the same.

SHAWN DESOUZA-COELHO

--

"Whenever you're ready," I said, sitting behind my table in Rehearsal Hall 1. My book was open in front of me, and Chris Blake was standing to my left at his entrance, a well-worn script and pencil in his hands. He flipped to the next page and ran his fingers through his short curly hair, as if to comb away his fatigue. We were well into the evening, and the tired sun was clocking out.

Onstage, there were two benches, downstage left and upstage right, the scene set up exactly as it would be on the two evenings Chris was to go on as Claudio in *Much Ado About Nothing*. Possessing the unlikely gift of foresight, Chris came to me for help the second he knew about the scheduling glitch that rendered the actual Claudio unavailable on those nights. I was more than happy to oblige because, regardless of the reason, be it death or the will of the actor or clerical error, being an understudy was always terrifying. There was just never enough time to do the job justice. So, if Chris wanted to learn, I wanted to help. It was that simple.

Chris entered and I spoke the first lines of the scene as Don Pedro. Also onstage was Leonato, but only through the sound of my measured voice.

"Come, shall we hear music?"

CLAU.   Yea, my good lord. How still the evening is
                  As hush'd on purpose—

"That's right," I said, seeing him point downstage as if to ask where he was meant to land. He moved there as he spoke.

                  As hush'd on purpose to grace harmony!

"See you where Benedick hath hid himself?"

CLAU.   O, very well, my lord: the music ended,
                  We'll fit the kid-fox with a pennyworth.

"Balthasar enters from the right tunnel."

"Over to here, yeah?" Chris asked, pointing to his left at the first step down from the deck.

I nodded, and continued on. "'Come, Balthasar, we'll hear that song again.' Blah, blah. On Benedick's 'Now, divine air!' you lie down on your side, leaning on your elbow." Chris scribbled the note into his script and then followed it. "As Balthasar sings you lie on your back. That's right. Don Pedro: 'By my troth, a good song.'"

"There's a move here?"

"Yes. You go to Leonato on the bench, downstage left. Blah, blah. You two are chatting silently. Balthasar leaves. Don Pedro: 'Come hither, Leonato. What was it you told me of to-day, that your niece Beatrice was in love with Signior Benedick?'"

CLAU.   O, ay: stalk on. stalk on; the fowl sits. I did
          never think that lady would love any man.

"Have loved," I corrected.

"Sorry," Chris said.

"No need to apologize. From 'O, ay: stalk on.' Also, you're at the other bench by now."

Chris adjusted and then continued.

CLAU.   O, ay: stalk on. stalk on; the fowl sits. I did
          never think that lady would have loved any man.

"Blah, blah. Don Pedro is downstage right. Don Pedro: 'May be she doth but counterfeit.'" Claudio paused for a moment. "'Faith, like enough,'" I prompted, sensing Chris's need.

CLAU.   Faith, like enough.

"Leonato: 'O God, counterfeit! There was never counterfeit of passion came so near the life of passion as she discovers it.' Don Pedro: 'Why, what effects of passion shows she?'"

CLAU.   Bait the hook well; this fish will bite.

"I have a note here about that line. Marigold wants it to be simple. 'The line does the work for you.'"

Chris took a deep breath and scribbled. "Just give me a sec," he said, flipping through his pages, as if to cement what we'd done so far.

"Sure."

As I waited, I thought back to Chris's arrival at the Festival this season, tracing the steps from then to now, and how he never could have expected to be standing where he was, an apprentice poring over the text for a part he would certainly play.

It had been only Colleen and me in the office when a doe-eyed man appeared in our doorway. He looked as if he didn't know if he was in the right town, let alone the right building.

"Hi . . . Um . . ." he began.

"Hi," I said. "What can I do for you?"

"The guy at the stage door let me in, told me this is the stage management office. I'm Christopher Blake."

It was only then I remembered that Robin had hired three new guys for the Festival's twenty-fifth anniversary production of *Richard III*, a production Robin had already packed with fifty actors: Maggie, Brian, Eric, Max, Martha, Barry, Alan . . . the list went on. Thankfully, I wasn't stage managing it. I already had *Much Ado* to contend with on top of my PSM duties. I'd learned my lesson.

"They're in the auditorium right now. I'll take you there."

I left the office with Chris in tow, and walked to the backstage area. I was slow in going because I could hear that a scene was already playing out between Brian's Gloucester and Maggie's Queen Elizabeth. We stopped by the stage right door, and listened.

GLOU.   I cannot tell: the world is grown so bad,
             That wrens make prey where eagles dare not perch.

ELIZ.   Come, come, we know your meaning, brother

Gloucester;
You envy my advancement and my friends':
God grant we never may have need of you!

"Let's stop there," Robin called from the house. I wasn't sure how, but I knew Robin was standing as he spoke. "This is what I was talking about earlier. Listen to them. The iambic pentameter is there to help you if you let it. When Shakespeare wrote these plays it was for predominantly illiterate men, so he wrote everything in a rhythm that helped the actor learn the text and deliver it. It's good. Good stuff." I glanced at Chris and smiled knowingly. He had a familiar look about him, that look Robin always left on people's faces in his wake, like footprints in snow, as if the words had never been arranged in that order before, but now that they had, the world made a bit more sense. After a moment, I signalled Chris to follow me.

In the house, Robin had already bounded down the aisle to the stage and was speaking in low tones with Maggie and Brian. Onstage, the other actors were standing by. By the time I had shown Chris to his seat, Robin was whispering to Alan. Next, he'd whisper to Barry and then to Max and so on. That was Robin's way. He'd put each marble in play and then watch them crash together. I told Chris to sit patiently and that eventually somebody would tell him what he was there for. Such was the plight of all apprentices, it seemed. He nodded and thanked me.

"Shall we move on?" I asked Chris.

Chris scratched the back of his head. "I actually think I'm done for the day. I think I need some time to digest what we've done so far."

"Of course."

"Sorry."

"Don't beat yourself up. Just takes time."

He paused as if to let his thoughts catch up to him. "Thanks, Nora."

"Anytime. It's what I'm here for."

As Chris got his coat, and I packed up, I told myself it was a shame that directors didn't work with understudies. I understood why, of course. Directors had a hard enough time getting one cast ready. But they'd never see the sheer tenacity of the good understudies. Watching Chris leave, I felt more than ever that he and those like him were the backbone of the company. For all of the star power Robin brought to the Festival, for all of his plans to build a film studio in the back of the Avon building, the shows were still the Festival's heart and soul, and they would always go on thanks to the staggering grit of the understudies.

Walking home, the crescent moon was half covered with clouds, and the air was still and warm. On a whim, I decided to take Ballantyne Avenue and head up Front to see my old home.

When I arrived at 75 Front St., I stood at the corner and found myself gawking at the house, noticing practical things about the place that the veneer of childhood had hidden from me. I wondered why there were two chimneys when the builders could have stacked the fireplaces. I wondered why there was an entrance leading to the kitchen.

Shortly after my sister Marg married her fiancé David, and before they moved to Calgary, the owners of 75 Front St., the ones who had bought it from my parents in '71, put it up for sale. Marg had seriously considered buying it, but Sue and I told her that it would never be the same. She'd never have the memories she did when she grew up there. If anything she'd ruin the memories she already had. Standing idly on the street corner for no more than a few minutes, I already felt the distance of time tattering mine. With that, I went home.

Turning down Douro St., I saw that the lights in my living room were on.

He must be watching TV.

Michael's cat purred as I entered. Michael himself came out of the kitchen with a glass of water and gave me a kiss hello. He and his cat had finally moved in with me. He didn't ask me anything, and I felt no need to explain. He knew that to be alone together, with no expectations, was enough for a stage manager.

When I had changed out of my work clothes, I sat in front of the TV with Michael. He was watching Johnny Carson's *Tonight Show*.

The studio audience was laughing and the celebrity guest hadn't come out yet. I took up my needles and yarn, and continued knitting an ivory sweater coat, my small thanks to Heather for all her help getting this house.

TIK-TIK. TIK-TIK. TIK-TIK. TIK-TIK.

My brother Dave was getting married later this year. He had met his fiancée, Susanne Elizabeth, in his residence at the University of Waterloo. Once she added the Polley to the end of it, she would have the exact same name as our sister Susanne Elizabeth Polley. With Marg marrying a David, our family was quickly becoming a Freudian wet dream. Dave's wedding was going to be in Sudbury, and I was going to miss it entirely. I felt terrible about it, but we all understood the necessities of my career.

TIK-TIK. TIK-TIK. TIK-TIK. TIK-TIK.

I examined my progress in the blue light of the TV. The coat was coming along nicely. Next up were the sleeves. I thought of Aunt Reta, still working hard at the Avon, who was the best knitter I knew. She'd have had them done before Carson brought out his first guest.

TIK-TIK. TIK-TIK. TIK-TIK. TIK-TIK.

This was my life, and for all of its heartache and stress, for everything I had to put up with or miss, I didn't want to be doing anything else. I was right where I needed to be.

TIK-TIK. TIK-TIK. TIK-TIK. TIK-TIK.

SHAWN DESOUZA-COELHO

 When I returned to the auditorium at the NAC, John was tapping his finger on the stage management table, lost in thought. It was late in the evening, and rehearsal had just broken. John looked very tired. I didn't blame him.

"Any change?" I asked, taking a cigarette out of my pack and offering him one.

"No," he said, taking it. "No."

That year, John had been appointed the artistic director of the new English theatre section of the NAC, a prestigious position he didn't take lightly. His flagship production was *Troilus and Cressida*, a Shakespearean tragedy that wasn't performed very often. He decided to make a name for himself through it, with real steam pouring onto the stage from the NAC's actual steam system, and a startling amount of male nudity. But John's verve cost him. His dad was dying in a nearby hospital, meaning that every December day John was being pulled in two different directions.

I opened my notebook, just as I had in nights before, as John took a drag of his cigarette, inhaling deeply. As smoke filled the air, joining the haze that had settled above us from the day's rehearsal, he said, "If he dies tonight, then have them review the skirmishes at the end of the play tomorrow."

Cigarette pinched between my lips, I wrote the itinerary down. "Anything you want me to look for?"

"Transitions. It needs to be one on top of the other."

"Transitions. One on top of the other. Okay. And the next day?"

John considered this for a moment. "The top of the show up to Act 2."

"Sure thing," I smirked.

John looked up at me, languidly. "What's funny?" he asked out of genuine interest. It was then I told him what had happened while I was writing down the blocking for the opening scene.

At the top of the show, every actor was dressed in a sweat suit, working out, but then eventually they each dropped to their knees and started simulating fucking the floor. This built to an orgasm in which they all died, and the play started with a battlefield filled with dead bodies. As I was documenting the blocking, I asked Stephen Russell, his shoulder-length black hair slick with sweat, where he ended up.

"Stephen says, 'Pardon?' And I think he must not have heard me. So I ask him, 'Where did you finish?' And he looks down at the floor and then back at me and says, 'All over the place.'"

John laughed quietly through a half-smile, and then resumed his stolid introspection. As I finished writing down John's instructions for the second day, I tried briefly to imagine how I would feel being in his situation, torn between the job and the last moments of my dad's life. No answers came.

"And the next day?" I asked. "Act 2 into Act 3? John?"

SHAWN DESOUZA-COELHO

He snapped to me, brushing away his thoughts. "Act 2 into Act 3. That works." He ashed his cigarette, adding, "Same time tomorrow?"

"Hope so."

--

"It happened again," I said, picking at the warm brioche sitting on my kitchen counter. Michael slapped my hand away, but not before I could get a small piece. I was the woodpecker to his trunk since I had gotten home. It was night, and we were both wide awake, of course. He had arrived maybe an hour before I did, but he was already starting on the next batch of dough.

"If you want some I'm willing to trade," he said, playfully.

I perked up, chewing the buttery pastry. "What'd you have in mind?"

"You do the dishes and—"

"Hah!" I didn't even have to count all the bowls, whisks, spatulas, and plates on the counter covered in butter, flour, egg, and whatever else he used in the brioche to know he was joking. "We have a good system going. You make amazing food and I eat it and tell you how amazing it is. Why ruin a good thing?"

"You know it's not for you," Michael replied, before continuing his whisking in silence.

As the stage manager of Robin's *Private Lives*, Michael oversaw the photo call, wherein various scenes in the production were photographed for publicity, posterity, etc. And Robin wanted to stage the scene where café au lait and brioche are served. However, there weren't any places in Stratford that sold brioche frozen or fresh, so Michael, being the expert cook he was, offered to make some himself. Meticulous as ever, Robin took Michael up on his offer. The resultant photographs were stunning, of course. Never could still-life seem more alive than in Robin's hands. It was in the eyes of every actor he'd posed and had the photographer Robert Ragsdale shoot. But, the problem for Michael was everybody loved his brioche so much they started requesting it for dress rehearsals and performance nights. They could have just used dinner rolls onstage, but rather than turn down Mags and everybody else, Michael agreed. Now, almost nightly, he was on brioche duty because of the time it took to prepare the dough for baking.

Michael added two eggs to his mixture and started beating the dough when he said, "You should have seen Martha tonight at the photo call."

"What happened?" I said, getting a glass of water.

"Martha's hunchback nun is in love with the priest, and Robin wanted to see the scene where she gets the letter from him. But, when she reads the letter, she's supposed to have an orgasm. So, there's Martha surrounded by designers, crew, Robin, Robert, me, everybody, and she reads the letter. The more she reads, the more she becomes sexually charged, and then at the end she simulates a picture-perfect orgasm! But that's not the best part. Afterwards Robert asks her to do it again 'for colour.'"

"No!" I smacked my glass down on the counter.

"Yeah! And she does!"

Almost to myself, I asked, "Didn't he realize how much that cost her?"

Michael and I spent a moment silently admiring Martha. Neither of us could ever imagine doing that.

"How goes the search for a baby?" Michael asked, referring to the fact that Robin wanted to use a real baby for the photo call for *The Winter's Tale*. It was my job to source this baby.

"My cousin said she'd let us use hers," I said, lighting a cigarette.

"Nice of her. What if you couldn't find one?"

"Doll."

"Or make one."

There was another, different silence then. I took a drag. Our cats meandered in the dining room, both looking for something, a spider maybe.

"No chance of that now," I said, finally. I'd never really discussed having children with anybody before. Michael and I had only been seeing one another for two years. He only recently left his wife, only recently moved in. It was too soon to be thinking about that. But then, I wasn't getting any younger.

"You decided?"

"Yeah."

"Okay."

It was genuine, his response, and I was relieved by it. It was all over the news that smoking while on birth control increased one's risk of getting breast cancer later in life. So, I quit taking the pill and was planning to get my tubes tied. And it really was okay because Michael knew the demands of my job, the near impossibility for a woman, let alone a stage manager, to have children and a career. To me, doing well at either meant doing one or the other, but never both. I had certainly yet to see both at the Festival.

I stubbed out my cigarette in the ashtray on the counter.

"So?" Michael said, adding butter to the dough and then beating it all together.

"So."

"So, you never told me what happened in rehearsal."

I slapped the counter. "Right!" I immediately cradled my head. "Ugh. What a mess. It was all just a mess. Robin just took over the whole thing, you know? We're doing the banquet scene and you know how we're setting the entire thing in complete darkness, right? Banquo is murdered and then there's a blackout for like eight seconds, and then lights flash up and suddenly we're in this huge banquet?"

"Huh," Michael said, impressed.

"Yeah, it's brilliant. He's brilliant. He's reminding everybody what their blocking is from *memory*, all two-dozen of them. And there's nothing on the stage for people to mark their positions with since it's all in darkness, so he's down there counting paces up the ramp with them or wherever. 'Three paces forward, six paces left should do it.' Brilliant. I mean he does things sometimes that just make me go, 'What planet are you from?' You know he had Douglas Rain fake a heart attack as Macbeth? Yeah! During the banquet scene, just to get everybody onstage more 'in tune' with what was going on."

"What did everyone do?" Michael said, greasing another bowl.

"Nobody had any idea what to do. I mean, it's Dougie. He's scary in all the right ways so nobody is going to just stop him while he's maybe trying something new. I wanted to, but I didn't. It still somehow felt like a scene, you know? So he's just on the floor, saying all of the lines, and nobody is doing anything, but everybody from Peter to Chris to Maggie is looking at one another like they've just seen the sky open."

"Peter . . . Roberts?"

"No, Donaldson. New guy, second season, playing a bunch of small roles. So, they're all looking at each other like, 'What the hell is going on? What do we do?' And that's exactly what Robin wanted. He wanted them to react that way to Macbeth's outbursts. So, the next time we do the scene, that's what they give him. Isn't that just out of this world?"

"Mmhmm."

"And, *and*, then he had Dougie do it again! This time with a twisted ankle. And they all fell for it again!"

"A testament to Dougie."

I took a drink of water. "For sure."

"But what happened in the cue-to-cue?" Michael asked, now slowly moving the dough from one bowl to the next. It was sticking to his fingers.

"Oh, I lost it. I completely lost it. I just couldn't handle it. Robin's calling the shots, which means I'm sitting there with my thumb up my ass waiting for him to say something. I have maybe twenty minutes to get two dozen people onstage, with sound, with lights, with every-thing. Robin and Maggie aren't seeing eye-to-eye. Maggie and Dougie aren't seeing eye-to-eye. And Maggie had missed the first three weeks of rehearsal because of her film shoot, so Dougie was rehearsing with Barb Stewart the whole time. I mean, *Barb* must have felt amazing; an understudy getting the chance to work with the actual actors? Unreal! Anyway, eventually it came down to the fact that I felt my blood was about to boil, and I knew that if I could just get out of there, I could come back and deal with all of it. So, I convinced the crew to come in

SHAWN DESOUZA-COELHO

and reset the props, and I got Robin to talk to them. Then he gave me this look."

"Look?"

"Yeah, like he understood what I was trying to do. It was bizarre. So, anyway, he talks to them, and I run out to the parking lot and just break down crying." Michael was motionless, rapt. "Nobody saw me, I don't think. And when I finished maybe three minutes later, I went back in and we got it done." I looked down at my empty water glass. "I just hate that when I get angry, I cry. It's so counter-productive. And I left because the first time I couldn't deal was with John, last year. *King Lear*. Nothing was going right in the cue-to-cue, and you know how everybody is waiting on you because it all comes down to you, so I lost it for a second and said, 'John, just give me five minutes.' And everybody was around, and I hated that I suddenly became the centre of attention. So, if I can, I'll leave."

"Well, you got it done. That deserves something." I looked up to find him holding out of a piece of brioche for me, sweetly. I popped it in my mouth.

"It's really good."

Michael smiled, and we sat for a moment in silence. He began piling dishes into the sink.

"Oh!" I shouted. "I thought of what I'd call my book!" Knowing neither its form nor its content didn't deter my excitement whenever the idea spurted back to me.

"What's that?"

"Ready?"

"Yeah."

"*Go, Elephants. Go, Waterfall.*"

Michael tilted his head, considering it, and then nodded approvingly. "I like it. Why elephants and waterfalls, though?"

"The two things I'll probably never get a chance to call."

"Oh," Michael smirked, knowing that if it was to happen anywhere, it'd be at the Festival. "I wouldn't be so sure."

1979 It was mid-July when I took Robin out to the parking lot at the Festival Theatre to drink his coffee and get some sun. It seemed like so little, but already I could see the heft of his upturned eyes lighten. The ground was still wet from a dawn shower. I smoked beside him, to give him company and watch him sip from his Styrofoam cup. His black tie stood out to me, loosened as it was around the collar of his pressed blue dress shirt, as if it were a single cloud on a clear day. Robin was stretched to his limit.

For the entire season thus far we had all taken care of Robin in some way. His lunches were brought to him and he was watched while he ate them. Ann Stuart, a former ASM with long curly hair and soft features, was now his assistant, and occasionally she would kick us out of the stage management office to make phone calls for him. Having *finally* learned my lesson, I was PSM but wasn't stage managing anything this season. I was still doing my part, though, taking Robin outside on breaks for rehearsals I wasn't part of. We did it all gladly because Robin was our twice-bright candle, our artistic director, our leader, my friend.

A few cars drove by down Queen Street one after the other as Robin and I passed the time in silence. The scent of rain lingered on every breeze. I took a drag of my cigarette. Robin was very still.

He didn't mind the attention we'd given him. He was sputtering along by now, and at least he had the sense to recognize it. He announced his resignation at the end of last season, but the Board convinced him to take a sabbatical instead. Yet, this season, he was still directing three productions. He was actually listed as "co-director," but everybody knew there was nothing 'co' about Robin's style. It was Robin's show, always. He was a man sick unto his work.

"I'm thinking of writing a book," I said idly.

"Oh?" He breathed deeply and I saw, briefly, the actor in him, stepping forward from the crowd of his other talents: artist, tailor, prop master, administrator, director, visionary. Those were an actor's lungs gulping in the air, capable of belting lines to the back row and beyond.

"A book on stage management," I added. "What it's like to stage manage in Canada."

"That could be very good. Very useful to quite a number of people."

"I think so."

I still couldn't figure out what exactly I was going to write, and maybe Robin sensed this because he then asked, "What else is available?"

"Not much, at least not about what we do here. It's all mostly about commercial theatre, which is useful but—"

"But doesn't quite capture it fully, does it?"

"No."

"Important stuff." He took a sip of his coffee, and looked up, squinting. "Well, it could only be you who writes it."

I didn't know what to say to that, so I said nothing at all.

"Michael has taken up knitting, has he?" Robin asked, turning to me.

"I've been teaching him here and there. Right now he's working on a sweater . . . I think."

Robin chuckled limply and then resumed his thousand-yard stare.

As the ASM for *Lear*, Michael would tell me that Robin was as alert as ever, banging away on his timpani to pace his actors, or fiddling with the sliders on his dimmer board to set the mood onstage. Yet, as I looked at the exhausted man standing beside me, a stranger to the sun since he always arrived long before it rose and left long after it set, I wondered from which depths he culled all that energy. It just seemed impossible to me that he could be constantly pushing.

A crow soared overhead, and I checked my watch. We still had a few more minutes. We spent them in another fond silence while I finished my cigarette and he his coffee, both of us knowing we'd be back out there in the evening or the next morning or the afternoon after that.

"Feeling better?" I asked when it was finally time to head in.

"Much," he replied, leading the way.

1980 When I arrived at Rehearsal Hall 1, I was nearly out of breath. In the doorway, I clutched the present under my arms and quickly scanned the room. Members of every department in the company were scattered around the space, mingling, chatting, smoking. Their reflections in the windows were vivid against the late-evening sky. There were no decorations hung, and no one was dressed up, though it was a special occasion. We knew Robin wanted to resign from the Festival quietly, but we just couldn't let him leave without sending him off, without thanking him for pushing us to the brink, for redefining the brink, for being the first artistic director in our history to list stage managers as part of the creative team, and for growing the Festival to unprecedented acclaim. Tonight was our closure.

I spotted Ann where the stage management tables would be, and went to her.

"Any word?" I asked, still taking in the room.

"No," she replied. "But he'll be here." She sounded almost hopeful. "You finished?"

"Hm? Oh! Yes." I tapped the box under my arm. "Finished it twenty minutes ago."

It was then that Robin entered, and the company began to cheer. For all of Robin's efforts to smile at the warm reception, he still looked tense.

"Nick of time," Ann said, leaning towards me.

"You're telling me."

I glanced down at the present and suddenly felt anxious, remembering the Guthrie Awards ceremony earlier in the season. The company presented Robin with a gift, and he didn't even open it. He was finished with the Festival, adulations and all. I hoped then that I wasn't overstepping my bounds.

For a long time Robin made his way through the room and greeted everybody who greeted him. When the champagne arrived, Nicholas Pennell, a middle-aged, blond, British actor, led everybody in a toast. Robin stood close by, kneading his hands throughout.

"Robin came five years ago, and we're all thankful that he did. The Festival has unquestionably changed, has become a different creature altogether. It will never be the same. To quote the Bard, to whom we all owe a great debt: 'The words of Mercury are harsh after the songs of Apollo. You that way: we this way.' Cheers."

"Cheers!"

In the receiving line that followed, my anxiety became memory as Robin opened my gift in front of me and showed it around proudly. It was a sweater vest I had spent many nights in front of the TV knitting, while Michael sat beside me, still learning to knit himself. The vest sported a patterned band around its bottom where I'd knitted the names of all thirty-six shows Robin had directed at the Festival during his short time as artistic director.

"Thank you, Nora," he said, kissing me on the cheek. "It's very lovely."

I was tearful in my delight, sad at his departure, but content that he could finally relax. If anybody deserved to, it was Robin.

This place can't close.

I had just come from the office where Peter Roberts, now the production manager of the Festival, still sat, poring tirelessly over the production schedule for this year's season. This process normally began in June of the previous year and took months to complete. It was January now, and we'd only just begun. The season, if there was going to be one, was only a few weeks away. In a bout of hopelessness, I told Peter I needed some air, and, shivering in the solitude of the backstage hallway, I discovered the stage and house lights were on. I stepped onto the deck, and the lights were warm. I called to anybody who might have been there, but no one replied, my voice instead swimming up through the auditorium. Whoever had turned on the lights must've left. I took in the sheer breadth of the space, from aisles one to eleven, and basked in the ghosts of everything that had come before. I stared at my feet and the floorboards beneath them supporting me as they had my grandfather Patrick's choir, which sang in the Festival's inaugural production of *Richard III*; the first generation of Polleys to tend this garden. I stared at the patina of the balcony pillars where, with water skin in hand, the oil of my fingers enjoined with Alec Guinness's when he had played Richard in the same production. And it was then it really hit me.

This place can't close.

I stood for a while with this thought, squinting at the spot where Richard Monette had stood up at the annual general meeting and called the Board pigs. The shock of his outburst had faded to a trill, but was still immortally present.

Robin had left a vacuum, one that Martha and the three other members of the Gang of Four tried to fill with a viable season, only to have it suffocated by the Board. Upon their summary dismissal, and with the possibility of the Board importing John Dexter, another British artistic director, to fill the void, Equity, our union, boycotted the Festival, citing injustice and nationalism as its rationales. And at the annual general meeting, Robin and I were in attendance when an actor took to the microphone to reiterate these rationales. I was there when Martha read from her diary so as to straighten the Board's account of the timeline of events. She was quiet, pointed, and strong. Robin himself clarified his position regarding John, sounding all the while as if he were reading a menu aloud to the room. The fight had left him completely. Then an actor motioned to depose the Board, and it was seconded. The motion was crushed by the Board on account of the hundreds of proxy votes they'd gathered prior to the meeting. Finally, when Richard had had enough, he stood up with his coat over his arm and belted out, "You *pigs*! We have spent our lives in this theatre, we have given of our time, and we care about art. You talk to us about money all the time. You have no morals. I don't know how you can sleep. And I care deeply and passionately about this place, and you must address yourselves to your consciences and to your hearts." Amidst the cheers and condemnations of the crowd, the president of the Board banged his gavel and asked Richard, a seasoned Festival actor, "What is your name, sir?" The meeting was promptly adjourned.

I could still hear Richard's voice faintly echoing through the empty house as I stood on the empty stage. Maybe it was just the boards creaking beneath my feet as I shifted my weight from one leg to the next, thinking the same thought over and over again.

This place can't close. Maybe we'll all be out of a job next season, when things settle down and whatever artistic director decides we're not his cup of tea. We'll all definitely be out of a job next season if John Hirsch is on board. The writing is on the wall. But we need this season. This town needs this season. It needs a Festival. This room cannot be empty because if this place closes, it will never reopen.

Having reminded myself of the stakes, I felt renewed. The thought of not being here next season didn't faze me. It was the same anxiety when Jean left and Robin came. But this time I refused to play along. I wasn't going to remind Hirsch I was here, that I was valuable. I wasn't going to walk around on eggshells. I was going to do my job and that job was to make sure there was a ground for Hirsch to throw eggshells on.

"Nora?" I turned to find Peter standing under the balcony. "Shall we?"

I nodded, taking one last look around before heading back to the office.

--

"So," I said to Mom as she sat on the chesterfield, Dad's arm around her. On Dad's lap sat his two-year-old grandson Matthew, dressed in blue-and-green plaid overalls. "What's it like having Dad around all day?"

Mom shook her head disapprovingly, her fading blond bob shaking with it. "He wants to help all the time."

"Can you blame me?" Dad chuckled. He was wearing a grey sweater

SHAWN DESOUZA-COELHO

with the words "The Old Vic" printed on its front. "You've been doing it all yourself for forty-five years."

Mom patted his knee. "Exactly." We all laughed at the gibe, sitting around my parents' basement rec room after brunch. Dad had just retired from the St. Lawrence Centre, and was now trying to fill his days with golfing, rug hooking, horse shows at the Royal Winter Fair, and trying to help Mom do a job she'd been doing alone and well for decades. "We'll be at the grocery store," she continued, "and I'll pick something up and he'll ask me, 'Why are you buying that? Why not this?'"

"I'm learning," Dad replied plainly, still not seeing the joke.

"Planning to go see some theatre with all your free time?" Dave quipped from the other side of the room, Susanne beside him, both of them sitting on folding chairs. They had driven in from Waterloo.

"Forget it. I'd rather work on my stroke."

"Rather *have* a stroke from the sounds of it," I retorted, taking a sip of eggnog.

Dad laughed and then we all lapsed into a cozy silence for a while. Christmas was one of the only occasions we were all in the same room together anymore. This year there were more of us than ever. Fred was sitting with Janice, the two of them having come in from Winnipeg. Beside them were Aunt Dorothy, Sue, and Neil, and upstairs in Marg's old room were Sonja, Jannine, and their nine-year-old sister, Heather. Marg was in the centre of the rec room, on the blue floral rug with her one-year-old daughter, Jennifer, while David looked on from the side. Michael was beside me on the other couch.

"Was that your recipe?" Sue said to Michael. He had brought seafood crêpes and quiche for brunch.

"No, no," Michael laughed. He was wearing a cardigan sweater I had knit him for Christmas. "I just read it in a recipe book."

"Well, you'll have to lend it to Sue," Neil joked. Sue was not impressed.

The house at Don Mills was beautiful in the winter. There was a massive evergreen on the front lawn; the perfect Christmas tree. It was taller than the home itself, and shone like a lighthouse. At the end of the street was a pathway that forked into the snowy woods on one side, and on the other was a small bridge leading over the Don River to the Donalda Club's eighteen-hole golf course, which Dad thought was too expensive.

I had to stop myself from staring at my dad then. It was pride, really. Here sat a man who managed to be the sole breadwinner of a family of seven for twenty-seven years in the *theatre*. So adored was Dad that the St. Lawrence Centre held a retirement ceremony for him in one of their theatres. At the ceremony, Dad asked all of his children to stand in the auditorium as he spoke about each of us in turn. He took a bit longer with Fred because not only was he the firstborn son, but he had also had given Dad Matthew, the firstborn grandson, and had therefore redoubled his position as my parents' favourite child.

"So this season . . ." Mom began.

Michael and I both shook our heads.

"Terrible, right?" I asked.

"It wasn't *terrible*."

"We were surprised it came together at all. A woman named Muriel Sherrin stepped in while Hirsch fulfilled his commitments in — where was it?"

"Seattle," Michael replied.

"Right, Seattle. Anyway, more than half the actors were new."

"Oh, that explains it," Mom said as if she'd heard the answer to a riddle. "Really wooden performances."

I nodded knowingly.

Abruptly, Michael turned to me with his hand on mine and asked, "Do they know?"

"Know?"

Around us ears perked up.

"About the award."

"Oh! No."

"What award?" Dorothy asked.

"Well, two awards, actually," I replied, balking at the sudden attention. "The Festival gave me a Guthrie Award and the Canada Council gave me a grant to write my book."

"Congratulations," Dad smiled.

"Yeah."

"So now you have to write the thing."

"Yeah."

"How do you feel?"

How do I feel?

I didn't know how to tell them that I had applied because of the finality of it all, because I felt the Festival's tide had turned, and I was certain now it wasn't carrying me with it. I was worried, anxious, but strangely empowered by this. The Festival had been the ceiling of my life for twelve years, and now it was opening up like a spring bloom. What that meant for my career as a stage manager, I didn't know. But looking above me into the vast expanse of the future, I knew I had something to say and that there was still time for me to say it.

In place of all of this, I told everybody, quite simply, "It's going to be tough."

 John Wood sat beside me, his hand to his chin, watching his *Richard III* unfold. Queen Elizabeth, the Duchess of York, Dorset, Anne, and Lady Margaret were onstage in the rehearsal hall at the NAC, standing before an imagined tower of London. Brakenbury had just entered, and Lord Stanley would follow shortly. He would let slip that Anne had become queen.

BRAK.   Right well, dear madam. By your patience,
          I may not suffer you to visit them;
          The king hath straitly charged the contrary.

ELIZ.   The king! why, who's that?

John had tried the scene over and over again in different configurations, but it just didn't work. I had figured out a solution, but wrestled with myself, not knowing how he'd take the advice.

BRAK.   I cry you mercy: I mean the lord protector.

ELIZ.   The Lord protect him from that kingly title!
          Hath he set bounds betwixt their love and me?
          I am their mother; who should keep me from them?

The problem wasn't that I felt it not my place to say anything. John trusted me in ways a stage manager could only hope to be trusted by her director. We had both grown as professionals together over the eleven years since Theatre Calgary. He trusted me when I told him to cancel the first preview of *Troilus and Cressida* because the production wasn't ready for an audience. He trusted me to look after his rehearsals when his father was dying. Two days after opening night, his father did die, and John said he stayed alive long enough to read the reviews, knowing how important it was to him. No, the issue now was that my solution was in fact Robin's idea, something he'd done back in '77 for his *Richard III*. I didn't know if John would consider it theft to use it.

YORK.   I am their father's mother; I will see them.

ANNE.   Their aunt I am in law, in love their mother:
          Then bring me to their sights; I'll bear thy blame
          And take thy office from thee, on my peril.

"The worst that can happen is he shoots me down and we continue on," I told myself behind motionless lips. I leaned over to John and whispered, "I've seen this done before." He tilted his head closer to me. "I know what you can do."

"Okay," he said and then called, "Thank you," to the room moments before Lord Stanley's entrance. The actors doffed their characters and stood at the ready for further instruction or critique. "Give me five minutes," he told them. He leaned in closer to me and in a low voice said, "Let's hear it."

I told John the idea, and he sat with it for a moment. I sat up, expectant. He then nodded in approval, and spent the next few minutes speaking with the actors onstage. Returning to his seat, he told them to run the scene again.

YORK.   I am their father's mother; I will see them.

ANNE.   Their aunt I am in law, in love their mother:
          Then bring me to their sights; I'll bear thy blame
          And take thy office from thee, on my peril.

BRAK.   No, madam, no; I may not leave it so:
          I am bound by oath, and therefore pardon me.

Brakenbury exited and Lord Stanley entered.
Here it comes.

STAN.   Let me but meet you, ladies, one hour hence,
          And I'll salute your grace of York as mother,
          And reverend looker on, of two fair queens.

Upstage near the centre, Anne stood stupefied by the sudden recognition on everybody's faces, now turned as they were towards her, sunflowers to a newly minted sun. It seemed as though everybody but her understood what Lord Stanley meant by "two fair queens." Then every character onstage, including Elizabeth, bowed to her in a deep, reverent curtsy, almost to the floor, and Anne suddenly knew: she had become queen. John nodded slowly, approvingly, as the pregnant moment passed, and the scene carried on.

STAN.   Come, madam, you must straight to Westminster,
          There to be crowned Richard's royal queen.

When rehearsal had broken, John thanked me for the tip, and I confessed I was a bit hesitant to tell him in the first place.

"Why?" he asked.

"It was something Robin had done. I didn't know how you'd feel about it. Didn't know if you'd consider it stealing from him."

John chuckled as if I'd said something crazy. "I'm not worried about stealing from someone. It's all been done before anyway."

Only a few weeks later I stood shivering in the crowd on Parliament Hill watching Pierre Trudeau arrive for the signing of the Charter of Rights and Freedoms. As soon as he hit the steps, the crowd erupted in cheers, delighted he had finally got much of what he wanted. Then Queen Elizabeth II herself arrived, and everybody from the spectators to the Mounties lining the corridor to Trudeau himself showed her such reverence. In the back of my mind, Robin flashed to life. How well he understood people.

--

I was sitting in the dining room having a cigarette after dinner at Chris Blake's brother's house. Colleen and Chris didn't have many guests, so the house did just fine for an evening reception. The chintz curtains were drawn and the scarlet red carpet softened everybody's steps. I wore a deep purple dress designed to match the corsage on Colleen's raw-silk champagne-coloured wedding dress. I was her maid of honour, and she and Chris had just been married.

"Thank you so much for coming, Nora," Colleen said, sitting beside me, having pried herself from a conversation she was having in the hallway. She almost slumped in her chair, she was so beat.

"Of course. As soon as you told me, I refused to miss it. I made them put it in my contract that I could fly out to Toronto."

Colleen laughed serenely. "When do you head back?"

"Tomorrow morning."

She nodded. "And how's the show going?" My eyes widened and I shook my head. "Tell me!"

"Robin stuns me sometimes."

"How so?"

"Do you know *The Dresser*?"

"Mm, no," Colleen answered, waving to Michael as he passed by with Chris, who was still looking dapper in his ash-grey three-piece suit. They waved to us on their way into the living room.

"It's a play about an actor's dresser who takes it upon himself to keep the actor's life in check. Bill Hutt plays the actor. Anyway, Robin's playing the dresser because he thinks he needs to get back in touch with the actors. He thinks he's intolerant of them now or something. But, he's the most forgetful actor I've ever met. I'll be sitting backstage in the wings of the Playhouse, having just called beginners, and I'll turn and see Robin. I'll look at him and say, 'Robin, you forgot your sweater.' 'Fuck.' And then he'll smack his head and run back to the dressing room. Or, 'Robin, you forgot your watch.' 'Fuck.'" Colleen was slack-jawed. "Isn't that just bizarre? It's like he's using a completely different part of his brain."

"That's so strange."

"Colleen?" Colleen's sister called from the living room.

Colleen put her hand on my shoulder. "I'll be right back."

"Take your time."

I took a drag and looked to the doorway through which Colleen left, hearing the somewhat stifled chatter of Colleen's family. Looking forward again, I gave a start. One of Colleen's sister's little girls was standing a few feet from me. She had a real *Children of the Corn* vibe to her: dark bowl-cut hair, bangs and all. I shuddered to myself, not knowing how long she'd actually been there. Then she spoke.

"God doesn't want you to smoke."

"Sorry?" I asked, taking the cigarette from my mouth.

"God doesn't want you to smoke."

Uh . . .

"Sorry."

The little girl scampered off, leaving me in the dining room with my cigarette and God's disapproval. I took a drag and inhaled slowly.

I cannot believe how bad these women are at scene changes. It's astounding. The combined talents of Donna Goodhand, Carole Shelley, Sheila McCarthy, Susan Wright, and Martha Henry, and they can't find a spike mark to save their lives.

"Let's run it again," Robin said calmly.

This was John Murrell's *Waiting for the Parade*, the first play of the Grand Theatre Company's long season, and we were trying to transition from a clothing shop to a train station where the ladies stood behind a table filled with baskets of fruit and knitted socks for the troops.

"Whenever you're ready," I told Donna, a thin woman with long brown hair that reached down to the middle of her back. Donna reset and finished the scene. As she did, the other ladies began moving the furniture and baskets around onstage, again missing the spikes, the little pieces of tape used to mark locations onstage. Ann Stuart was giggling beside me so quietly only I could hear her.

"No, Susan, put the leg—" I began in awe.

"Sorry!" Susan shouted. She was a voluptuous, gregarious redhead.

"Try it again," Robin called once more.

The Grand in London, Ontario, was where the diaspora of Festival company members arrived after either boycotting the Festival or, like me, simply not being asked back. Never missing an unprecedented beat, when Robin took over the company at the Grand, he completely changed its usual one-play-at-a-time stock season into a repertory one like the Festival, demanding once again that we all burn as bright as him in the process. I was PSM as well as stage managing two shows, confident I could handle it this time if only because, while the stakes were certainly higher, the Grand was so much smaller than the Festival.

Once the ladies had set up for the transition, I gave them the scene. As they struggled yet again with the placement, waddling about the stage, I felt as if we were watching a flock of confused ducks.

"No!" I called. "It goes like—"

"Is it the upstage leg?" Susan yelled, agitated.

Of course it's the upstage leg! Because that's the one you can see!

"Yes, it's the upstage leg."

When they had finally finished, the furniture was somehow still off its mark. Ann was red from bottling her laughter.

"How is this even possible?" I muttered. "The spike marks are five inches square."

Robin scratched his head helplessly. "Shall we do it again?"

--

At a defunct train station in London, Robin's film crew scrambled to set up another take before lunch. Having spent much of the morning with my hands in my pockets, I wanted to tell Robin I wouldn't be back after the break, but he was busy surveying the camera-dolly set up on the train tracks with his attractive, muscular camera guy. On the platform, two-dozen women dressed in World War II–era clothes stood waiting in the slivers of shade gifted by noon and the red brick of the station hut itself. Among them were Sheila's Eve, a sweet school-teacher; Carole's Janet, the stern self-appointed supervisor of all volunteer efforts; Martha's Margaret, a melancholic old woman; and Laura Burton, the company's musician turned background actress for the day. They looked bored too, or maybe I was just seeing myself in them.

Robin had squared a production deal with the CBC to air *Parade* on television, so we rehearsed both the stage and film productions in tandem. Unfortunately, there wasn't really much for a theatre stage manager to do in the latter because there was no job on set comparable to it. As the day progressed, I became intensely aware of my own utility as I only could in a place where I was ostensibly useless.

When Robin had finished his survey I stopped him.

"Nor," he said, shielding his eyes from the sun. For some reason he'd taken to calling me Nor, as if Nora wasn't short enough. I never asked why because I knew he wouldn't tell. It was just Robin's way. To this day I didn't know why he left that note for me back in '75. I probably never would.

"I don't seem to be making much of a contribution here. I think I'll just stay at the theatre for the afternoon."

Robin was shocked. "No, no, you must come back!"

"There's nothing for me to do here. I feel like a spare prick at a wedding."

Robin's voice became suddenly sincere. "But when I say cut and look up, you are the only one who is still looking at me."

I couldn't help but chuckle.

Oh. Yes. That's what I do. I just watch you.

--

EVE.   Tell me about your work, down at the plant?

CATHERINE. Not much to tell. I make sandwiches. I sell Orange

Kik and jujubes four times a day. It's somewhere to go, something to do. And I need the money.

EVE.   Working around all those men — it doesn't make you nervous?

CATHERINE.   Men have never made me nervous.

EVE.   They've never made me anything but.

There was a pause, and Eve looked at the mirror in Catherine's hand. In many ways Susan was the perfect Catherine, the kind of woman who ate men for lunch and when asked by a waiter if she wanted anything else would say, without flinching, "Yeah. A blowjob." Catherine had just put a silver streak in Eve's hair. Robin was on the edge of his seat, mouthing their words. I knew the look: pensive, explosive, present. Something wasn't working.

EVE.   May I look at —?

CATHERINE.   *Not yet.*

There was another pause.

EVE.   Last week Harry joined the Mounted Constabulary.

CATHERINE.   The what?

EVE.   The Calgary Mounted Constabulary! Ta-ta! A bunch of old men with horses and chaps and pith helmets. From dusk to dawn they bravely patrol the Reservoir. On guard against enemy infiltration! I asked Harry, "Who would want to infiltrate a reservoir?" I thought he was going to hit me.

"Let's stop here," Robin interrupted, bolting to his feet.

"Sorry," Sheila said. She was a petite woman with red hair who had been having trouble with her character since the very beginning, and that was what she assumed Robin had stopped the scene for.

Taking Sheila by the arm, Robin led her aside and whispered a marble into her ear. She raised her eyebrows and squeezed Robin's arm. He glided back to his seat, but didn't sit.

"From a bit further back," he said.

"Last week Harry joined," I prompted to Sheila.

She nodded.

EVE.   Last week Hawwy joined the Mounted
            Constabuwawy.

Susan's eyes shone as she gave her next line, and she couldn't stop giggling for the rest of the scene. My mouth opened like a drawbridge.

CATHERINE.   The what?

EVE.   The Cowgawy Mounted Constabuwawy! Ta-ta! A
            bunch of old men with howses and chaps and pith
            helmets. Fwom dusk to dawn they bwavely patwol
            the Wesewow. On guawd against enemy infiwtwation!
            I asked Hawwy, "Who would want to infiwtwate a
            wesewow?" I thought he was going to hit me.

Robin had told Sheila to drop her "R's" and suddenly the character came alive. Robin gave no indication that he had just cracked the code for Sheila, but I knew he was over the moon. We all were. When the scene ended we all had a good laugh and they talked about what felt different.

--

"Jump!" Robin bellowed at Sheila and Susan, who had been at it for five minutes already. The war was over, their characters were to celebrate, and this was Robin's way of instilling that spirit. Martha snuck a cigarette off my table and lit it. She had been having back troubles recently, so she didn't participate in the exercise. Fortunately, her character didn't participate in the festivities either.

I leaned in to Martha, keeping my voice low. "Are we working on the film right now?"

"Stage," Martha replied.

"Okay, that's what I thought." In truth, working on both the stage and film versions was confusing me more and more each day, not least because I had to keep two separate books.

"Robin," Sheila pleaded, laughing and panting. "I . . . can't keep . . . jumping . . . I'm gonna pee myself!"

"Keep jumping!"

"I can't!"

"Don't stop! Don't stop!"

"Robin!"

"Don't stop jumping! Oh! My God! Sheila!" Robin was shrieking. I wanted to shield my eyes. Ann wanted to shield hers. Sheila's face lit scarlet as her pants darkened. "You did it! My God, you really did it!"

It was then Susan began to laugh, the kind of quaking laugh that no bladder could ignore. Susan had peed herself too. I hung my head.

I'm going to have to clean this up, aren't I?

--

CATHERINE.   Your boy could be home from Halifax any day now! And Billy —

EVE.   And the othew one! They won't keep him much longew! Suwely not! Now that it's all ovew!

CATHERINE.   And Billy!

SHAWN DESOUZA-COELHO

MARGARET.   You know what I think?

EVE.   Ding-dong!

CATHERINE.   Ding-dong!

JANET.   This is absurd!

MARGARET.   I think we should all get down on our knees —

EVE.   Ding-dong!

MARGARET.   And thank God — whose mercy —

Margaret clutched her side and fell to her knees amidst the celebrations marking the end of the war. She was having a heart attack. The other characters grew hysterical at the sight of it, panicking loudly until Robin abruptly called the scene to a stop. For a moment he stared at Martha and seemed oddly submerged in his own labyrinthine mind. Then he resurfaced, and we began again with a different scene altogether.

--

"O Romeo, Romeo!" Susan belted, dressed in a black caftan, standing on the chesterfield in the middle of the living room, beer bottle in hand. "Wherefore art thou Romeo?"

"Susan—" I cautioned, thinking, stupidly, that I or anybody else could interrupt her.

"Deny thy father and refuse thy name," she continued until the whole cast and crew of *Parade* was listening. She then pointed to me. "Or, if thou wilt not, be but sworn my love, and I'll no longer be a Capulet! Norni!"

"Nora," I corrected, moving close enough to catch her if she fell. We didn't have the luxury of understudies.

She took a sip of beer. "Norni, be my Romeo."

"I don't think—"

"Norni, was he everything you ever dreamed of and more?"

I flushed red, suddenly wanting to push Susan off the chesterfield instead. I could hear Sheila's laughter from the corner of the room where she stood with an equally enthused Donna.

Robin had found a use for me on set after all. His idea was to shoot an entire scene between the five women with Janet walking around a table barking orders while the other four spoke in whispers and rolled bandages. The camera would never move. Rather, the focus would change depending on who was speaking, and it was my job to whisper the next speaker to the hunky camera guy.

"Norni, if you're done puttin' your tongue in his ear, be my Romeo!"

I shook my head incredulously, deciding it was easier to just play along. "Uh . . . Shall I speak more, or shall I . . . speak at this?"

"You're not fuckin' Romeo," Susan dismissed, laughing heartily. She turned to Sheila, who was now crying. "Shirley! Be my Romeo!"

--

I looked over at Michael, still blissfully asleep, and felt a pang of regret. He was stage managing at the Festival, and had just come into town the night before after a long rehearsal day. I wanted to wake him, to spend time with him, but I had rehearsals today and I was acutely aware of the importance of rest, having had very little myself for quite a while.

Unlike others in the company who believed wholeheartedly in Robin's gospel that the Grand was going to be a three-year project, I decided to keep my house. I believed in Robin. I just believed in having some semblance of security more. But on nights when rehearsals ended late enough, I stayed in London. So, Michael and I took turns commuting. Aunt Dorothy taught me how to drive expressly for this purpose. Michael went with me to test drive cars, and I finally settled on a used, blue Honda Civic.

I didn't feel too bad about learning at thirty-five. My dad was forty when he learned. Driving just didn't make sense in a walking town like Stratford.

I watched Michael for a moment longer, the gentle rise and fall of his chest and the fluttering of his eyes beneath their lids, and suddenly realized how hard this was becoming. Michael was right beside me, but seemed so very far away. I wished I could stay but instead got dressed and left.

--

CATHERINE.   Your boy could be home from Halifax any day now! And Billy —

EVE.   And the othew one! They won't keep him much longew! Suwely not! Now that it's all ovew!

CATHERINE.   And *Billy*!

MARGARET.   You know what I think?

EVE.   Ding-dong!

CATHERINE.   Ding-dong!

JANET.   This is absurd!

MARGARET.   I think we should all get down on our knees —

Martha doubled over in pain, clutching her back. The room fell silent. I didn't move. I could see Ann wanted to, but I stopped her.

"Martha?" Carole murmured. "Are you okay?" In a low voice she then urged the room for help as the other women stood by, nervously looking on.

"Okay!" Robin yelled as he stormed the stage, elated with what he'd seen. "*That's* what you do! When somebody is hurt you don't all yell and scream. When somebody is *really* hurt you get very quiet. Everything gets very quiet."

Martha got to her feet, the magician's assistant, and the other women were stunned into embarrassment and laughter. It was the same chicanery with Dougie in *Macbeth*, and it was just as brilliant now as it was then.

After rehearsal had broken, Ann asked me, "How did you know Martha was faking it?"

"I didn't."

"Then . . . ?"

"Robin didn't get up. If he doesn't get up, I don't get up."

Ann drank the advice in, and I nodded. She was right to do so.

--

The audience's applause was rapturous as Sheila, Susan, Carole, Donna, and Martha each took a bow after the final performance of *Parade*. Crowds had clamoured to see it, and John Murrell himself said it was the perfect production, that the play never had to be done again.

I saw to it that the women were honoured properly. From the stage-left wing, I cued on five men in the company, each dressed in tailcoats and holding a rose bouquet. They glided onstage, stopping downstage to make sure the women could see them. Then, they handed each woman the flowers, gave each one a kiss, and whispered for each to take one more bow. The women were beside themselves with tears as they bowed for a second time.

Later in the evening, one of the men, Peter Donaldson, told me Robin caught them dressing backstage. Robin asked what they were doing, and so Pete told him. Robin said, "Oh, no. You can't do that." Pete said, "Oh, yes we can," and continued getting dressed. Robin left, fuming. He didn't like playing favourites or singling anybody out.

--

SHAWN DESOUZA-COELHO

We backed into the loading dock of the Festival's scenic shop at the corner of Waterloo and George Street. I got out of the truck, shivering instantly from the still cold. White snow and a late night lay beneath me and around.

"Everything ready to go?" I whispered to Roy Brown, our pillar of support on the '73 Russian tour and now head of props at the Avon and the Third Stage, who had been waiting for us by the receiving door. In the darkness, he was little more than a silhouette.

"Just about," he replied, pulling the door open.

Sitting there, covered in a fine layer of dust, was all the furniture we needed for our next show at the Grand, relics from Robin's time at the Festival. Under John Hirsch it was all unused, which meant all of it was ripe for the picking.

We began loading the furniture into the truck, fighting the ever-growing fatigue inside us. Somehow, though, we gave no thought to the fact that the Grand season had come to this. Audience attendance had dropped drastically since *Parade*. So much so that Robin ordered the box office workers to call patrons and ask why they'd turned away. The answer he received was that subscribers didn't like the new system, plain and simple. Whereas Robin wanted people to think about what shows interested them and make a decision about the work, subscribers told us they just wanted to go to the theatre and sit in the same seat they always had for the past five, ten, fifteen years. That didn't sit well with Robin. And none of it sat well with us. We all knew Robin's ship was going down. Yet nobody thought of abandoning it. Instead, we established a system, with Ann on the receiving end in London, to "borrow" as much as we needed right out from under Hirsch. Of course, like parents protective of their kids, we kept this all from the acting company so they could focus on the actual acting.

After the last piece was loaded, I smacked the back of the truck, thanked Roy, and we pulled out.

--

"Michael . . ." I said into the receiver, for a moment afraid he might not have heard me. "Please . . . get me out of here."

We'd walked in the park for a while after he'd arrived in town, the sun poking through the clouds, neither of us talking. Eventually we stopped and sat on a bench opposite a rose garden. Nearby, a squirrel munched on something it had found beside the pavement.

"There's only one bank in town that will cash our cheques," I whimpered, finally. "One. Everybody has to take their stuff home every night because we don't know if by morning the bailiff will have bolted the doors shut. A part of me thinks Robin knew it wasn't going to work. He had to. I mean you don't raise the budget and cut the subscriptions. And now we're doing *everything*. I—" I cradled my head in my hands. I couldn't say another word. If I did, I was afraid I'd never stop, and then I'd end up quitting. I'd abandon Robin's leaky ship entirely. Michael didn't speak either. Instead, he put his arm around me and we watched the squirrel run headlong through the rose bushes, thorns and all.

--

LAWYER.   I do beg your pardon! That was inexcusable. It was
          the wrong cylinder! I did label them all so carefully,
          but the maid must have mixed them up when she was
          dusting. I am truly grieved. Ah, here we are. This is it.
          I can't apologize enough, ladies . . .

Okay, that was weird.

CARLOTTA.   We all make mistakes.

As the actors onstage were lost in their own world, I turned to John Neville with a questioning look. He was a talented British actor with a long face and big, kind eyes. Wearing his dressing gown, he sat beside me in the wings of *Dear Antoine*, the last production of Robin's

SHAWN DESOUZA-COELHO

last season as artistic director at the Grand, and nodded in agreement. We'd both just seen the lights flicker.

LAWYER.   Not a German lawyer! Just press this, monsieur, if you would.

The lights flickered again.
Shit. This is the last thing we need.
"Stand by, John," I whispered, thankful he was there.
He nodded, and the lights flickered on and off again, this time with enough delay to question whether they'd make the transition at all. "Standing by," John reiterated, as if in response.

In this scene the surviving relatives of Antoine have all arrived to hear the reading of his will via a phonograph onstage. A lot depended on the recording we'd made of John's Antoine, so instinct told me to plan for its failure. I had asked John to sit next to me during the cues when the recording was playing in case something screwed up. That way he'd be able to say the lines from offstage and the play could carry on. He told me he'd be happy to.

LAPINET.   Shall I?

CARLOTTA.   Go on.

I took a breath and then called the sound cue for Antoine's speech as Lapinet set the cylinder to play.

ANTOINE'S VOICE.   Hullo, friends. First of all, let me thank you for coming out here, especially if it's in winter. I hope it isn't snowing too hard. Thank you, Estelle. I caan seeeee yooooouuu iiinnnnn myyyyyyyyy miiiiiinnndddd'ssssss eeeyyyyyy-eeee, all frail and small, and looking a little pale.

Shit.

"It's not on my end," the sound operator said over headset. The lights flickered again. The actors onstage did their best not to call attention to any of it, but the audience had begun to rustle, a pile of leaves in a niggling wind.

> I'm sure your grief is great, but I know that you look yooooouurrrrr best in blaaaaaackk. Thaaaaaank yoouuuuuu, Carlotta and Valllleeeerrrie. Thaaaaank you—

"Kill sound," I shot into the headset. To John, I said, "Pick it up from wherever."

ANTOINE.   Thank you Carlotta and Valérie. Thank you, Anémone. I shall ask to have you sent for too—

I placed my hand on John's shoulder. He stopped. The lights had just gone out, and remained so for almost ten seconds.

"Bring up the house lights," I said when power was restored. "We're stopping the show."

The actors filed off stage, each disappointed but understanding, each with a question I'd answer later by telling them it was just too unsafe to continue, not only for them but also for the audience. For now, we watched as Robin entered and apologized for the technical difficulties. He then offered the audience tickets to return to any performance of their choosing. Their response was middling. We all really hoped they would.

Later when we learned that a brownout rolling across London had been the cause of our technical difficulties, it seemed to some of us that our Grand season, even in its winter, just couldn't catch a break.

--

"This is your half-hour call," I informed John and Martha in the dressing room. "Half-hour."

"Thank you, half-hour," they replied, and then resumed their conversation.

"This is your—" I began at Susan's dressing room, but stopped when I realized she wasn't there. Just then Barry passed behind me, still in his dressing gown. "Have you seen Susan?" I asked him.

"No, I'm afraid not."

I checked the sign-in sheet on the wall. Sure enough, it hadn't seen Susan either. I checked outside, back and front, to see if she was having a smoke. She wasn't there either. I checked my watch and rubbed my forehead.

Maybe she went in as I went out.

With this in mind, I checked her dressing room again. She still wasn't there. I then checked the green room. Nothing. Washroom. Nothing. Having run out of places to look in the building, I sent whomever I could to every bar and restaurant within sprinting distance to check if Susan had stopped in for a drink or a bite. When they all came back empty-handed my frustration turned to worry. Susan was nowhere to be found.

I combed the backstage area, telling myself she'd turn up, willing it so. Others did the same, all of us thinking the same things.

Did something happen to her last night? This morning? Were there any accidents I missed on the news?

At the five-minute call, I found Robin and told him Susan still hadn't arrived. His eyes narrowed, as if weighted with irritation and concern. He adjusted his tie and said, "Here's what we're going to do . . ."

"Unfortunately, ladies and gentlemen," Robin said to the audience as he stood onstage prior to the show, "Ms. Susan Wright is not well and has not yet appeared at the theatre, but we're still going to do the performance." The audience shuffled and mumbled, some clearly unimpressed. Those were the unfortunate ones who had attended the brownout performance, the unfortunate ones who were now in attendance for Robin's decision to stand in for Susan. He would walk around carrying the script in hand the entire time. I felt mortified for him, but with no understudies, there was no other choice.

To our surprise, though, the audience loved it. Sure, the play was indecipherable *without* Robin standing in for one of the female characters, and was possibly made more so because of that, but for whatever reason the audience accepted it wholesale. The actors had to gently nudge Robin here and there when he sat at the wrong times, but other than that, the first act went smoothly.

During the interval, Susan burst into the backstage area, and before anybody could get a word in she yelled, "Don't say anything! I'm getting dressed!"

Thankful Susan was alright, I was now confident the audience would be completely baffled in the second act.

--

Martha stood behind me during the final moments of *Dear Antoine*, her small smile growing. In the scene, each character has something to say, so Robin gave them each a spotlight in which to say it. And, in the wings, beside the stage, able to see every nuanced expression of the actors' faces — a joy the booth at the Festival could never give me — I called the final sequence of the show.

"Quick! Quick! Let's get out! At least we headed **off** the pastor!"
And as the actors spoke . . .
"A pastor for Antoine! How **he'd** have loathed that!
And I called the cues . . .
"He was a Catho**lic**, wasn't he?"
Cues tethered to words and syllables . . .
"Isn't everybody? In unimportant things Antoine took the line of **least** resistance."
Cues heard only in their outward form . . .
"I'm sure you'll find the new playwrights very interesting. There's an amazing movement beginning to take shape! An irresistible gust of fresh air sweeping all the **old** claptrap away."
I felt like I was out there . . .

SHAWN DESOUZA-COELHO

"I'll do you my duck pasty! It's my triumph. And then a nice sweet leg of lamb and, to finish, my apricot cream with brandy."

Onstage . . .

"Then I'll bring some champagne! And that will give us a chance to talk about Antoine!"

Beside them . . .

"Oh, isn't living fun! Don't you **think** we're lucky!"

With them . . .

"Lucky, why?"

"Coming **to** the same funeral!"

"**And** what was the play?"

"*The Cherry Orchard.*"

And that all of us were . . .

"Don't know it. Antoine never mentioned it to me. **Or** maybe I've forgotten."

Breathing as one.

From the darkness shrouding the stage, the audience applauded. And, as the actors bowed, I knew it wasn't for me they clapped. It wasn't for my closed book, my little lamp, or my tiny desk that they poured forth congratulation. Yet, night after night, Martha's smile made me feel otherwise. Night after night, it bridged the gap between my effort and their adulation, and made me feel that for every pillow we'd forgotten, every tissue we'd soaked, every set we'd stolen, and every ovation we'd won, this was the best year of my entire career.

1984 I was in my living room when I heard Tom Hooker had died. I suddenly felt as if I was sleepwalking. The room seemed so strange as I realized how useless the furniture would be when I was someday gone. I sat perfectly still, looking through the window as cars drove by one after the other after the other.

The doctors hadn't confirmed a diagnosis. They just called it 'immune malfunction.' For years Tom went from pillar to post trying to understand why he felt so sick all the time. He saw a psychiatrist who told him it was in his head. He saw a nutritionist who told him he had too much vitamin C. I wrote letters to him in the hospital a couple of times, knowing that, near the end, somebody would have to be there to read them to him. By the time he died he was completely blind.

I remembered Tom there and then in my living room, filling the walls with images of him.

"I didn't come here for this—"

"Nora—"

"I didn't come here to be belittled—"

"Nora—"

"It was so demeaning, Tom."

I wanted to yell at him, but I knew it wasn't his fault. There was also just no more fight left in me. The tank had been emptied at the Grand only a few short months ago. He had recognized it the moment I walked into his office, where he helped Muriel Sherrin run the Toronto International Music Festival. Tom had asked me to stage manage the events at Roy Thomson Hall, and with the Festival still under Hirsch's control, I needed all the income I could get. Tom gestured towards a chair, with thin hands. He looked so delicate now, like an autumn leaf.

"Tell me again what happened," he said as he closed the door and I sat.

I stared at the white cement wall to my left, one hand steadying the other. "We're running late, so I knock on Bobby Short's dressing room and say, 'Sorry to bother you, Mr. Short.' 'Not at all,' he says. He's already dressed to the nines in his tux. 'What's the delay?' he asks me. So I tell him we normally have two follow spotlights on him, but one of the operators is a bit lame so the stairs are difficult for him. I tell him we have the house, and if it's alright with him, we'll just start with one spotlight and then add the other once the operator gets there. Simple, right?" Tom nodded and my vision grew blurry as I fought the angry tears back. "So Bobby Short agrees. He doesn't want to keep the audience waiting. I go up and tell the crew what the plan is, and you know what a crewmember says? 'Fuck no.' Yeah. 'Fuck no.'"

"Who was it?"

"I tell him that's what we're going to do. I tell him we're going to start. He says, 'No. We're going to wait 'til the other guy gets here.' But it's not just that," I added, hoping Tom knew I didn't ignore his question to be rude. It was just that that one crewmember was meaningless, only a stand-in for a prevailing ideology. "There isn't a single thing I've done here that hasn't been contested by the crew. If I ask for a certain number of chairs, they check with somebody else to make sure I'm right. I could tell them the grass is green, they'd go outside to make sure. And what's worse is that they'll go above me to the supervisor and tell him what I want and he'll agree with *me*. Still, they question me. And it's not because I'm unqualified, Tom. It's not because I can't do the job. It's because I'm a woman."

Tom surveyed me for a while, unsure what to say. As my gaze met the floor, I wasn't sure what could be said either. I had contemplated writing my vitriol into the show report, the document that states whether or not any issues arose during the performance, but Muriel and Tom were powerless. Sure, they could reprimand the crew, but then the crew would just ostracize me more.

Muriel herself had never seen a show report either, until I sent her one at the beginning of the festival. I was disillusioned by this too. To think that she had spent an entire season running the Stratford Festival and not one person had given her a show report. I wondered what the hell was going on over there. This was Stage Management 101.

Finally, Tom asked, "What happened after that?"

"I told them there's an audience waiting, that Bobby Short is waiting and he's happy to start. I told them front of house is wondering what we're doing. He looks at me and says, 'Nope.' And that was that. I should have fought him, but Tom, I can't anymore. I just — I can't anymore. It's just not worth it. You called and asked me to help out, and I'm thankful you did, but it's just not worth it anymore."

Tom leaned back in his chair. "What are you telling me?"

"I — I need to go. I can't be here."

"Okay, Nora." There was no hesitation in his response, and from it relief hummed in my bones. A moment later he added, "For what it's worth, I'm sorry all of this happened."

"Me too, Tom. Me too."

SHAWN DESOUZA-COELHO

Tom, one of the greatest stage managers this country had ever known. Tom, the perfectionist who didn't need a ruler to remind you. Tom, the great list maker who didn't need you tell him so. He didn't want your attention or your adulation. He wanted to do his job, whatever the job. He took the blame for screw-ups big and small. He trained an entire generation of stage managers, myself among them. He listened to everybody: actors, stage managers, directors, whomever. He listened because that was the job. He cared because that was the job. Tom, the stage manager who phoned the entire company when Leo died, out of duty and friendship. Tom, the stage manager I'll only ever be half as great as, even now that I'm all grown up.

In my living room, my thoughts then went to Paddy, the two of them forever inseparable to me as mentors in my fledgling years at the Festival. After Paddy was excommunicated, he went to Vancouver. He still drank too much. A friend told me once that he had to pull Paddy out of the gutter one night and take him home. Eventually Paddy went to England and found work as a night desk clerk. I still got the odd call from him. It was always sad. He was such a smart man. Alcohol does that to so many people.

The drone from the receiver startled me. I blinked at the inhuman smoothness of the plastic in my palm, and then hung up. As I did, I hoped the person was calling everybody in the company to tell them the news. I hoped the person on the other end knew Tom. What a privilege it was to know Tom Hooker.

**1985** "What are ya drinkin'?" Susan asked, pointing to the cast and crew of John Murrell's *New World*. The steakhouse we'd ended up at was dusky, and I struggled to find a place for my rosin ball as the actors lobbed drink orders at Susan. It was the size of a bowling ball, hollow and made of a translucent material that had the texture of hardened glue; a memento from the production. Ann was holding one too. Susan had already shoved hers under her chair, atop a layer of peanut shells that seemed to coat most of the floor.

"Nora?"

"Uh . . . Diet Coke," I replied, deciding to do as Susan had done and just shove the ball under my chair.

"Same," Ann added.

"Two Diet Cokes," Susan repeated for memory's sake. She turned to Bill Hutt, who was sitting in the corner. "And for you, Mr. Prime Minister?" Bill rolled his eyes and we all laughed. His blond hair had a tinge of red, a design choice meant to show that the pair were brother and sister in the play. Since Susan's head was topped with a vivacious red, the *most* Robin could do was hint at their kinship. Martha comforted Bill with a pat on his shoulder. "Well?" Susan urged.

"One of anything, Mr. Speaker," Bill replied.

"That's Madam Speaker, thank you very much."

He chuckled. "Not anymore."

We had just closed a production run in Toronto at the St. Lawrence Centre, which was the second leg of a tour beginning at the NAC. While we were in Ottawa, Bill was recognized by the House of Commons; a great honour. Ann, Donna, and I went to Parliament to be there with him and witness the momentous occasion.

"Cheers!" we all yelled, about to clink our glasses together.

"Wait, wait," Susan interrupted. "Robin, make a toast."

"Oh, come now," Robin retreated, setting his drink down. My eyebrows raised at the novelty of what I was seeing. I didn't think it was possible for Robin to feel sheepish, but there he was.

"C'mon."

"No, no."

Susan tagged Bill. "Help me out, Brother." Bill declined with a small wave. "Fine, fine. I'll make one. Um . . ." Susan paused for a moment, lost in thought. Jerking her hand forward, she said, "To laughter."

"To laughter!" we all cheered.

CRASH!

Susan screamed as she leapt from her seat and our half of the bar went nearly silent. We scanned our glasses to see if anything had broken. I then leaned over and looked on in amazement at the rosin ball underneath Susan's chair. It had shattered into a dozen pieces. Seeing what I saw, Susan burst into laughter, picking up a piece of the ball and shouting, "How funny is that?" Turning to the bartender in search of help, she called, "Nurse! Nurse!"

At one point in the production a rosin ball — one of a few set onstage — was in fact designed to shatter on cue. It was a specially made one, sitting on a table all by itself, and inside the table was a mechanism that shot a rod up with enough force that, rather than dislodging the ball, it would shatter it instead. Strangely, Susan's souvenir wasn't the special one.

We laid the pieces of the ball on the table and, as if it were Humpty Dumpty, throughout the night took turns trying to put it back together. Ann and I had become vigilant, placing our intact mementos in our laps for the remainder of the evening.

It was an oddly nice night out for January, quiet and windless, so Ann and I decided to walk to Union Station. From there we'd take the subway up to St. Clair West, where Ann lived with her husband of ten years, Ross, who was a professor at York University. I was staying with them while we were working at the St. Lawrence Centre. Along the way, the hardened snow crunched under our feet and we took in the city lights. There were more high-rises than ever, and it made me feel really small. As I looked down Front Street, I could see the CN Tower silhouetted under the fingernail moon.

I looked over at Ann as she broke the warm silence. She had begun talking about her time at the University of Toronto, how she had gotten into theatre there, and how she had entered the PhD program just so she could stage manage a new play by Robertson Davies, who was also a professor at the university at the time. She told me that when she started working at the St. Lawrence Centre as an apprentice in '75, my dad was probably the only one who knew her name. I told her what had happened with Nathan Cohen at the production of *The Memorandum* I sort of produced, and we were both a bit taken aback by the fact that we were talking about things that happened maybe fifteen years ago. At thirty-six, the "recent" past seemed suddenly so distant.

"When do you fly out?" Ann asked, as we crossed Yonge St.

"Next week."

"I caught Bill with the script a few nights ago."

I giggled. "Did you?"

"Yeah."

"I don't blame him," I said. "Clarence Darrow is not an easy role for a sixty-something-year-old. Tom once told me — Did you know Tom?"

"Tom?"

"Hooker."

"Oh, yes. Well, no, not really. We had adjoining offices a couple of years ago, but other than that, not really."

"That's too bad. He was a good man. Anyway, I can't remember what show it was, but I made some dumb mistakes once when I was prompting, and I told him I was angry that the actor was getting mad at me." Ann smiled as if I'd just traced her experience in the air. "And Tom told me that an actor's greatest fear is losing their lines, and that fear gets much worse as they get older."

"Because it's harder for them to remember things."

"Exactly."

We were both silent again, our thoughts in tune. The city gently hummed, and steam churned from the manhole covers. Once we arrived at Union Station, we paid our sixty-five-cent fare, and hopped on the subway. It wasn't until we got out on the other side that Ann spoke.

"It's stupid that you weren't asked back."

"It's Hirsch, really. That's all. I'm just too closely associated with Robin."

"And I'm not? I was his personal assistant for a time."

Ann had a point. Though the alternative reason why I hadn't been asked back was that I just wasn't good enough to work there anymore, which I knew wasn't the case. Then again, I once thought I was a pretty good ASM, until Ann and I worked the Grand together and I saw exactly what a good ASM was. I didn't think I'd ever see anybody better. Watching her instincts deftly guide her from rehearsals to performance filled me with both pride and professional jealousy. Watching her stage manage her own shows filled me with selfish longing. It was well deserved and long overdue, but I couldn't help but feel I'd lost something precious to me.

"Do you miss it, the Festival?" Ann asked as we turned up Bathurst St.

"I do." My voice was wistful. Having now worked from east to west and in between, I was certain the Festival was still a place without compare in Canada. And, in spite of its politics, it was still a place I'd love to work at again.

When we arrived at Ann's brown brick house, her Siamese cat greeted us in the foyer, and we lingered there with it for a time.

As I walked to my room to get changed for bed, Ann said, "Good show."

"Good show," I replied, and closed the door.

--

Standing on the cottage porch I heard Mom give a little cheer inside. Dad must've won a trick for them. He'd collect the cards, and Bob and Ruth Killer would shoot one another a furtive glance. As I stared out at the stand of spruce trees in front of me, I could see clearly backward to the four of them still sitting in the middle of the room, dressed in polos and shorts. They'd been at it for an hour already.

The bridge club was a Polley family tradition that began long before I was born, back when my parents were in high school. It consisted of Dad, Mom, the Killers, the Halls, the Carrs, and the Galloways. At first it was just weekly bridge, but as time went on and they got older, they started doing everything together. They went on vacations together to tropical destinations. When Dad and Mom moved to Toronto, they would all come down for the Royal Winter Fair. When Dad and Mom rented the same cottage every year, it quickly became one of a row of cottages occupied by none other than the Killers, the Halls, and the Carrs. They had even made plans to be buried beside one another in Avondale Cemetery in Stratford.

Though I grew up around it, bridge never interested me. Maybe I was just waiting for somebody like Jack Hutt to invite me to Murray's Restaurant in the Park Plaza Hotel and ask me to apprentice at bridge for $65 a week. I had been inside watching them for a while only to take my mind off Michael and the running tally of distance and time slowly separating us like water freezing in a crack. When that didn't

SHAWN DESOUZA-COELHO

work, I had decided to come outside where the air was fresh with birdsong and the smell of conifer needles.

I spied Aunt Dorothy chatting intently with Matthew on a nearby brown bench. Behind them the wall of spruces continued on. The pair were more than seven decades apart in age, but both of them looked rapt by the conversation. Dorothy had her arm over the bench, her snow-white perm shifting slightly in the wind. Matthew, who was tiny enough to curl his legs up on the seat, looked as if he were explaining something to her that only his childhood wisdom could know.

Just then I spotted Jannine galloping up the laneway towards the cottage. She'd grown, I thought.

"Where's Michael?" she asked as she passed me on the way in.

"Oh, he's working," I replied, trying not to sound annoyed.

"Where?"

"Calgary now."

Jannine raised her chin an inch and then went inside. I was thankful she left it at that. I still hadn't decided how I felt about any of what I thought was going on.

A little while later Dad came out and stood with me. We didn't speak much until he pointed to the big blue tarpaulin on the Halls' property beside ours. Each of its four corners was tied to a different tree to form a makeshift carport.

"I hate that he does that," Dad said, taking his glasses off and putting one temple tip in his mouth.

"Well, he needs a roof to park his car under."

Dad gestured to the sky. "That's not enough? It ruins the whole picture."

"Did you tell him you don't like it?"

"No. That wouldn't be very neighbourly, Ah."

1986

8:00 a.m.

Okay, Nora. Get out of bed.

8:05 a.m.

Nora. Get up!

8:10 a.m.

Nora Catherine Polley!

The world is a thick haze when I open my eyes. I blink and turn over to see Michael's impression in the sheets. I stare at the ceiling and steel myself.

Morning, PSM scheduling. Cymbeline *rehearsal. Maybe eat something. Rehearsal again. Spot the conflict. Performance of* The Boys from Syracuse. *Why do I keep doing this to myself? No, remember, this is Alan's fault. He was supposed to direct* Cymbeline, *but he withdrew and Robin volunteered. Now, look around the room, ladies and gentlemen. Who did you think they'll ask to stage manage the show? Of course it's—*

"Just be happy you're back," I mumble, if for no other reason than to truncate my downward spiral. I let out a deep yawn and get up slowly. Once I'm dressed, I follow the smell of coffee downstairs.

Michael is in the kitchen, pouring some coffee into a mug. "Good morning," he says, handing it to me. I take care that my fingers don't touch his. Behind him, through the open window, the aubades of small birds stream in with the July sunlight.

"Good morning," I reply and we sip in silence.

His cat enters the kitchen, circles his bowl, and starts snapping at his food. Michael is at the Avon this year, so we don't see one another very often at work. I'm not sure how I feel about it. Some days I think some time apart is good for us.

"I'm heading to the theatre now," he says, setting his mug down in the sink. "Do you want me to wait for you?"

I glance out the window. "I'll just walk."

"I'll see you at lunch then?"

"Today's going to be a busy one."

"Okay."

After Michael leaves, I sit in the kitchen for a few more minutes before putting my mug in the sink beside his.

Damn it.

I stare at the handle, now separated from the mug. I must have dropped it in the sink without realizing it. I throw both the handle and mug in the garbage, grab my wallet, and head out the door.

9:00 a.m.

At the Festival Theatre stage management office, I set my wallet down and smile. It's in this moment, before the chaos begins, that I'm free to feel thankful, even if the only reason I'm back is maybe because John Neville's first task as artistic director was to spite Hirsch by rehiring company members who weren't asked back under him.

"Good morning!"

I turn to find Patricia Ashworth walking in. She's the PA this season, a short woman with long blond hair. "Good morning," I reply before adding, "Shall we?"

We set to work on the schedule, which by now has become almost mechanical and comforting, like sweeping the floor. Sometimes we miss a spot, but the task itself hasn't really changed from the time when Dad pushed coloured pins into corkboard. I've also had nearly a decade to hone my technique. If only I'd been this capable with Heather Kitchen a decade ago. I feel like she wouldn't have had to help me keep my head so much. She turned out just fine, though. She's the PSM at the Third Stage this season.

"Morning!" Ann says brightly, a little while later. She sets her bag down at her desk, and we hardly have time to reply before she's heading out to the stage to do her presets for *Cymbeline*. I'm thrilled to be working with her again, not least because she knows how to handle Robin.

When 10:40 a.m. hits, I get my *Cymbeline* book and toolkit and head to the stage. The daily schedule is nowhere near done, but that's to be expected.

10:45 a.m.

I step out from underneath the balcony as Ann lugs a large trunk across the deck. I shake my head and she chortles, setting it downstage centre. She's pregnant, and it's only now starting to show. She hasn't told anybody yet because she knows the second the news hits, everybody is going to tell her a pregnant woman shouldn't be lifting heavy furniture. In other words, they'll tell her to stop doing her job.

I make my way up the aisle and set my effects down on the stage management table as Robin enters from the back.

"*What's this?*" Robin booms from the back row. He's prim in every sense of the word. Ann has just positioned the bed with one of the crewmembers who is now backstage. She's staring blankly at Robin.

"Pardon?" I reply.

Robin descends halfway. "The furniture. It's all off."

"Is the furniture on the spikes?" I call to Ann.

She inspects every set piece on the deck. "Yes, they're all on their spikes."

"Then the spikes are off," Robin says.

Excuse me?

"What do you mean?" I ask.

Robin looks twice at me, as if I've just questioned an order. "The spikes are all off," he repeats.

"They're the same as they were yesterday."

"I'm not talking about yesterday. I'm talking about today."

I'm barely hiding my disbelief at what Robin is implying. "The spikes haven't changed."

"The positions are different."

You seriously think somebody came in overnight and changed the spike marks?

"It needs to be fixed," Robin demanded.

Take the blame, Nora. Just take the blame.

"Ann, let's move the furniture." I snap open my toolkit and rip out the spike tape, refusing to play Robin's game. "Where should the spikes be, Robin?"

As Robin commands us around the stage, I'm glad Ann understands that this is how Robin stops an argument: there is no argument. He's right and he always is. Nobody comes in and moves the spike marks overnight for one particular scene, but Robin is convinced that the furniture is in the wrong position, and maybe he's right. Maybe this isn't where the furniture should go, but that's where it was yesterday and the day before and the day before that one. So, now he's telling us where he's going to put it, and this whole stupid back and forth is his way of saying that he's just changed his mind.

Satisfied, Robin takes a seat, and the actors file in for rehearsal. All I can do is try to put the nonsense behind me as I throw open my book and Ann returns backstage to begin the day's scene work.

1:35 p.m.

I return to the office with Ann, who is as tacitly perplexed as I am at Robin's outburst. When we arrive, my intention to continue scheduling and nibble on some semblance of lunch is postponed by the crowd huddled over my desk. Even Colleen is there. She's the production manager now, so her office is upstairs.

"What's going on?" I ask.

At the centre of the mass comes a familiar voice. "I made a little something for you."

My mouth falls open as the crowd parts. It's Chris Blake, back this season, but as marketing manager, and he's pointing to my desk. On it is a scale model of the Festival Theatre's parking lot, maybe a foot and a half square, complete with little toy cars, bushes, and even lines drawn on to show the parking spots.

"There's the stairway going up to the stage door! Chris, why?" I don't ask to sound offensive. I'm just so startled by the gesture and the time this no doubt took to create.

"I know this past year's been difficult for you," Chris says, while Ann and the others fan back to their desks, "so this is your very own parking lot for whenever you need one in the future."

My thoughts suddenly career back to eight years earlier and the parking lot that played styptic to my helplessness, inadequacy, and tears during Robin's fraught *Macbeth*. I then flash forward to last year and Dorothy's heart attack. Her funeral was at the Dack Gingras Funeral Home on Caledonia Street. I brought beer because Dorothy requested it. She said she just wanted everybody to have a good time.

SHAWN DESOUZA-COELHO

I placed the bottles in the casket behind her head, and mourned her with a million quiet memories.

"Thank you so much, Chris," I say, hugging him. I'm still stunned that anybody would do something like this for me.

"Robin!" Colleen calls to the door, waving him in. I turn to find him craning his neck inside the office.

"Check it out," I say, thinking he'll get a kick out of it. I tell him what I remember — about *Macbeth*, about the knowing glance he gave me — and he looks at me like I've just screwed up some very basic math.

"I'm not sure I have any idea what you're talking about," he says plainly, before leaving as quickly as he came. Something tells me he's lying. I could have sworn he knew what I was trying to do when I asked him to distract the crew all those years ago. But, as with all things Robin, I know the truth of his thoughts is locked away for good.

I spend another moment taking in the model. "It's great, Chris. Thank you."

When Colleen and Chris leave, I carefully place the model above my desk, on a shelf, telling myself to cherish it while hoping I'm never again boiled to the point where I have to use it.

BRRING! BRRING!

I pick up the phone. "Stage management."

Oh for Christ's sake.

The man on the other end sounds shocked, and I know why. "Yes," I say, "this is the stage management office at the Stratford Festival. Sorry . . . Thanks . . . Bye."

"Another one?" Patricia asks, amazed.

I hang up the receiver. "Another one." Last season there was a production of *Measure for Measure* where, during the pre-show, the stage was set up to look like a leather bar. The actors were dressed as prostitutes and transvestites, all mingling with the audience. Some patrons were invited onstage to dance, and one young actor playing an escort even handed out cards with his name and phone number written on them. Maybe the recipients were just curious, or maybe they really were looking for a good time, but all of them were shocked to find they'd reached the Festival Theatre stage management office and a disgruntled stage manager.

There's a rumble in my stomach loud enough to spur Patricia to run and get me a sandwich. "It's fine," I tell her, adding, "You know what they say about stage management and lunch, right? Never in the same sentence. I've only got fifteen minutes left anyway."

With that, we continue working on the schedule.

2:00 p.m.

Back in the auditorium, we're set up for the scene where Susan's Queen, who will be costumed and made up to look like the Queen Mother herself, creates the poison intended to kill Imogen. The stage is set up to look like a laboratory, and the Queen will wear a white lab coat.

"Whenever you're ready," I call to Susan.

"Thank you," she replies before setting herself and beginning.

> QUEEN. I wonder, doctor,
> Thou ask'st me such a question. Have I not been
> Thy pupil long? Hast thou not learn'd me how
> To make perfumes? distil? preserve? yea, so
> That our great king himself doth woo me oft
> For my confections? Having thus far proceeded, —
> Unless thou think'st me devilish — is't not meet

"Meow," I drone, providing the sound effects for a cat that is supposedly scurrying around the room. We won't have an actual cat onstage, thank God. It'll just be assumed the cat is somewhere out of view.

> That I did amplify my judgment in
> Other conclusions? I will try the forces
> Of these thy compounds on such creatures as

I watch as the Queen nonchalantly pours milk into the cat's dish and then a few drops of something else before setting the mixture on the floor. She doesn't even bat an eyelash; she just carries on with her speech.

We count not worth the hanging, but none human,
To try the vigour of them and apply
Allayments to their act, and by them gather
Their several virtues and effects.

I chuckle quietly to myself, wondering if anybody will realize she's just poisoned her cat as casually as she would put on a coat.

4:00 p.m.

BRRING! BRRING!
I check the clock as I head to the phone. 5:05 p.m.
When did an hour pass? It feels like I just got here.
By some miracle Patricia and I finished tomorrow's schedule on time. Really, it was her, which is fine because when I'm pulled in two directions and we need to go in three, I know *somebody* is there covering that other third. It's days like these that remind me stage management is a team effort.
"Stage management," I say once I've picked up the phone, thinking it's a call about a conflict.
You've got to be kidding me.
"Yes, this is the stage management office at the Festival Theatre. Okay . . . Bye." I set the receiver down. Patricia is stifling her laughter. I simply shake my head. "I cannot believe people are still calling."
BRRING! BRRING!
I rub my forehead. "You answer it," I tell Patricia.

6:00 p.m.

In the green room, my hunger nags even as I sate it with a sandwich and coffee. I'm sitting near the back, and the space is alive with energy as the actors and crew of *Syracuse* chat. There's now an endless sea of grey clouds behind me; one of those days that gives the impression of rain. I find myself focused on the bodies entering the room; each one makes me think of Michael. I teeter here with my food between the urge to look away and the compulsion to continue, knowing that even if Michael did walk in, I still wouldn't know what to say.

When I've eaten as much as habit will allow, I head down to begin my pre-show work.

6:45 p.m.

In the washroom, I change into my blacks: a black T-shirt and jeans. Arriving in the office, I set my street clothes down and sit at my desk. I make sure my book is in order while I dry-swallow two Aspirin.

"Headache?" Patricia asks.

"Not yet."

7:00 p.m.

Actors begin arriving for the show, each stopping at the sign-in sheet on the callboard beside the office on the way to his or her dressing room.

"Evening, Norni!" Susan says as she walks by the office.

"Make sure you sign in," I quip.

"Yeah, yeah."

Rarely a day goes by when we don't have to remind at least one of them.

7:25 p.m.

"Good evening, ladies and gentlemen," Ann says over the paging system, "for this evening's performance of *The Boys from Syracuse*, this is your half-hour call. One half-hour." It's not a half-hour to show time. Rather, it's an English half-hour: half-hour to the beginners call, which is five minutes before curtain. "If you have not signed in, please do so now at the callboard."

7:30 p.m.

Ann checks the sign-in sheet to certify that we have the full company. Not so long ago this verification process was done through the stage doorman, but that proved unreliable one too many times, the middleman signing in actors who were actually nowhere to be found. Ann's voice beckons through the paging system once more.

"Would Messieurs Davies and Thomas please sign in at the callboard? Messieurs Davies and Thomas, please sign in at the callboard. Thank you."

Two this time. I wonder what the record is.

Once the truant actors have signed in, Ann announces, "Ladies and gentlemen, the house is now open. The house is now open."

The front of house manager informs stage management of the percentage of seats full. I go around to each dressing room and relay the information. I also do it just to say hi because the actors won't see me again until after the performance. I could go home and they wouldn't even know.

7:40 p.m.

"Ladies and gentlemen, this is your fifteen-minute call," Ann pages. "Fifteen minutes."

"I'm heading up," I tell Ann as I pass by the ASM console with my book in hand. Around her, dressers and stagehands flit up and down stairs and in and out of doors like a French farce. "See you on the other side."

"All right," she replies, turning back to the checklist on the counter in front of her.

The walk up to the booth is always a bit harrowing as I cross the planks strewn across the lighting grid a couple of stories in the air. I'm thankful they finally installed a railing, at least. Below me, I can see the house filling up. Just under my feet, the many different-coloured streamers tied from the top of the grid to the stage floor underneath are dazzling in the pre-show light.

7:50 p.m.

I can't hear the paging calls from the booth, so I just assume Ann has given the five-minutes. I place my book on the desk, turn on the lamp in one corner, and settle in. I adjust the seat so I can reach the cue light box over my head with ease. I smile at it always because it means Tom's legacy lives on.

7:55 p.m.

I put my headset on, assuming the call for part one beginners has gone out. "Hello, hello," I say plainly to all channels at once. I'm not sure which god I have to thank, but the Festival has finally purchased single-muff headsets, so I no longer have to worry about things sliding when they aren't supposed to.

"Hello," I hear in return.

Good, good.

8:00 p.m.

"Put your warns on," Ann says to me over headset to let me know the house is ready and that I'm free to issue a warning for the cues at the top of the show. She issues a "standby" to the backstage, tunnels, and on the monitor page system.

"Warning Lights 11, 12, and the Orchestra," I intone over the headset before setting the cue light switches for the right door, up-centre, left door, right tunnel, balcony, and left tunnel. "Warns on," I repeat back to Ann.

Through the window, high above the stage at a wretched angle, I can see that the audience has settled. I'd feel like God if I didn't know I wasn't actually in control of anything. There were actors long before there was anybody to stage manage them, and the show ends when they are done, not when I call the last cue.

Still, I can't help but feel like I'm in outer space when I'm up here, cut off from everybody and everything. Between myself and the actors is a plate of glass and fifty-eight feet. Between myself and the lighting and sound operators is six inches of floor. Between myself and the ASMs and crew is a tethered earmuff. It's certainly not how I prefer to call shows.

"It's all yours," Ann says.

My voice becomes lithic. "Lights 11, go." The house lights dim halfway. "Lights 12, go." The house lights dim almost entirely.

One, two, three.

"Orchestra, go." The overture begins, directed by the incomparable Bert Carriere, a musical director and institution at the Festival for years and years now. As the orchestra plays, my work continues as I say, "Warning Lights 12.5, 14 auto-follow 14.5, 15, the Bell, the Streamers, and the Bomb." The overture ends. "Streamers, go." All at once, the streamers zip up to the grid like a tape measure. "Bomb, go," I say during the applause, referring to the firing of the Festival's cannon outside to signal that the performance has begun. "Lights 12.5, go." I flick the up-centre switch down. "Bell, go," I continue, referring to the bell rung in the loft.

One, two.

"Lights 14, go."

Out from under the balcony walks Butch Blake's Diogenes, wearing a yellow tunic and red sash. He's holding a lantern. My fingers are still primed on the switches for the left and right doors and tunnels. I watch as Diogenes says he's looking for an honest man. I shake my head.

When you find him, send him my way.

8:18 p.m.

Shit. She mixed up the lines.

Keith Thomas's Dromio is onstage with Susan's Luce, arguing in song about what good a man is, but she just screwed up the words. Bert tries to compensate by shutting down all the instruments except the piano. My heart is in my throat for Susan as she stammers around the stage while the pianist smashes keys trying to guide her back to the correct spot. But, I'm also laughing because Susan is just so damn funny trying to find her place. I reach over to the God mic, the one that will shatter the auditorium with my voice as it trumpets out from speakers now in the voms, but before I can do anything more, Susan speaks.

"Bert, Bert, Bert!" Bert cuts the piano. There are little pockets of laughter throughout the audience. "We need to go back to the top!"

The top of what? The song? You're in the third verse.

Susan and Keith step back to their starting positions.

"From the top of the song," I say over headset.

The music begins again, this time only with the piano. As the song progresses, and Susan finds her footing, Bert adds in the other instruments. When the song is finally finished, the audience's applause is enormous. It's probably bigger *because* of what just happened. If my career has taught me anything, it's that audiences love that stuff.

I cue the next scene, and after Susan leaves the stage, I whisper over headset, "How's she doing?"

"Fine," Ann says. "She's laughing it off."

"Of course she is." If anybody can laugh off something like that, it's Susan Wright.

SHAWN DESOUZA-COELHO

10:30 p.m.

"How about that?" Ann says as I pass by her on my way to the office.

"Indeed," I reply, knowing I'll have to put what happened in my show report. Calls of "good show" pass between actors as they head to their dressing rooms to change. Some of those good graces are lobbed through the office door as people walk by, and I feel appreciated. After another fourteen-hour day with no overtime pay, I'll settle for a kind word here or there.

It's only when I sit down and write about what happened that I realize I almost had to prompt Susan over the God mic. I wonder what Susan would have done then. I can hear her laughing down the hallway. I smile. She probably would have screamed something up to the booth like, "Heads up!" or "Grandma?" She was a consummate professional, but she also knew just how to lighten the mood.

Through the door, I see Colm Feore walking out with Goldie Semple, the voluptuous sandy blond who played the scantily clad Courtesan in the show. They work well together, those two. They're laughing about something, maybe something that happened in a scene between them. I've always wondered about the private lives of actors onstage, and whether their corner of the world feels anything like ours.

11:30 p.m.

I slip into my house as quietly as I can, but end up bumping into the coat rack by the front door. I pause, listening for Michael. Only the distant sound of a barking dog greets me. I can see his cat's neon eyes glimmering at me in the darkness of the dining room. I turn the light on and he saunters away indignantly, as if I'd just disturbed him. I set my wallet on the kitchen counter, make my way upstairs, undress, and crawl into bed. Michael's already fast asleep. I turn away from him, too tired to even think. I'm glad for that because I'd only turn his words over and over again: "I'm in love with someone else."

1987

So this is where we are. Huh.

At the corner of Douro I turned right and headed up Waterloo. It was late Monday morning and, as I walked, I noticed a car trying to park behind St. John's Church. The driver couldn't seem to figure out where the lines were. I toyed with the idea of stopping to help, but instead kept on with my chin down. The truth was I felt like a tardy thief, dressed for a job interview, but running late. I didn't want to be seen by anybody because this morning was my first step to leaving the theatre behind. I just couldn't do it anymore.

At Ontario I turned left, and there it stood like a beacon to me. The sign above its doors was a beautiful red wood with letters finely carved into it: Crabtree & Evelyn. At the centre was the company's logo: an intricately detailed apple tree. I took a moment and adjusted my short blond hair in the reflection in the store window. People ambled sparsely behind me, and I hoped they couldn't tell how anxious I was. I couldn't remember the last time I'd sat for a job interview. I'd sort of just floated from one theatre job to the next for years now, always asked to participate somewhere. Yet, here I was doing the asking at a Crabtree & Evelyn where I imagined myself doing nothing more than selling lovely-smelling soaps to people. I smiled almost giddily at the placid, pleasant thought. I opened the door, and, as the chimes above the frame rang out, I went inside.

I sat by the phone in the stage management office, watching the time tick closer to 7:00 p.m. The rest of the team carried on with their pre-show work with one eye towards me. Any moment now Howard might call and I'd have to kick them out of the office in order to talk to him. The conversation always seemed so dire.

Howard Rollins was a wonderfully successful American television and film actor that Neville had contracted to do *Othello*. A broad man, he played the title role, but I always felt he just wasn't equipped for it. He didn't get it, the stage work. In rehearsals he'd speak Shakespeare's words in ways I'd never thought possible, and not in a good way. Night after night the show was either twenty minutes longer or shorter depending entirely on his performance.

These evenings when I sat on my hands waiting for him to tell me if he'd show up or not had become something of a ritual for me. I hated every second of it. I even asked the management, "Are we going to support Howard through this production in the hopes that we will make it to the end? Or are we looking for a reason to replace Howard, who is obviously not doing the best job in the world?" Their answer was clear: Howard stays.

I watched the clock until my periphery faded. 7:00 p.m. was the point of no return. Tiresome repetition had taught me that if he called at six to tell me he wouldn't be coming in, I definitely had enough time to talk him down. But if he called at seven, then I didn't have enough time to both talk him down *and* replace him for eight in the eventuality that I failed to do so.

His understudy, Joseph Ziegler, needed time too. He had the unfortunate task of being a white man understudying Othello. Initially, there wasn't an understudy at all since Howard was the only black actor in a company of a hundred. But I needed an understudy for Othello to rehearse Iago's understudy, so Joe volunteered because he'd never get to play the part otherwise. I had even voiced my concern to Neville, who was directing the show, and he said, "He'll never be off. And if he is, I'll come down and do it." To this day, Neville hadn't once followed through. At least four times now, Joe had had to go on for Howard. We'd fit him into a wig, paint his face black, and change the sheets on the bed from white to black as well because keeping them white meant Joe's body paint would rub off on them as he murdered Desdemona.

6:45 p.m. I must've sighed aloud because Maggie Palmer, a thin stage manager with long dark hair, turned to me and reassured me, "He'll call." She understood, as I did, that it's not knowing that hurts the most. If an actor doesn't make it onstage or into the rehearsal hall or to a fitting or wherever, of the many things we think could have happened, the actor's death is among them. Depending on the actor, it was higher on the list of possibilities.

6:47 p.m. *For the love of—*

BRRING! BRRING!

I snatched the receiver up. I spoke calmly. "Stage management."

"Nora…" Howard said, his dulcet voice cracking. I could tell he'd been crying.

It was as if the world had been put on pause. Everybody in the office turned to me, some midstride, others with their pencils still on paper, poised to write. I nodded, and they each promptly gathered their things to wait outside while I tried to talk Howard into giving us one more night.

"Cheers," Michael and I said, clinking our wine glasses together. I sipped and the white wine nudged me, as if it was morning and it was time to

SHAWN DESOUZA-COELHO

get up. I needed that. It was oddly chilly inside, so I could see the steam from the pasta on our plates curling in the air. The two of us had decided to spend our day off together for a change. It was a welcome change. We were reminiscing about how our relationship had started.

"As I recall," I said, setting my wine down, "it was me playing the records . . . and making all the moves."

He scoffed. "That doesn't make any sense! I have a *way* better record collection than you. Besides," he added, buttoning his words with a fork full of food, "I made the first move."

I chuckled. "Yeah, because I set the stage for you. You would have been stupid not to."

"Ever the stage manager."

"Indeed."

Our cutlery tinkled with our dishes as we ate and drank, neither of us saying very much else for a time. I found myself glancing upward on occasion, feeling like some fog had settled above us. Twice Michael asked what I was looking at, and twice I didn't have an answer for him, only an instinct.

"You know what I just remembered?" Michael said, wiping his mouth with his napkin.

"What?"

"Do you remember when I made all that brioche? For *Private Lives*?"

I nodded.

"Maggie used to pick at it even after the scene was done. She used to accuse me of making her fat."

I chuckled at the thought of a clandestine Maggie Smith picking at warm brioche under the cover of darkness. "I remember you telling me that. I was actually thinking not long ago of sending her a card or something, to see how she's doing. Maybe I'll bring that up."

"No, don't."

"I know, I know. Still, it'd be nice to hear from her again."

We laughed a little, and then fell silent once more. It was then the air in the room shifted, as if everything had suddenly moved two inches to the left, including us. Michael looked different, like somebody I'd barely known, let alone loved.

I stood in awe at the beauty of the store. The floors were hand-stencilled with flowers and on all sides there were huge, dark wooden cabinets. I shifted my weight from my left foot to my right and through scent alone travelled from an orange grove to a lemon tree. I could only imagine where in the world the other side of the store would take me. Maybe to a fjord where mint grew wild. There were no customers, but in a back corner of the store a short, brunette woman popped up from behind a shelf like a mole. I waved and was about to say something, but then the manager, a blond woman of middle age, came out of her office at the other back corner and greeted me.

"Nora!" she said, her voice bright. "So nice to see you." The brunette woman ducked back down behind the shelf.

"Sorry I'm late," I said, clutching my wallet tightly.

"Not at all." We shook hands. She smelled like a pine forest. She motioned to the shelf just behind her and the series of small spray bottles laid out neatly there. "You have to try this new fragrance," she added, clicking the cap off one and misting the air between us. She breathed deeply, and motioned for me to the do the same. It smelled like a spice rack, but I smiled through it. "Isn't it great? There's a hint of coriander in there." I smiled, as if I'd noticed.

I just want this job. If smelling like an old cupboard is the worst of it then bring it on.

She clicked the cap back on and set the bottle down. "Let's have a chat, shall we?"

"Sure thing."

I followed her into her office and she shut the door behind us.

"How are you, Howard?" I asked, his strained breathing filling my ear and the empty office.

"Not too good, you know?" His voice was soft and distant, as if he were holding the phone at arm's length.

"What's going on?"

"I . . . I — I don't think I can do it tonight."

I suddenly felt so very tired. "Why? What's the matter?"

"It's my friend, you know?"

SHAWN DESOUZA-COELHO

"What happened?"

"He was in a fight at this bar. He was just havin' a drink. At this bar, he was just havin' a drink and then this guy comes up to him and starts causin' trouble."

"Oh?"

"This guy starts causin' trouble, and they get into a fight and my friend, he . . ."

"Howard? Are you there? Howard?"

"Yeah, yeah. There was just this kid ridin' by on a bicycle. He didn't have a helmet on. Little kid . . . didn't have a helmet on."

"What happened to your friend?"

"I don't think I can do it tonight."

"What happened to your friend?"

"This guy starts hittin' him, and he fights back because he's got some fight in him, and they start throwin' down and he ends up gettin' stabbed. He called me from the hospital. Told me he's alright. Stitches on his forehead, all along his arm, all over. I don't think I can come in tonight. I just . . . It's too much, you know? Too much . . ."

"Howard? Howard?"

"I've been thinking . . ." Michael started, setting his hand on his glass. "I've been thinking of going into directing."

"Makes sense to me," I replied, knowing a lot of stage managers used stage management as a platform for other careers in the theatre.

"The University of Alberta has a good program. I know some people who went through it and they said it's a great place, great teachers. I'd get to stage three full productions."

I paused. "Which means you'll be gone for . . ."

"I mean they only accept two people per year, so competition is stiff."

He must not have heard me. Am I whispering?

"Which means you'll be gone for a year."

"Two."

"Two?"

"Yeah."

"Two . . ." I took a drink.

Can I do two more years of this? I mean Marg has been living out there for I don't know how long and I see her once or twice a year. That's not so bad, right? I still love her like I always did. And he won't be working around the clock, not like at the Festival. Everything is a bit tamer after the Festival. Maybe we can handle it. But he was in Calgary already, and Montreal, and Toronto, and Blyth . . . Now he's in Stratford, right across the table from me, but he might as well be on the moon. I can't tell anymore if he's moving or I am or the world is just spinning too fast for either of us to hold on.

All of this I thought, but didn't say. Instead, I said, my voice cracking in spite of myself, "I need you to tell me the truth."

"So, tell me a little about yourself."

The last time I sat for an interview like this it was with Jack Hutt in Murray's Restaurant back in '69. The diner smelled of coffee and cigarettes and Jack treated me like an old friend. Now, I was sitting opposite a woman who bathed in ylang-ylang, her question much more formal than Jack's because she didn't know me at all. She picked up my résumé from a pile of papers strewn atop her wooden desk. Around me wooden cabinets stood beside the filing kind, and a part of me felt that this was what it would be like to work inside a tree.

"Well, I grew up in Stratford just down the road from here. Though, that doesn't say much since everything is just down the road from here." I let out a nervous laugh. She simply smiled and waited for me to continue. "Well, you can see on my résumé that I've worked with the Stratford Festival for a good part of my life."

"I do see that. Why the change after all this time?"

"Oh, you know. I think the Festival is great and all, but I'm just looking for something low pressure." I caught the look in her eyes, as if she were asking me to correct myself. "I mean that's not to say that this job is low pressure, but just lower pressure I guess. I don't do well with pressure." Again, the same look. "I mean I do well with pressure, I'm just looking for a job with no pressure."

Am I sweating a lot? I feel like I'm sweating a lot.

SHAWN DESOUZA-COELHO

"Do you have any sales experience?"

"No, not really. I worked in the box office at the Festival when I was a teenager, but most of my time as a stage manager was spent in a dark room. So, no, not much sales experience." I paused for a moment and then hastily added, "But I'm a fast learner."

"Great." I could tell my answer was anything but. "So why Crabtree & Evelyn?"

"Well, I love the fragrances here. And everything's so beautiful. I can see myself working in a place like this where there are beautiful things to look at, you know? Like I said, I spent a lot of my time in a dark room looking at a script. Not very interesting. Here, though, it's bright and colourful and cheerful." I winced deep down at that last word, feeling like I'd somehow given her too much. "Did I mention how much I love the smells here? Yeah, oranges and lemon and, I think I smelled . . . was that . . . sage . . . out there too?"

She nodded, impressed. "Good nose." I couldn't tell sage from a burning tire. Michael used sage in a recipe once, maybe. That was how I remembered it was a spice that existed. "And where do you see yourself in five years?"

I tried briefly to imagine myself working at Crabtree & Evelyn in five years, misting the air with all kinds of bottles, wafting my hand over candles, but instead my mind went blank and I said something about not wanting to plan too far ahead and living in the present moment. It was clear from how abruptly the interview ended that that was not the right answer.

I left the store and somehow the fresh air seemed stale. It smelled like Stratford, a small town in Southwestern Ontario where in the summers the surrounding farmland blew the scent of dung into your throat. I was in the store for all of fifteen minutes, so the street was just as empty as it had been when I went in. I lowered my chin, still hiding, only now it was because I felt like a failure.

"Howard, come in," I pleaded. It was now 7:10 p.m., and if I was going to have enough time to get Joe on for the start of the show, I had to know Howard's decision.

"I can't, Nora," he replied apologetically. Whatever it was going on inside him was tearing him in two.

"I can pick you up. I could be there in seven minutes." I was willing to try anything and I wasn't lying. Howard lived in the white house on Douglas for the season because Neville had decided not to use it for his tenure as artistic director, since he already owned a house.

"I wouldn't be givin' it my all, you know?" I wasn't shocked by his dismissal. I'd offered before and he'd turned me down. If he was going to come, it would be on his own terms.

"It doesn't have to be your all. You just have to do what you can." To this he said nothing. "Howard, you don't want to be at home by yourself. You need to come in here where you have something to do, where you have people to talk to." Something told me the winds were changing, so I added, "Being here will take your mind off your friend. It's what I would do."

There was silence for a minute or so. I could still hear him breathing so I didn't say anything to interrupt whatever thoughts were battling away in his head. Meanwhile, a war raged in my own with salvos of thoughts I wasn't proud of. Never did I think them all at once, but rather in snatches throughout the entire year, thoughts I'd felt had been forced out of me by the sad routine of this production.

You have no idea what you're putting this cast through every time you do this, you selfish prick! I have to be here waiting on you hand and foot to make a decision when I should be preparing for the show. And what about Joe? Do you realize that whenever you decide not to show up, we have to take him out of Troilus and Cressida *and put understudies on there too? Did you ever think about who you're letting down here, Howard? Did you ever think that you're one of the reasons this production is a nightmare, and that the only thing we look forward to is the food a company member brings in for the interval? You're not the reason we do this show, Howard. We do it for a container of cookies.*

Spurred on by Howard's continued silence, my scornful thoughts spiralled out to the rest of the Festival . . .

And the stupid fiefdom Robin's created out of the Young Company in his own secretive way. How are you going to tell them not to associate with the rest of the company, Robin? What gives you the right? And of course David William is livid again over in Troilus. *And Neville! Why would you leave your assistant director high and dry on the first day of rehearsal? Jeannette Lambermont had no idea what she was supposed to do. I had to give her a dictionary and tell her be ready to look up words just so she'd have some place to start. And on the top floor of this shit tower is Michael—*

Finally, Howard said, "I don't know."

"*Howard*," I urged as gently as I could. "*It can only help.*"

After another moment he said, "Okay, Nora," and then hung up the phone.

I sat for a moment with the receiver in my hand, staring at the parking lot above my desk. In place of solace I found only ambivalence. I couldn't help but feel like I was enabling Howard by talking him down from the ledge yet again. But I was also saving Joe from the panic-inducing task of understudying Othello. I set the receiver down, and then opened the office door.

"The program is only two years long," Michael explained. "It's maybe a bit longer with the thesis I need to write."

"You know what I'm talking about," I said pointedly.

"If it's about the distance, I'd come back whenever I could. And you could come visit me. You could visit Marg too. Isn't Fred moving up there this year?"

I know you're leaving because there's somebody else.

"We've made it work before."

I could take it if it were just sex.

"I'm forty this year and I just — I just don't want to be a fifty-year-old stage manager."

I could take it if you two were just screwing around.

"I've always been interested in directing and I think if I'm ever going to do it, it has to be now."

But you love her, and that I just can't handle. When I look at you, all I see is her.

"We could alternate holidays. You spend one in Edmonton, I—"

"I'm going to London for a few days," I said, almost like I was noticing rain. "When I come back, I don't want you living here." Michael collapsed into his chair. I didn't pay much attention to his expression because I had gotten up and gone to the bedroom to pack my suitcase. Oddly, I wasn't crying.

As I walked home from my botched interview, I thought about turning around to shop for something for Ellen. She was only less than a year old, but it was never too early to start showering a child with gifts. I was her proud godmother, after all.

Ellen was Ann's beautiful miracle child. She and Ross had stumbled upon her conception after many years of trying. Ann brought her to the opening night of *Othello* to greet the cast. I could still see her sitting on the red rug centre stage, wearing a onesie that looked like a tux. I laughed thinking about it. Ellen was the best part of that show.

When I reached my front door, I gripped the handle, but didn't move. Nearby, a bird cackled in a tree.

What am I going to do? I can't do it anymore. I can't work at that place anymore. They need somebody who will be there for them, who has patience and empathy, and I've run out of both. Nobody ever comes to you with good news. Pile it on, boys! Pile it on. They were "fascinating." That's what Dad would say. Nobody could party like theatre people. I totally get why: because they're all fucking crazy. And you'd have to be crazy to work with them. You'd have to be crazy to work eighteen hours without any chance of overtime. You'd have to be crazy to sit still and watch people abuse one another and themselves. You'd have to be crazy to play their bullshit political games.

In the hall, the rest of the stage management team was standing by anxiously. I gave a little thumbs-up to let them know how things had transpired. With relief, they flooded back into the office. I thought of Joe then, who would soon be getting ready for *Troilus and Cressida* over at the Avon, and the anxiety he must feel every performance, never really knowing if tonight was the night.

SHAWN DESOUZA-COELHO

When Joe had gone on a couple of times, I recognized and congratulated his Herculean efforts with a really nice bottle of wine and a card that read, "What five words strike terror into Joe Ziegler's heart?" Inside it read, "Hello, Joe? This is Nora."

Michael tried to talk sense into me, but he knew that I wasn't going to change my mind. I could tell he wasn't trying very hard in the first place. Maybe he recognized this as his ticket out, that I was giving him a free pass to leave me.

TIK-TIK. TIK-TIK. TIK-TIK. TIK-TIK.

Only my headlights guided me as I drove the dark and winding road to London. The moon was nowhere to be found and I tried not to think about very much. I didn't turn on the radio either. Instead, I just listened to the sounds of the zippers on my suitcase tinkling around in the backseat and my tires scratching the pavement, picking up stones and whipping them underneath the car.

TIK-TIK. TIK-TIK. TIK-TIK. TIK-TIK.

It was when Stratford had disappeared entirely from my rear-view mirror that I began to sob, so quietly that, if the radio had been on, I myself might not have heard it.

TIK-TIK. TIK-TIK. TIK-TIK. TIK-TIK.
TIK-TIK. TIK-TIK. TIK-TIK. TIK-TIK.

BRRING! BRRING!
    Is that—?
BRRING! BRRING!
    I went inside, set my wallet and that horrible interview down, and answered the phone.
    "Stage management. I mean . . . Nora Polley." I smacked my head, unable to believe what I'd just done.
    The voice on the other end laughed. With very little preamble it said, "I'm calling to tell you that Richard Monette wants you for his *Shrew*."
    "Wants me?"

"For his *Shrew*, yeah."

"Okay."

Shit! Why didn't I think about it first? No, I can't.

"But only if that's *all* I do," I added.

Nora, what are you doing?

"Yeah, that's fine," the voice replied. "Just fine."

After a little while longer, I hung up. With my hand still on the receiver, I stared out through the window. A car sped by. A crow swooped down on my lawn.

Nora . . . what are you doing?

SHAWN DESOUZA-COELHO

1988

Enter Clowns and Town.

"**Lights 9** *Go*," I said over headset, and with two hands above me, I **flicked** the balcony, right tunnel, and left tunnel switches down on the cue light box. I'd almost forgotten this feeling. But as the acrobats, tumblers, and riotous music filled the stage and town of Padua in Richard's *The Taming of the Shrew*, all of it came back to me like leaves in spring. "**Fireworks** *Go*." *CRACK! CRACK! CRA-CRACK!* The streets were alive! I **flicked** the left and right tunnel switches up again, as well as the trap, right door and up-centre. "**Lights 10, Sound 3** *Go*." All five fingers **flicked** down and I felt alive too. She saw it all, watching me as I watched the stage. "**Lights 11, Sound 4** *Go*. **Lights 12, Sound 5** *Go*. **Lights 13, Sound 6** *Go*." Every move a moment memorized; the only way to call it. I **flicked** the right door and up-centre switches up again. **"Lights 14, Sound 7** *Go.* **Lights 15, Sound 8,** *Go.* **"** **Down** on the right door switch. **"Sound 9 and 10,** *Go.* **"** And then the crown jewel of the transition: **down** on the up-centre switch, followed quickly by **"Lights 17, Sound 11** *Go.* **"** From under the balcony came a scaled down red Alfa Romeo roadster. **"Sound 10.1,** *Go.* **"** *VROOM! VROOM!* It did a three-point turn. **"Sound 15,** *Go.* **"** *SCREEEECH!* It parked under the balcony, facing upstage as Lucentio and Tranio hopped out. I checked my stopwatch, noting the elapsed time. Four minutes and forty-five seconds.

Good. Right on track.

Everything was slow to me then, as it had been the entire season. It was like time was being pushed through a needle, and I could pick out every word and gesture it carried with it. I felt my senses expand beyond the darkness of the lamplit booth where Jeannette and I sat: below to the operators

Exit Clowns and Town.
Enter Lucentio and Tranio.

LUC.   Tranio, since for the great desire I had
To see fair Padua, nursery of arts,
I am arrived in fruitful Lombardy,
The pleasant garden of great Italy,
And by my father's love and leave am armed
With his good will and thy good company,
My trusty servant well approved in all,
Here let us breathe and haply institute
A course of learning and ingenious studies.
Pisa renownèd for grave citizens
Gave me my being and my father first,

A merchant of great traffic through the world,
Vincentio come from Béntivolii.
Vincentio's son, brought up in Florence,
It shall become to serve all hopes conceived
To deck his fortune with his virtuous deeds.
And therefore, Tranio, for the time I study
Virtue, and that part of philosophy
Will I apply that treats of happiness
By virtue specially to be achieved.
Tell me thy mind, for I have Pisa left
And am to Padua come as he that leaves
A shallow plash to plunge him in the deep,
And with satiety seeks to quench his thirst.

TRAN. *Mi perdonato*, gentle master mine.
I am in all affected as yourself,
Glad that you thus continue your resolve
To suck the sweets of sweet philosophy.
Only, good master, while we do admire
This virtue and **this** moral discipline,
Let's be no stoics nor no stocks, I pray,
Or so devote to Aristotle's checks
As Ovid be an outcast quite abjured.

adjusting their clothes; through the window shielding me from my actors; out into the auditorium where elbows rustled elbows and armrests creaked under the pleasure of the viewing public. Every step taken on the deck was checked by my marrow. I even knew the secrets of whispering feet backstage. It felt like I knew the locations of every man and woman in every hall and wing. I could feel the flag atop the Festival Theatre rattling softly in the lazy summer breeze.

Dressed in black with long frizzy hair, Jeannette rattled too, so minutely I could call it biology, her every movement changing the air. I smiled, feeling her eyes still aimed at me though they were fixed on the stage.

I reached up to **warn** the right door as I said, "**Warning Sound 18, Lights 18 and 19,**" over headset.

Jeannette was Richard's assistant director, and Richard used her to her fullest, leaving her to conduct rehearsals in one space while he worked in another. Richard believed in people, believed in her. She needed that, especially in this all-boys club where every word and gesture played foreground to the perpetual question: Is it because I'm a woman?

"**Lights 18**," I said, as I turned the page in my script, the sound of bending paper vitalizing in its familiarity. "*Go.*"

They won't take my advice. Is it because I'm a woman? They question my every suggestion. Is it because I'm a woman? I have to work twice as hard just to not be invisible. Is it because I'm a woman?

The skin of my fingers bowed against the right door switch above and I **flicked** it down, finding the click oddly satisfying. I leaned slightly forward to see characters flood the stage. I checked my stopwatch once more. Eight minutes and twelve seconds.

We're running sixteen seconds behind.

I **flipped** the right door switch up on the syllable, and then **flipped** it down as I warned, "**Lights 19**," in wait for the exasperated reactions of the others to Baptista's tinny proclamation. There was one, and another. "*Go.*"

Let's hope it corrects itself.

It was always touch and go, the timings of scenes. It was

LUC.

Chop logic with acquaintance that you have,
And practise rhetoric in your common talk,
Music and poesy use to quicken you,
The mathematics and the metaphysics
Fall to them as you find your stomach serves you. X
No profit grows where is no pleasure ta'en. X
In brief, sir, study what you most affect.
Gramercies, Tranio, well dost thou advise.
If, Biondello, now were come ashore,
We could at once put us in readiness,
And take a lodging fit to entertain
Such friends as time in Padua shall beget.

Enter Baptista, Katherina,
Bianca, Gremio and Hortensio.

TRAN.
BAP.

But stay awhile, what company is **this**?
Master, **X** some show to welcome us to town. **X**
Gentlemen, importune me no farther,
For how I firmly am resolved you *X* know;
That is, not to bestow my youngest daughter
Before I have a husband for the elder.

GREM. If either of you both love Katherina,
Because I know you well and love you well,
Leave shall you have to court her at your pleasure.

KAT. To cart her rather. She's too rough for me.
There, there, Hortensio, will you any wife?

HORT. I pray you, sir, is it your will
To make a stale of me amongst these mates?

KAT. Mates, maid, how mean you that? No mates for you
Unless you were of gentler, milder mould.

HORT. I'faith, sir, you shall never need to fear.
Iwis it is not halfway to her heart.
But if it were, doubt not her care should be
To comb your noddle with a three-legged stool,
And paint your face, and use you like a fool.
From all such devils, good Lord deliver us!

GREM. And me too, good Lord!

TRAN. Husht, master, here's some good pastime toward.
That wench is stark mad or wonderful froward.

LUC. But in the other's silence do I see
Maid's mild behaviour and sobriety.

TRAN. Ah, hah!

LUC. Peace, Tranio.

never the same each night, but when one scene dragged a few seconds, it was easy for the next scene to do the same until brick by sluggish brick the whole production ended up taking three, four, or even five minutes longer than rehearsed. In this regard, I was powerless because, for the most part, I took my cues off the actors. I couldn't call an entrance sixteen seconds earlier just to pick up the pace. The actors needed to feel the pace drag and make up for it in and between their lines. It was their show, always.

I chuckled quietly to myself, my hand sliding up and down edges of my script. Jeannette laughed too. Lucentio and Tranio were downstage at the edge of the left tunnel while Goldie's Katherina commanded the stage. The verve, the power, the grace: she stole every scene she was in. Jeannette's clothes rustled as she shifted position. I wasn't sure why, but I was suddenly struck with how relevant and problematic it all was, the taming of a shrew. Here was a

TRAN. Well said, master. Mum! And gaze your fill.

BAP. Gentlemen, that I may soon make good
What I have said — Bianca, get you in.
And let it not displease thee, good Bianca,
For I will love thee ne'er the less, my girl.

KAT. A pretty peat! It is best
Put finger in the eye, an she knew why.

BIAN. Sister, content you in my discontent.
Sir, to your pleasure humbly I subscribe.
My books and instruments shall be my company,
On them to look and practise by myself.

LUC. Hark, Tranio, thou mayst hear Minerva speak.

HORT. Signor Baptista, will you be so strange?
Sorry am I that our good will effects
Bianca's grief.

GREM. Why will you mew her up,
Signor Baptista, for this fiend of hell,
And make her bear the penance of her tongue?

BAP. Gentlemen, content ye. I am resolved.
Go in, Bianca.

Exit Bianca.

woman reaching the top of her field, the first woman at the Festival who would have made the transition from assistant director straight to director next season when she helmed her own production of *Titus Andronicus*. Yet, time and time again she was driven to over-assert herself, only to be ignored after having done so. I knew the cycle well. Richard helped her stand outside it, though.

Every rehearsal, it felt like Richard emptied himself into the work entirely by including personal touches, scenes that reflected moments from his own life. In a scene later in the play, after Colm's Petruchio takes Katherina to his home, each of them smash plates by throwing them offstage under the balcony. It was both funny and crushingly sad to know that it was real and it had really happened to Richard as a child. But, being new to directing at the Festival, he just didn't know how to talk to his actors. It got to the point where he threatened, silently, only to Jeannette and myself, to cut an actor because he wasn't doing what Richard wanted in a scene. Jeannette told Richard she would talk to the actor. He trusted her enough to let her, and that was all it took to smooth things out. It turned out the actor wasn't married to his choices anyway.

And for I know she taketh most delight
In music, instruments, and poetry,
Schoolmasters will I keep within my house
Fit to instruct her youth. If you, Hortensio,
Or Signor Gremio, you, know any such,
Prefer them hither; for to cunning men
I will be very kind, and liberal
To mine own children in good bringing-up.
And so farewell. Katherina, you may stay,
For I have more to commune with Bianca.

Exit Baptista.

KAT. Why, and I trust I may go too, may I not?
What, shall I be appointed hours, as though, belike,
I knew not what to take and what to leave? Ha?

Exit Katherina.

GREM. You may go to the devil's dam. Your gifts are so
good here's none will hold you. There! Love is not so

If it wasn't for Richard, who knew where I'd be. An orange grove somewhere, maybe. He believed in me too, at a time when I couldn't believe in the theatre at all. If I wasn't doing this show, I'd probably be sitting alone at home in a living room once big enough for two, but now somehow too small for one.

When I told my parents what had happened between Michael and me, that he was now living on his own in Stratford and we weren't seeing one another anymore, they were disappointed but understanding. I'd finished crying about it, so they didn't feel the need to either. It was just another bump in the road.

Through guilt, I found myself in charge of the Apprentice Training Program. I had told the Festival I would come back if Richard's show was the only one I did. I thought there was no way they would let me fly. After all, there was no such thing as a stage manager guest artist. So, when they gave me their wholehearted approval, I felt like I'd somehow taken advantage of them. With my nagging conscience getting the best of me, I volunteered to run the training program. I was glad I did, though. Through this program I worked more with understudies and learned just how terrible actors had become at reading aloud.

I held weekly readings of Shakespeare's plays every Saturday in Rehearsal Hall 1 for anybody interested. Once the actors arrived, we divided up the smaller roles so people wouldn't be talking to themselves and split up the bigger roles between two or three people. At the first meeting, I put all of the character names in a hat and each actor drew one. The women were fine with drawing a male character's name, perhaps knowing the likelihood of them ever playing Romeo or Hamlet or Prospero was minuscule. But, for some reason, the men outright refused to read for female characters. For some reason the men got it into their

HORT. great, Hortensio, but we may blow our nails together, and fast it fairly out. Our cake's dough on both sides. Farewell. Yet, for the love I bear my sweet Bianca, if I can by any means light on a fit man to teach her that wherein she delights, I will wish him to her father.

So will I, Signor Gremio. But a word, I pray. Though the nature of our quarrel yet never brooked parle, know now, upon advice, it toucheth us both — that we may yet again have access to our fair mistress and be happy rivals in Bianca's love — to labour and effect one thing specially.

GREM. What's that, I pray?

HORT. Marry, sir, to get a husband for her sister.

GREM. A husband? A devil.

HORT. I say a husband.

GREM. I say a devil. Think'st thou, Hortensio, though her father be very rich, any man is so very a fool to be married to hell?

HORT. Tush, Gremio. Though it pass your patience and mine to endure her loud alarums, why, man, there be good fellows in the world, an a man could light on them, would take her with all faults, and money enough.

GREM. I cannot tell. But I had as lief take her dowry with this condition — to be whipped at the market-place every morning.

HORT. Faith, as you say, there's small choice in rotten apples. But come, since this bar in law makes us friends, it shall be so far forth friendly maintained till by helping Baptista's eldest daughter to a husband we set his youngest free for a husband, and then have to't afresh. Sweet Bianca! X Happy man be his dole. He that runs fastest gets the ring. How say you, Signor Gremio?

GREM. I am agreed, and would I had given him the best horse in Padua to begin his wooing that would thoroughly woo her, wed her, X and bed her, and rid the house of her. Come on. X

Exit Gremio and Hortensio.

TRAN. I pray, sir, tell me, is it possible That love should of a sudden take such hold?

LUC. O Tranio, till I found it to be true, I never thought it possible or likely. But see, while idly I stood looking on,

---

heads that they'd have to do high voices or something. Not knowing how to respond to that, I grouped the male roles in one hat and then the female roles in another, and we started over. Then, once the female roles ran out, as I knew they would since we were doing Shakespeare, the women ended up drawing male characters anyway. Then we read.

From the booth, I watched Hortensio patiently, as if he were telling me some deeply guarded secret. It was a gesture I stalked, not a line. Seeing it, I called, "**Warning Sound 16,**" priming the operator for his next cue. I breathed slowly, savouring the moment in spite of the distance. Always, I wished to be down there with the actors, breathing the same air as them. "**Sound 16** . . ." There was always a special thrill that came with calling a cue off an actor's tiniest move. "*Go.*" I consulted my stopwatch. Fourteen minutes and thirty seconds.

"Does it seem slow to you?" Jeannette asked as we watched Lucentio and Tranio take centre stage.

I nodded. "Thirty seconds behind now."

"Hm. Off night."

"They'll have to pick it up somehow."

"Yes."

I found the effect of love in idleness,
And now in plainness do confess to thee,
That art to me as secret and as dear
As Anna to the Queen of Carthage was —
Tranio, I burn, I pine, I perish, Tranio,
If I achieve not this young modest girl.
Counsel me, Tranio, for I know thou canst.
Assist me, Tranio, for I know thou wilt. X

TRAN.   Master, it is no time to chide you now; X
If love have touched you, naught remains but so —
Redime te captum quam queas minimo.

LUC.   Gramercies, lad. Go forward, this contents.
The rest will comfort, for thy counsel's sound.

TRAN.   Master, you looked so longly on the maid,
Perhaps you marked not what's the pith of all.

LUC.   O yes, I saw sweet beauty in her face,
Such as the daughter of Agenor had,
That made great Jove to humble him to her hand,
When with his knees he kissed the Cretan strand.

TRAN.   Saw you no more? Marked you not how her sister
Began to scold and raise up such a storm
That mortal ears might hardly endure the din?

I turned the page, and ripped the following page apart from it. "**Warning Lights 20**," I called, scratching off the offending glue from the corner. Jeannette turned to me with raised eyebrows, and I chuckled in disbelief, thinking how possible it was for a million-dollar production, complete with extravagant costumes and spectacular pyrotechnics, to be derailed by a wayward speck of glue. Keeping my attention on the stage, I warned, "**Lights 20**," and then watched for Tranio's response. "*Go.*"

As a stage manager, I always found reading plays in my head difficult because, on the job, I never read who was talking. When a play was up on its feet, that work was done for me. It was clear who was talking because somebody actually was. Plays made more sense to me when read aloud. It was stunning, though, seeing the actors at our Saturday morning gatherings chew their way through a speech, as if the words were stale gum. Granted, it was a cold read for

LUC.
Tranio, I saw her coral lips to move,
And with her breath she did perfume the air.
Sacred and sweet was all I saw in her.

TRAN.
Nay, then 'tis time to stir him from his trance.
I pray, awake, sir. If you love the maid,
Bend thoughts and wits to achieve her. Thus it stands:
Her elder sister is so curst and shrewd
That till the father rid his hands of her,
Master, your love must live a maid at home,
And therefore has he closely mewed her up,
Because she will not be annoyed with suitors.

LUC.
Ah, Tranio, what a cruel father's he!
But art thou not advised he took some care
To get her cunning schoolmasters to instruct her?

TRAN.
Ay, marry, am I, sir — and now 'tis plotted.

LUC.
I have it, Tranio.

TRAN.
Master, for my hand,
Both our inventions meet and jump in one.

LUC.
Tell me thine first.

TRAN.
You will be schoolmaster,
And undertake the teaching of the maid —
That's your device.

most of them because when else would they have had the chance to read any of Shakespeare's plays aloud, let alone some of the lesser known or performed ones like *Timon of Athens* or any part of *Henry VI*? The Festival hadn't even performed *Timon* once in all the time I'd been here. I also surmised that people just didn't read aloud anymore, period. Gone were the days of sitting around the hearth listening to stories read by one or another. So I'd chime in with corrections to their pronunciation here and there, but never did I fault them. Everybody was there to learn.

It was gratifying, really, being part of their growth as actors, especially when they flourished. Sometimes an actor would blow me out of the water, making me rethink everything I knew about Shakespeare's language. Then there were other actors who floundered to the point of depressing me. I watched them give it everything they had, watched them beat their heads against the wall of Shakespearean verse until their brains were porridge, all the while knowing they would never be great Shakespearean actors.

LUC. It is. May it be done?

TRAN. Not possible. For who shall bear your part
And be in Padua here Vincentio's son,
Keep house and ply his book, welcome his friends,
Visit his countrymen and banquet them?

LUC. *Basta*, content thee, for I have it full.
We have not yet been seen in any house,
Nor can we be distinguished by our faces
For man or master. Then it follows thus —
Thou shalt be master, Tranio, in my stead,
Keep house, and port, and servants, as I should.
I will some other be — some Florentine,
Some Neapolitan, or meaner man of Pisa.
'Tis hatched, and shall be so. **X** Tranio, at once
Uncase thee, take my coloured hat and coat.
When Biondello comes, he waits on thee,
But I will charm him first to keep his tongue. **X**
So had you need. **X**

TRAN. In brief, sir, **sith** it your pleasure is,
And I am tied to be **obedient** *X* —
For so your father charged me at our parting:
'Be serviceable to my son', quoth he,

"They are flying now," Jeannette remarked on the sudden change in the show's pace. I detected it too.

"Maybe they finally noticed."

"I think they just started listening."

"Indeed."

Jeannette's observation was astute. It was a problem every production at the Festival fell victim to at one point or another. The routine took control and what was once alive petrified into mere bodies waiting for their turn to recite lines. I was just as susceptible to this, for I too had lines and cues, which was why I always reminded myself that there were people opposite these switches. **"Warning Lights 21 and 22,"** I said, as I **flipped** the left door switch to tell the nuns waiting there to stand by for their entrance. Tranio and Lucentio began to exchange clothes in the street. **"Lights 21 . . ."** The audience roared, and I smiled. The best was yet to come. **"Go."** With great pleasure, I **flipped** the left door switch. The nuns strolled by and gasped. **"Lights 22 Go."** The audience loved it. Jeannette loved it. I loved it. And, once the nuns had had their much-unwanted fill and left, I took a deep breath. My

Although I think 'twas in another sense —
I am content to be Lucentio, X
Because so well I love Lucentio.

LUC. Tranio, be so, because Lucentio loves.
And let me be a slave t'achieve that maid
Whose sudden sight hath thrilled my wounded eye. X

Enter Biondello.

Here comes the rogue. Sirrah, where have you been?

BION. Where have I been? Nay, how now, where are you?
Master, has my fellow Tranio stolen your clothes,
or you stolen his, or both? Pray, what's the news?

LUC. Sirrah, come hither. 'Tis no time to jest,
And therefore frame your manners to the time.
Your fellow Tranio here, to save my life,
Puts my apparel and my countenance on,
And I for my escape have put on his.
For in a quarrel since I came ashore
I killed a man, and fear I was descried.
Wait you on him, I charge you, as becomes,
While I make way from hence to save my life.

finger on the up-centre switch, I followed Tranio's words to my cue and **set** it, knowing there was a living, breathing actor now standing by. I felt complete in my responsibility to maintain the rehearsed liveness of this production night after night, satisfied in the understanding that the switch wasn't above me as I now **flicked** it. It was in me, in my blood, sanguineous and consanguineous at one and the same time. I was satisfied in the understanding that, in me, a third generation of Polleys would continue to tend this wonderful, messy garden.

To thank Richard for pulling me back in, for saving me really, I gave him a gift on opening night. It was a pin I had made in the shape of a horse's head, white with an orange mane, modelled after the one that was added to the front of Petruchio's Vespa for the wedding scene. Richard loved it. He told me he'd wear it on his lapel for the opening of every production he directed: on the outside if it was a comedy, and on the inside if it was a tragedy. I was touched.

BION. You understand me?

LUC. I, sir? Ne'er a whit.
And not a jot of Tranio in your mouth.
Tranio is changed into Lucentio.

BION. The better for him, would I were so too!

TRAN. So could I, faith, boy, to have the next wish after, X
That Lucentio indeed had Baptista's youngest
daughter. But, sirrah, not for my sake but your
master's, I advise you use your manners discreetly
in all kind of companies.
When I am alone, why then I am Tranio,
But in all places else your master Lucentio.
Tranio, let's go.

LUC. One thing more rests, that thyself execute —
To make one among these wooers. If thou ask me why,
Sufficeth, my reasons are both good and weighty. X

Exeunt.

"Warning Lights 23 to 25, Sound 17 to 19.2," I called, raising two hands and, with three fingers, priming the up-centre, left door, and left tunnel switches. The plastic was warm and even as I spoke I listened to the tinny voices on the Tannoy. I listened to Jeannette breathing. I listened to her hair parting as she ran her fingers through it. I listened to the heartbeat of the front row. My breathing was even, and I was wholly present, but could already see my way through the labyrinth of cues leading us from here to the end of this next transition, from here to the end of the play. I felt like I could see everything. "Sound 17," I cued. "Go." Like clockwork, the car radio turned on. "Lights 23, Sound 18 Go." VROOM! VROOM! "Sound 19 Go." The car gone, its engine shut off. I flicked the up-centre switch. "Lights 25 Go." I flicked the left door and left tunnel switches. Tumblers and acrobats filled the stage, carrying a small, round table, setting it up-centre with three chairs and a parasol. I quickly set

the left door switch again. **"Sound 20** *Go*. **Sound 19.1** *Go.*"
I **flicked** the left door switch. Petruchio entered on a Vespa,
followed closely behind by Grumio on a bicycle. **"Sound
20.1** *Go.*" The audience rollicked as the pair crashed into
one another. I checked my stopwatch. Twenty-one minutes
and forty-five seconds.

We're back on track.

Enter Petruchio and his man Grumio.

Mushy peas . . . Mushy peas . . .

"Hey, Nora," Maloo said, looking out the window as we drove down the empty London street after a long night of rehearsal for Robin's production of *The Philadelphia Story* at the Grand. "What are we looking for again?"

"Mushy peas," I sighed, driving south on Richmond St. towards the downtown core.

"Mushy peas?"

"Mushy peas."

"Right! Mushy peas."

"No. Mushy peas. You know, the thing that 'looks exactly like it sounds'?" I'd never heard of the dish before, but Robin's description of it was still etched in my mind.

"Oh, my mistake. Mushy *peas.*"

Our laughter at the lunacy of both the words and our task fogged the glass. The street lamps laved everything in yellowy-orange, January snow and all. Our coats rustled like sandpaper as we craned our necks, searching one building after another, each a silent monument to our failure at this late hour. I glanced at the clock. 1:00 a.m.

"To answer your previous question," I directed at Maloo while I scanned the road, "working for Robin is a 24-hour job."

Maloo took in the car. "Clearly."

I turned right at York St. and noticed Maloo was actually smiling. She was unbelievable.

Melissa Veal, or Maloo, as people took to calling her, was my ASM for this show at the Grand, where Martha Henry had taken over as artistic director. She was a little over a decade my junior, from a smaller town than I, with short and curly brown hair. Maloo had never worked with Robin before, but was eager to learn how. She was one of the few who risked falling flat because she knew it was a vital part of the process. When prep week started, she was frank about her computer illiteracy and relieved when I told her I didn't care if her lists were done in crayon as long as they were done. Besides, I had barely learned to use computers myself. The Festival now had one in the office, and sometimes I had to wipe the dust off it before using it.

In rehearsal a few days before, she came into the room with a finished prop and began showing it to the actor who was going to use it. Robin and I clocked this at the same time, so I rushed over, took Maloo aside, and explained to her that any other director would have applauded her initiative, but not Robin. Robin had to see the prop first. Every decision about the play, no matter what the department, had to go through Robin. Maloo took the note in stride, with a smile that couldn't help but soften even the most hardened person. Sure enough, though, we didn't end up using the prop, and went with something else instead.

"Anything else I should know?" Maloo inquired.

"Um. Only move if he does."

"Meaning what?" I then told her about *Parade* and Martha's faked back spasm. The look on Maloo's face was priceless. "He's crafty."

"Smart," I corrected.

"*Smart*. What else?"

"Don't ask a yes or no question, because that's all you get."

"Okay."

"And write your questions down so you don't waste his time trying to remember them."

"This is good."

"And he always—" I turned right, up Ridout St., and thought I spotted a restaurant. Instead, I found Hanford's Tire Automotive Centre. Disappointed, I thought for a moment about taking my blue Civic in. I also thought about buying a new car, but not because anything was wrong with this one.

"Nora!"

"I thought I saw a place."

"Finish your thought."

"I don't remember what I was saying."

"You said, 'He always . . . ' He always *what*?"

"Oh." I tried to remember, but my mind felt as empty as the street. "I don't recall."

"Nora!" Maloo was astonished into laughter.

"It'll come back to me. I just need to focus on something else."

"Maybe we're going about this all wrong. This is a British thing, right?"

"I assume so."

"Maybe we should look for British things? Like a fish 'n' chips spot or something."

"Maybe."

"I think I saw a place down by the mall."

"How do we get to the mall from here?"

Maloo pointed behind us. "Head south, I think."

As we did, Maloo asked me how long I'd been stage managing.

SHAWN DESOUZA-COELHO

"Twenty years, this year." I found myself looking curiously at the wrinkles on my hands. "Started in 1969."

She gave a breathless, "Wow," and then asked what my favourite experience was in all that time. I told her about Martha and the water pitcher, how she scrubbed the dirt of Angelo off her skin. I told her I'd never felt like I was in the right place until that moment. Maloo drew inward, as if suddenly lost in a world all her own. I went on.

"Martha actually asked me something I've never been asked before."

"Oh?"

"She asked me, 'What show would you like to do at the Grand?' I thought she was asking me what show I wanted to stage manage next season, so I said, 'I don't remember what shows you're doing.' She said, 'No, no. Not what would you like to stage manage. What show would you like to *do*? Something not on my list. An original idea.'"

Maloo looked impressed, the question's novelty not lost on her either. "So what'd you come up with?"

"*Burn This*."

"*Burn This*?"

"It was on Broadway two years ago. John Malkovich played Pale. Do you know him?"

"I think so. He was in *Dangerous Liaisons*?"

"Yes. It was a great play. Mine would star Colm, and Sheila would be the ballet dancer. She's already got the figure for it. John was stunning, though. He wore this long wig, and the way he tossed his hair . . . There wasn't a dry seat in the house."

Maloo giggled, and then pointed right as we drove south on Wharncliffe Road, squinting as she read a sign. "Archie's Seafood. Maybe that place has mushy peas."

"Mushy *peas*," I muttered, rolling the words around in my mouth like hard candy. "Mushy *peas*."

"Mushy *peas*."

"Where are we? Wharncliffe and Cove Rd. Okay, we'll tell Robin."

"What about the mall?"

"We'll still check it out."

Before Christmas, Maloo and I were at the mall when we decided to get Robin a Christmas card. It was a picture of us sitting on the mall Santa's lap, looking childish and entirely out of place. The man in the Santa suit certainly didn't expect two grown women to join in the festivities. He laughed, though, when I told him I wanted Kevin Costner for Christmas.

"Nothing here," Maloo inspected as we drove around the lonely-looking mall.

"No."

"Oh well. Archie's Seafood it is. Now, finish your thought."

"My thought?"

"From before. You were saying Robin always . . . *something*."

"Oh." I squinted for a moment, but then shook my head. "I don't remember."

"Nora!"

SHAWN DESOUZA-COELHO

 As the afternoon sun combed Rehearsal Hall 1, Richard Monette sat forward in his chair, transfixed on the prone Rosalind and Celia eavesdropping on the balcony.

JACQ.   By my troth, I was seeking a fool when I found you.

ORL.   He is drowned in the brook; look but in and you shall see him.

Jacques and Orlando were wrapping up their tête-à-tête, and I found myself sitting forward too, trying not to mull over the many varied ways in which Lucy Peacock's Rosalind could hurt herself irreparably.

JACQ.   There I shall see mine own figure.

ORL.   Which I take to be either a fool or a cipher.

Around the room, actors lent their attention to the scene. John Stead, a newcomer to the Festival acting company who was also in charge of choreographing the fights for *As You Like It*, watched Rosalind intently. Tall, brawny, with blue jeans and dusky boots, he seemed to radiate confidence. He would stop the scene if anything went wrong.

JACQ.   I'll tarry no longer with you. Farewell, good Signor Love.

ORL.   I am glad of your departure. Adieu, good Monsieur Melancholy.

As Jacques left the stage in the direction of the left door, Orlando exited in the direction of the right tunnel. Then the air solidified, and I gripped my pencil tighter.

ROS.   Forester! — Do you hear, forester?

Orlando re-entered as Rosalind flung her legs over the balcony's front edge, the first time she'd ever done so since the idea was pitched, maybe the first woman to ever do so in the Festival's history, and she began her hasty climb down to the floor. John didn't move, so neither did we. Instead, we all watched as Rosalind dangled in the air for a moment, and then landed on her feet with a thud. A bit spent, she continued the scene amidst the silent admiration of the company.

ORL.   Very well. What would you?

{ Interval }

Nora Polley

... standing in front of 75 Front Street, her childhood home, 1954.

... receiving a Tyrone Guthrie award to help in the writing of her book, then titled Go, Elephants. Go, Waterfall, 1981. The Beacon Herald.

... accepting the Jean A. Chalmers Apprenticeship Award from artistic director Jean Gascon, 1969. Photo by Douglas Spillane.

... attending an opening at the Avon Theatre, 1966.

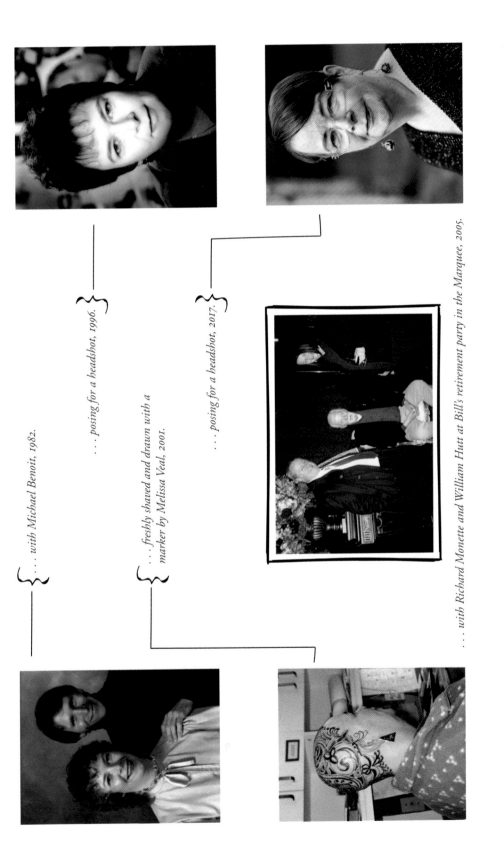

. . . with Michael Benoit, 1982.

. . . posing for a headshot, 1996.

. . . freshly shaved and drawn with a marker by Melissa Veal, 2001.

. . . posing for a headshot, 2017.

. . . with Richard Monette and William Hutt at Bill's retirement party in the Marquee, 2005.

... away from her desk at the Festival Archives, 2015.

... at the Loyal Service Dinner with the Festival Archives team, 2014. Front left to right: Roy Brown, Christine Schindler, Liza Giffen, Maggie Woodley, Nora Polley.

... at the Loyal Service Dinner, 2009. From Nora, moving clockwise: Robin Phillips, Jannine Coburn (unseen), Joe, Sue Coburn, John Wood, Jeannette Lambermont-Morey, David William.

... on the last day of her career as a stage manager, October 31, 2009.

Victor Charles Polley (age 19), 1935.

Family

From left to right: David, Margaret, Fred, Nora, Sue, Elizabeth, and Victor, 1961.
Photo by Peter Smith.

Dorothy McTavish (age 11), and
Gertrude Elizabeth Polley
neé McTavish (age 1), 1919.

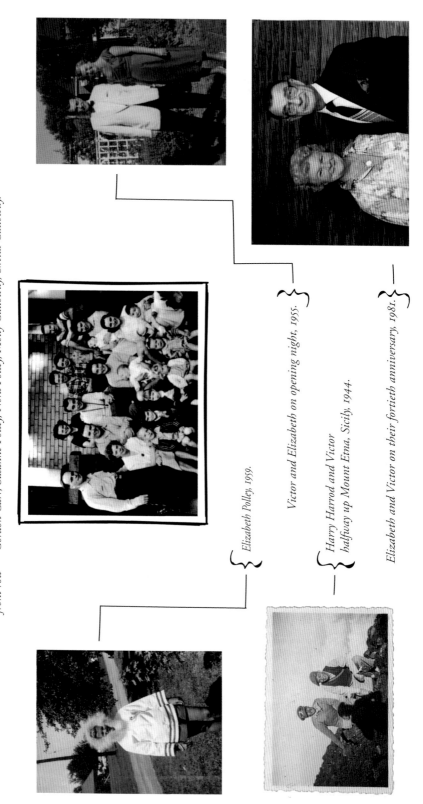

The Bridge Club, 1950. From left to right: back row — Elizabeth Polley, Victor Polley, Charlie Bill Hall, Dorothy McTavish, Howard Galloway; middle row — Robert Killer, Audrey Carr, Scottie Carr, Tony Galloway holding Nora Galloway, Ruth Killer holding Jane Killer, Kay Hall holding Ken Hall; front row — Gordon Carr, Susanne Polley, Nora Polley, Molly Galloway, Sheila Galloway.

Elizabeth Polley, 1950.

Victor and Elizabeth on opening night, 1955.

Harry Harrod and Victor halfway up Mount Etna, Sicily, 1944.

Elizabeth and Victor on their fortieth anniversary, 1981.

Francis Patrick Polley (centre) with the choir of the Festival's inaugural Richard III, *1953. From left to right: Ernie House, George Leinueber, Bob Morehead, George Boundy, Glen Richards, Ross Heimpel.*

Nora and her extended family at the cottage, 1985. From left to right: back row — Sue Coburn, Nora Polley, Victor Polley, Fred Polley, David Polley, Elizabeth Polley; front row — Heather Coburn, Jannine Coburn, Sonja Coburn, Dorothy McTavish, Lisa Polley, Matthew Polley, Janice Polley holding Kate Polley.

Marg, Dave, Nora, Fred, and Sue, with Victor and Elizabeth on their fiftieth anniversary, 1991.

Nora, Marg, Janice, Sue, Dave, 2016.

Directors

John Wood, posing for a headshot.

Robin Phillips, on break from rehearsal during Stratford's golden years. Photo by Jane Edmonds.

Jeannette Lambermont-Morey, in conversation. Photo by Jane Edmonds.

Richard Monette, at home. Photo by Kerry Hayes.

Robin Phillips and Marti Maraden, in rehearsal. Photo by Jane Edmonds.

Robin Phillips working with voice coach Lloy Coutts, in rehearsal. Photo by Jane Edmonds.

Richard Monette, the actor.

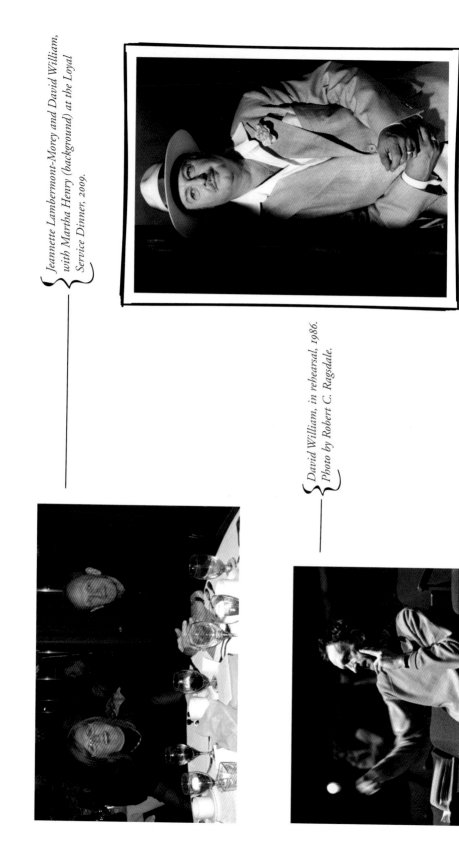

Jeannette Lambermont-Morey and David William, with Martha Henry (background) at the Loyal Service Dinner, 2009.

Richard Monette, as Domenico Soriano in Filumena, 1997. Photo by Cylla von Tiedemann.

David William, in rehearsal, 1986. Photo by Robert C. Ragsdale.

Stage Management

The Nora Polley
Stage Management Booth
in recognition of her 45 years of service
to the Stratford Shakespeare Festival
2009

*The Festival Theatre stage management booth,
now named after Nora.*

*Paddy McEntee, one of Nora's earliest mentors,
poses in front of the train taking them from Warsaw
to Moscow, 1973. Photo by Paddy McEntee.*

*Nora and Melissa Veal with
Mickey Mouse at Disney World, 1989.*

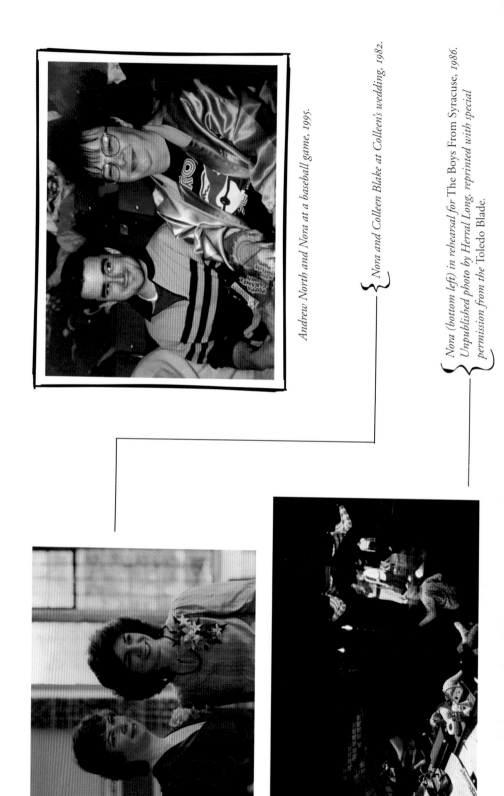

Andrew North and Nora at a baseball game, 1995.

Nora and Colleen Blake at Colleen's wedding, 1982.

Nora (bottom left) in rehearsal for The Boys From Syracuse, *1986. Unpublished photo by Herral Long, reprinted with special permission from the* Toledo Blade.

Production stage manager Maggie Palmer's weekly schedule for the 2015 season, showing the week of March 2 to March 8, with all the complexities and corrections involved therein.

Actors

Brian Bedford (Angelo) and Martha Henry (Isabella)
in Robin Phillips's Measure for Measure, 1975.
Photo by Robert C. Ragsdale.

Leo Ciceri in his final role
as Iachimo in Cymbeline, 1970.
Photo by Douglas Spillane.

"A little withered bird": Cordelia (Sara Farb) in
King Lear's (Colm Feore) arms, with members of the
company, in King Lear, 2014. Photo by David Hou.

Measure for Measure, 1969.
From left to right: Kenneth Welsh (Barnardine),
Bernard Behrens (Pompey), William Hutt (Duke),
Robin Marshall (Abhorson). Photo by Douglas Spillane.

Eric Donkin as King Lear in King Lear
at the Neptune Theatre, 1977.

*The cast and crew of the European tour gather
outside of their bus in Poland, 1973.
Photo by Paddy McEntee.*

The School for Scandal, *1970. Robin Gammell
(Joseph Surface) and Mervyn Blake (Sir Oliver Surface)
with the library chair, on the left. Photo by Douglas Spillane.*

William Hutt as Feste in Twelfth Night *wearing
the sweater Nora knit for the production, 1980.
Photo by Robert C. Ragsdale.*

Past Festival Romeos gather for a group shot.
From left to right: Antoni Cimolino (1992),
Bruno Gerussi (1960), Richard Monette
with horse pin (1977), Colm Feore (1984).
Photo by Jane Edmonds.

Keith Thomas (Dromio of Ephesus)
and Susan Wright (Luce) in
The Boys from Syracuse, 1986.
Photo by Robert C. Ragsdale.

Lucy Peacock as Rosalind
in As You Like It, 1990.
Photo by David Cooper.

Lucy Peacock as Rhonda in
The Blonde, the Brunette, and
the Vengeful Redhead, 2006.
Photo by David Hou.

William Hutt in his final role as
Prospero in The Tempest, 2005.
Photo by David Hou.

Peter Donaldson, a real salt-of-the-earth
kind of guy. Photo by Peg McCarthy.

ROS.   I pray you, what is't o'clock?

ORL.   You should ask me what time of day: there's no clock in the forest.

ROS.   Then there's no true lover in the forest, else sighing every minute and groaning every hour would detect the lazy foot of Time as well as a clock . . .

"Fucking fantastic!" Richard stood and cried after the scene had concluded. His bright, gravelly voice filled the hall. "Did that feel good?"

"Totally," Lucy replied, hands now on her hips, her short dark hair kempt. She stood to me then like an ancient redwood: sturdy and unbreakable.

"Well, it looked great. Let's take fifteen and pick it up when we return."

"Fifteen minutes, ladies and gentlemen," I called to the room. "Fifteen minutes. Thank you."

As actors filed out, a proudly grinning John patted Lucy on the back. Richard lit a cigarette and turned to me, pointing to where he thought Jacques should exit.

"No," I said, telling him why that wouldn't work.

"But what if—" he tried after taking a drag.

"No."

"And—"

"Nope." It was then I noticed John leaving, his grin all but gone, replaced with something vague and sullen.

"I don't suppose—"

"Won't work either."

"Fuck, Nora! Tell me!" I pointed to the stage left tunnel and, almost audibly, something clicked in Richard's head. "Perfect!"

I was already out the doors, after John, when I suddenly remembered my teenage years, sitting in the green room back when I worked in the Festival box office, overhearing Richard making plans for a scene with Plummer. He was only a stranger to me then. Now, my conversations with him were unlike any I'd ever had with a director. Richard wasn't just any other director, though. These halls had become his home, just as they'd become mine. So followed our banter.

Outside, the heat was polite, and with my hand for a visor I found John on a shaded bench near the Festival garden.

"Oh, hey, Nora," he said as I approached, glancing at me and then back to the flowers. "How are ya?"

"Fine, and you?"

"I'm alright. Lucy's really somethin', isn't she?" Agreeing, I sat. "When she told me she was pregnant, I thought, 'Okay! This scene has some *real* weight to it now.'" I chuckled, and he cocked his head to one side, realizing what he'd just said. "You know what I mean."

"I told her to take the stairs if she feels uncomfortable, but she wants to do the work."

The two of us then silently imagined Lucy further along in her pregnancy, making the descent for two. I was awestruck. Like Ann, she wouldn't let anybody tell her how to do her job.

"Ya know . . . I . . . I don't think this is for me," John offered, finally. I turned to him. "I'm a fight guy, ya know? I don't like having to be in the show. It's not what I want." He gestured in a wide circle above him. "All this, it's not what I *really* want. Which isn't to say I haven't had a great time. I have. It's been totally wild. Somethin' else altogether. But it just feels like somethin's missing, ya know?"

I nodded. It was only three years ago I'd been emphatically ready to leave this place behind. "What do you think you'll do instead?" I asked, needing him to know how wrong I was.

"I'm not too sure."

"Well, would you come back next season?"

He thought about it for a time, looking into the centre of every flower in the garden for an answer. Eventually, he said simply, "I don't know, Nora . . . I just don't know."

I pointed gently then to the building behind us, the building that was once a tent and, before that, an idea. "This place, if you give it a

SHAWN DESOUZA-COELHO

chance, it will become a huge and important part of you. But, you really have to give it a chance. Give it another season."

We sat for a little while longer, my words mixing in with John's thoughts like cream in coffee until eventually it was time to head back in. It wasn't a problem that could be solved all at once, but the half-smile on his face as we walked to the front doors assured me he'd be back at least for today. That was enough for me.

Making our way through the doors, John turned to me and said, "Hey Nora, I heard a rumour."

"Oh? What's that?"

"I heard that . . . uh . . . Kevin Costner's gay."

"Fuck off, John."

"Hah! Good golly, Miss Polley!"

1991

"He woke me up at two in the afternoon!" Susan Wright cried, cigarette in hand in the passenger seat beside me. She took a drag and blew smoke through the cracked window as droplets from the deluge outside pattered on her jacket sleeve. In her other hand was a white mug with a big letter *B* on it, filled with coffee. She had borrowed it from Brent Carver's house in Stratford where she was staying. It was late autumn, and the country air was chilly as we — Richard, Susan, and I — whipped along the road to London and the rehearsal at the Grand for our production of Willy Russell's *Shirley Valentine*. I concentrated on driving, knowing it was likelier for me to spontaneously combust than to get a word in between Richard and Susan. She was telling him about the time she had arrived late to *Dear*

Antoine because of a late wake-up call from a gentleman she'd picked up at the bar the night before. "*Two in the afternoon!*" she cried again.

"Bet he regretted that," Richard chimed from the backseat.

CLICK.

Susan took the cigarette lighter from the dash, handed it to Richard, and he lit a cigarette with it. "Oh yeah! I tore his place apart looking for my clothes. I ran out the door screaming all kinds of shit, straight to the theatre. He'll never sleep with an actress again, that's for sure."

He handed the lighter back to her and she replaced it. "You sound almost proud."

"Well that would make me his last, the one that broke him for all others."

"There's a musical. *The Vainglorious Vagina.*"

"Hah! I'd pay to see that. And near the end of every month all of the characters' costumes would have a tinge of red."

SHOOM!

A huge sheet of rain draped the windshield. I set the wipers on their highest setting. It did the trick.

I had recently purchased another car, a white Civic hatchback, so the results of every button press were still a bit of a surprise to me. Any new-car smell had long faded, though. Now, it smelled of coffee, cigarettes, and rain.

"Jesus," Richard said, staring out the window. "Good thing we left when we did."

"Yeah," Susan added. "Good thinking, Nora."

"It's my job," I said frankly.

"*The Vainglorious Stage Manager!*" Richard announced.

"No such thing."

"Who would want to see that anyway?" Richard said. "Just a bunch of people dressed in black silently judging you. Might as well pay for tickets to a funeral."

Susan found this hilarious, and, I had to admit, the thought of a musical about stage managers was probably the least interesting thing I could ever imagine seeing. Still, Richard continued riffing on the idea.

"It would be one day in rehearsal. We would open with a lone stage manager setting up the tables. It's quiet." His voice softened, and the rain threatened to overpower him. "Quiet. Only her footsteps. Then the actors arrive one by one, but we can't hear them. Once they've all taken their seats, the stage manager notices . . . There's no director! She checks her watch." Susan took a sip of coffee. "Then she sings softly, sweetly, soprano . . . *Why the fuck are you late?*" Susan spat her coffee back into the mug, she was laughing so hard. I laughed too, but stifled myself so I didn't veer into opposite traffic. "*Oh, tell me why the fuck are you late?*"

Susan picked up the tune, the two of them alternating lines. "*Was the company drinking . . .*"

"*Were you stuck at home thinking . . .*"

"*I've not an inkling . . .*"

"*So why the fuck are you late?*"

"Wait, wait!" Richard shouted. "And then! The director bursts in! A real handsome guy, with the charm of an Adonis, and the chiselled features of a David."

"I can see it won't be an inside hire," I said to him in the rearview mirror.

"You keep that up and we'll go back to the worst of Robin Phillips!" I tilted my head, wondering what on earth that could have meant, as Richard continued describing his imaginary musical that nobody would ever pay to see, least of all myself. "He really belts out that first line. *Noorraa Poolleeyy!*"

"Don't use my name."

"Too late. *Nooooorraaa Poooolleeyy!* Ever heard Pavarotti sing "Nessun Dorma"? That's what it sounds like. *Noooorraaa Poooolleeyy!*"

"Does he . . . Does he . . . *Shit*," Susan strained through her laughing, wiping tears from her eyes. "Does he start singing in Italian?"

"Of course! How could he not? The sight of his distraught stage manager brings it out of him. What he can't express in English he *must* say in his native tongue. Besides, Italian's just sexier anyway. So, he bursts in and there are gasps! Nobody expected this! His shirt is ripped to shreds, showing his rippled chest—"

SHAWN DESOUZA-COELHO

"Oh, please," I chortled, suddenly feeling an eternity away from London.

--

A few days later, it was strangely sunny when I came home from Susan's memorial. It felt like everything in the world had become weird and different, as if replaced with an exact replica of itself, only I didn't own any of it. The door handle wasn't mine. Neither was the living room. Then a putrid stench ripped the veil away. When my cat, Ivy, slinked closer, mewing, I understood where the smell was coming from. I picked her up and took her upstairs to the bathroom to clean the darkened brown fur at the base of her tail.

Ivy and my other cat, Holly, were a birthday gift from Louise Guinand and Brenda Henderson, a lighting designer and ASM, respectively, I had worked with quite a few times. The cats were rescues, so they had no names. But because my birthday was near Christmas, I named them Holly and Ivy.

Not long after I got her, Ivy's tail broke. I took her to the vet and she said there was nerve damage, probably due to a fall. Soon, Ivy would have a metal rod inserted in her tail to help her nerves regenerate, but as she flinched at the sight of the shower and tried to clamber away in vain, it was clear that that day couldn't come fast enough.

As the water turned brown, Holly poked her orange head through the door, curious. I began whispering to her that Ivy had an accident, but she left midsentence. I couldn't blame her. Ivy's screeching was horrendous, made worse as I struggled with a particularly knotted spot. In my frustration, I briefly contemplated cutting her whole tail off then and there.

It had been a long time since I'd owned a cat. Michael's didn't count since he was Michael's and went with him to Alberta, where they probably still were now. We hadn't spoken for quite a while. I wasn't sure we ever would again. And it seemed last year was the year the universe decided to try to make up for it.

Before Holly and Ivy showed up, my parents decided to gift me the money they were saving for the wedding and children we were all certain I was never going to have. I used it to pay for a new roof and a washer and dryer while building an addition on my house. I decided to mount a plaque in the laundry room saying, "Funding for this facility was provided by Victor and Elizabeth Polley." I modelled it after the Festival, where donors could "buy" an auditorium seat, thereby having their names permanently engraved on a plaque on that seat's armrest.

"There," I whispered to Ivy, turning the water off. "All clean." I set to work drying her. This time she purred, and I was thankful for the relief her relief brought me. When she was dry, I stroked her nape and sent her on her way. I then sat for a while in the bathroom, just staring into the wall, into nothing, hearing Brent Carver sing softly in my head.

Earlier that day I'd stood backstage at the Festival Theatre, thankful to be asked to stage manage Susan's memorial. The alternatives were to sit at home and do nothing or sit in the house and do nothing but watch the procession of loved ones recount their memories of not only Susan, but her parents as well. They had all died together. I just couldn't handle all that.

In the front row were two of Susan's three siblings, Anne and John. Janet, her third sibling, was unfortunately in Winnipeg, doing a show. Close by, Richard held a hand to his mouth, his face wet with tears of all kinds. Onstage were Sheila McCarthy and Peter Donaldson, who were now married and had a beautiful girl named Mackenzie, for whom I had knitted a little pink sweater when she was born. They took turns reciting hilarious sayings from Susan and her parents.

"When seeing Goldie Semple playing the skimpily clad Courtesan in *The Boys from Syracuse*," Sheila began, "Susan's dad told her later . . ."

"Now that's acting!" Pete finished.

Behind them was a La-Z-Boy recliner and a small table with a TV remote on top. When I was told a La-Z-Boy was needed, I knew the Festival wouldn't have one in stock, so I called Hudson's and told them who I was and what I needed to borrow one for. They delivered it right to the stage door. They didn't ask for a deposit or anything. Instead, they said we could keep it as long as we liked, and to just let them know when they should come pick it up. When they left I found myself muttering, "This is a good town. These are good people."

With every story and memory the room felt warmer and sadder at the same time. Then Brent took the stage and stood before an auditorium of people unable to imagine what was going through his head, Susan and her parents having died in a fire while staying in his home. For a moment he was silent, and then in the purest of voices, he sang "When the Red, Red, Robin Comes Bob, Bob, Bobbin' Along" by Al Jolson. I told him beforehand that if he needed accompaniment, it wouldn't be a problem at all. Brent said he didn't need any, that he would sing it a cappella.

Turning off the bathroom light, I went downstairs. Amidst the ethereal silence of my strange furniture, I realized I had left my wallet in the car.

I went outside to get it, seeing the wallet on the seat through the passenger side window. But when I opened the door and reached for it, my body tensed as if I was looking down from a great height. Tucked under the seat, to the side closest the door, was a white mug. I leaned closer and nearly fell. I picked it up like it was the only thing in the world that belonged to me, though the letter *B* on it reminded me it didn't. I stared at it for a while, feeling the cold porcelain against my fingers as my face grew very hot and I fought back tears. I took the mug inside.

In my kitchen, I washed it; a rare moment in my life. Susan would have laughed at its rarity. She loved to laugh. I wondered then if she did the dishes or, like me, paid someone else to do all her cleaning for her. I didn't know the answer. I put the mug in a cupboard at the side, near the front, and it was only after I closed the cupboard door that I remembered my wallet was still in the car.

"Yes," I said, pointing from behind the lectern to a middle-aged woman in the second row near the right.

The woman stood and waved. "Hi, I'm Doris Grant," she said demurely. For a moment, I thought she might be in the wrong place. "I was doing a show early last year and we were well behind in our rehearsals. I won't name any names, but the director decided to work the actors relentlessly, keeping them long after they were completely exhausted. The actors weren't in any position to say anything. To them it was a big director. But eventually I couldn't take it anymore, so I broke the rehearsal and told them to go home. The director scolded me for it, threatened to have my head and all that. Anyway, do you think I did the right thing?"

Doris looked at me then, along with nearly two dozen other stage managers, and waited for my response. Winston Morgan was among them in the back row, sporting short brown hair and a moustache. He was an experienced stage manager himself who had begun a unique program in Canada called Stage Managing the Arts, or S.M.Arts, which was a platform for stage managers to share their experiences and knowledge with each other. He was the one who had asked me to be here. And it was here, in the Equity headquarters in Toronto, in a small room with beige walls and a white floor, that I had nervously begun the morning speaking about my career path, the differences between running shows at the Festival and elsewhere, and what computers might do for our work. I mentioned Susan's name, and the room inhaled: a testament to her legacy. But it was as Doris waited that I suddenly felt odd. She was looking at me as an expert, and I saw myself as anything but. Yet, to her complex question of right or wrong, I had to respond. So, I gave her the truth.

"I wasn't there," I apologized. "I don't know if you were right or wrong. If it struck you as the right thing to do, then it was the right thing to do." Doris considered this for a moment, and then sat down pensively. "Is there another question? Yes."

"Hi," the young woman said, her voice spritely and quick. "What do you do if an actor has bad breath?" The woman flushed red as some of the audience tittered at the implication. She corrected herself. "I mean, if two actors are in a scene and one of them has bad breath, and the other actor complains to you about it: What do you do?"

"Good question," I replied, using it as a way of talking about diplomacy. "This happened to Richard, and it's more common than you think. On the first day of rehearsal for a show he brought two bottles of mouthwash to the room, gave one to both leading actors and said, 'I've found that when we have kissing in a play it's always really good if I just give this to both of you and you can do something about it so you both know that your breath is sweet.' It's important not to put anybody on the spot."

"Thank you!"

"Any other questions?"

A hand shot up in the front row at the left edge. I pointed to the man, one of the very few in the audience, and he stood. "What's the worst thing that ever happened to you on the job?" His soothing voice didn't match his stocky build.

"The worst thing? Tough to say . . ." I quickly combed my memory. There were lots of terrible times, but each balked at the title of "worst." Finally, I replied, "Well, it wasn't on the job exactly but . . ." I then recounted the events at the Russian border in '73, being in the presence of soldiers with assault rifles strapped to their backs. I told them I'd never been more scared in my entire life. It wasn't the answer he was looking for, but an enjoyable one all the same. Truthfully, I wasn't sure *what* answer he was looking for.

Shortly before lunch, I asked everyone to share a word they believed best described the role of the stage manager.

"Patient."

"Assertive," Doris said. I felt a tinge of pride in her response, given her dilemma.

"Practical."

"God," the man to my left said.

"Invisible."

That's a good one.

"Sister."

"Mother."

On it went as stage managers called out the label they felt best suited their position and experience. I was delighted by the validity of them all.

"What's your word?" Winston called from the back row.

I smiled. "Consistency."

--

"Scrambled eggs, with very crisp bacon, and no home fries, please," I said, placing the one-sheet menu back on the table.

Madelyn scribbled my order down in her notepad. She was a stocky woman in her forties with a big smile, and I knew her name

SHAWN DESOUZA-COELHO

because it was on the sign out in front: Madelyn's Diner. "White or brown toast?" she asked.

"Brown, please."

"All right." With another little jot she pointed with her pen to Andrew North, this season's PA, sitting across from me with straight dark hair and a broad, open face. "And for yourself?"

"Um . . . Western omelette, please."

"Alright. Coming right up." Madelyn scooped up the menus and headed behind the counter.

Andrew sipped his coffee, and I looked into the kitchen, open to the public as it was. The staff were blurs as they prepped plate after plate. It was Sunday morning, so the diner hummed.

I don't come here often enough.

I turned back to Andrew. "You were saying?"

"Yes, so . . ." he began, trying to find his place again. His voice was almost nasal. "I think a computer program would help with that. There's no reason that in this day and age you should be double-booked."

"Isn't that just so stupid? Unbelievable." To think I was going to miss the first show in my twenty-three-year career because of a scheduling oversight. *Shirley Valentine* had been scheduled at the same time as *Romeo and Juliet* because Janet, Susan's sister, was in the former but not the latter. The people upstairs thought that meant they could do the shows at the same time. No thought was given to the fact that both shows were stage managed by the same person. Luckily, I knew about the conflict early on, so I had time to train somebody.

"My point is," Andrew went on, "the technology is there to prevent it. We just need to use it."

"I'll be honest, computers are like magic lamps to me. I rub them the right way and sometimes they grant me wishes."

"Perfect."

"Is it?"

"Well, yeah, because you're going to be the one using it. We'd have to create it so that it was like the original process, only better, because now we won't have to be done at three or four just so we can play Spot the Conflict."

We sat contemplating the almost surreal possibility of not sitting on our hands waiting for scheduling conflicts to file in one by one and the almost euphoric idea that we wouldn't have to scramble to rectify them once they had.

Madelyn brought our orders, popping our soap bubble imaginings.

Andrew picked up a bottle of ketchup and smacked it. "It just doesn't make sense to me that you and I should have to work all day just to prepare the next day. It's 1992 and we're still using pencil crayons. I have some database experience, and I was talking to Chris Wheeler in the electronics department, and he was saying he loved programming things, so I was thinking we could team up on it."

"You're going to have to ease people into this," I replied, admiring his tenacity but seeing right away the flaw in his plan. "You can't go from night to day and assume people are going to make this work." Andrew nodded in agreement, chewing. "But, anything that makes our job easier, I'm all for it. Good on you." I took a bite of my eggs and thought they were missing a little something. "What do you think you'll call it?"

Andrew swallowed. "ARIEL."

"Like the character in *The Tempest*?"

"Mm-hmm. It's an acronym. It stands for All Rehearsals In Every Location."

I pitched my head to one side. "I like it."

SHAWN DESOUZA-COELHO

 Richard took a step back from his office door upstairs at the Festival Theatre, arms crossed in admiration at the words now written there. They were an exquisite painting to him.

"Looks great," I said, having chosen those words.

It wasn't all that long ago I was working in the stage management office downstairs only to hear cries of "Oh my God!" bellowing through the hallways as Richard flew around the backstage area. "I'm going to do this!" he had screamed, and before anyone could ask what "this" was, he had already flown away.

"I love it," Richard said, his eyes never leaving the plaque and its lettering. It read: Richard Monette, Artistic Director Designate.

"I can't think of anyone more deserving."

 It was a late, sunny Sunday
morning, and, while I ritu-
ally ate with Andrew at this
time, Antoni Cimolino had
asked me to chat. Antoni was
a talented young actor at the
Festival who was also Richard's assistant director on this season's production of *Twelfth Night*. We'd chatted often, Antoni and I. He'd ask
my opinion on certain productions, and I wouldn't sugar-coat what
I thought. He appreciated my honesty, and since I didn't drink much
anymore, I was always a cheap date.

"I asked Colleen why Richard wasn't onstage in '88." He smacked
his head and laughed in disbelief. There was real warmth to his voice.
"He was sitting right there too. She was smart about it, though. She

said, 'Oh, we can't afford him.'" I took a moment to admire Colleen's tact. She was a wonderful producer and a wonderful production manager before that and a wonderful stage manager before that. It was a shame she left the Festival entirely when Richard became artistic director. Professional differences. Chris Blake had left a few years ago as well. With both of them gone, I took my parking lot home and stashed it away, feeling like it somehow didn't make sense anymore. Antoni continued, "And then I said, 'That's crazy! You can't afford *not* to have him onstage!' I don't know what got into me. I was too starstruck to realize that he probably really did want to go onstage, but just couldn't because of his stage fright." We laughed, and then let the diner's white noise take over for a minute or so. Krista, our twenty-year-old server and Madelyn's daughter, was greeting a customer by the door. "How are plans for 'Monette at Mid-century'?"

I set my fork down, as if needing two hands to discuss the revelry we'd planned for Richard's fiftieth birthday party. "It's going to be great. We're going to set up the tables with gold and silver balloons. Colm's emceeing. We've got some demo reel footage from his agent we're going to splice together with Disney musicals. We're trying to see if we can get a clip of *Le Ballon Rouge* in there too. He loves that movie. What else? Oh, we're going to get a board member to wear a pig's head."

"That's going to be so great!" Antoni declared. "Well, I managed to wrangle Stephen for our 'Nessun Dorma' three tenors lip-synch. Just need one more. I have someone in mind, I just need to talk to him."

"Great," I smiled, imagining the look on Richard's face come the day. We'd make it impossible for him not to know how much we loved him.

"Has Holly turned up?"

I shook my head, wincing to myself. I missed her more than I let on. She had run away a week ago, and I'd since spent my spare time solemnly taping posters to lampposts. Ivy's name just didn't make sense without Holly.

"She'll turn up," he assured me.

"Hope so."

The white noise crept in again, the chatting of patrons and the clanging of cutlery. Antoni looked at his eggs as if deciding whether or not to eat them. It was only as I finished my plate that he finally spoke.

"I'm worried about him."

I sighed. "Me too." I couldn't watch Richard all day, no matter how much I wanted to. And even if I did, I still didn't know what to do.

John Stead stood before the taped-out stage while Antoni's Laertes and Stephen Ouimette's Hamlet took their places, rapiers in hand, for the duel at the end of the play. "Let's take it at quarter-speed, guys," he told them.

Antoni and Stephen duelled slowly, as if moving through molasses, while Richard watched with crossed arms. He looked almost impatient.

"Good," John said before stopping them altogether. Stephen had flinched backward after Antoni had flashed the point of his sword across Stephen's face.

"Sorry," Antoni said, instinctively tilting the point downward.

"It's alright, brother."

John then moved Antoni aside, deftly showing him the proper motions. His stance told the story of a man at home with a weapon in his hand. I'd totally believed it when I'd heard he hunted bears up north with a bow and arrow. I totally understood why he'd returned as a fight director, and not as an actor.

I looked over at Stephen, his short hair thin and fraying. His tired eyes were fixed on John, tracing with his sword the counters to John's movements. My role as stage manager in fight calls left me small moments to think, and watching Stephen, I had to wonder how he was handling all this.

Richard's *Hamlet* was an attempt to right a wrong for Stephen, one that had followed him for over two decades. Stephen was promised the title role in '81 by the Gang of Four. That didn't pan out. Then Hirsch took over, saw Stephen in a play in Toronto five years later, loved him, and planned a production of Hamlet on Broadway with another director.

SHAWN DESOUZA-COELHO

Then that director died. Then Richard took over as artistic director and told Stephen he was going to make good on that original promise. Yet, it sometimes felt like Richard just wasn't there for Stephen.

It was early in the day and actors were still mingling when Stephen walked into rehearsal, lost in thought. He had the appearance of somebody who had done a great deal of thinking very late at night. Thumbing his script, he approached the director's table.

Richard exclaimed quietly, "Oh no, the actors wanna ask questions!"

To this, Stephen simply raised his eyebrows and then went to the side of the room and set his script down. I didn't know how to feel, or whether my role had any bearing at all on either Richard's neglect or Stephen's dejection. Regardless, a couple of minutes later we started rehearsing.

"Let's try it again," John said, offering the pair the floor.

"Quarter-speed?" Stephen asked.

"Quarter-speed."

Again, the viscous fight unfurled, this time through to completion. Then the actors fought again at half their normal speed. Then, once that was carried through, they fought at the speed they would in the show. Richard was silently tapping his foot the whole time. When the fight had concluded, John turned to Richard for his thoughts.

"John," Richard blurted out, "for Christ's sake, it needs to be more peppy! Ya know?" He clapped his hands, as if marking out the pep he had imagined. "Make it peppy!" John took Richard's comment in stride and was about to begin altering the fight when Richard told me to call a break.

Again?

"We're back in ten minutes," I called to those in attendance. "Ten minutes."

As Richard left I made some notes in my script, not having to look to know he was going to get some fresh air and to have another smoke.

"I got him to take a walk by the river on break yesterday," Antoni said amidst the diner's hum. He sounded as though he were asking if it was enough.

"How did it go?"

"Good, at first. Then he got irritated. It's hard on him, ya know? He's not in the best shape physically."

I nodded. "Anything helps. When Robin was still in charge, I took him outside to drink his coffee just so he could get some sun."

"What was it like working under him?"

"He had more energy than I think even he knew what to do with. I don't know when he slept. One of the cutters brought him food every day at lunch just so he'd eat." Antoni set his coffee down in disbelief. "It's a hard job. It always is at first." I chuckled. "I remember when I first became PSM, not that you can equate that with being artistic director, but still, I was stage managing two shows at the same time, under Robin no less, on top of PSM duties I'd never had before. So I was working twelve-, fourteen-, sixteen-hour days, day after day. And I remember there were times when I'd just zone out completely, and people right beside me would be calling, 'Nora? Nora?' and I wouldn't even hear them. It was exhausting, just exhausting. But that was partly because I wasn't used to it. I have no doubt Richard will figure it out. Of course, I still don't wish the job of artistic director on anybody. I certainly couldn't do it. It's good, though, what you're doing."

Antoni's mouth curled into a half-smile, and I knew he thought he could do more. With that, he finished eating, I lit a cigarette, and we paid the bill and left.

Outside, I squinted as I waved goodbye to Antoni. Getting in my car, whatever worries I'd harboured about Richard seemed to vanish as I glanced around at what little snow remained, as if the sunlight glinting off it were a balm for my ambivalence. I turned the engine on and pulled out of the parking lot, all the while seeing Richard's eager face.

Though the sky was wan and white powder dusted the cold ground outside, Richard stood brightly before the company in a smart-looking blue blazer. In Rehearsal Hall 1, he had begun his company address, his first as artistic director. It was something all artistic directors did, every season, a few weeks into rehearsal.

SHAWN DESOUZA-COELHO

"And I don't know why I did it," he said, "but in 1960, for those of us old enough to remember there was a 1960, I walked into the auditorium for a production of *King John* or *Romeo and Juliet*, and I started to *genuflect*. I swear! I caught myself and thought immediately: this is my church. I had three wishes then: to be an actor, to do Shakespeare, and to work at Stratford." He took in the crowd from stem to stern, and from where I stood I spotted Bill Hutt, his hair snowy white. He watched Richard with appreciative eyes because, at the age of seventy-four, having spent the last few years at the Shaw Festival in Niagara and the Grand and now believing his career was over, Bill had been brought by Richard back to the stage. "I got all three wishes and so much more," Richard continued, before joking about once calling the board a bunch of pigs and saying he now hoped he was welcome at the trough. He went on to describe the magnitude of his position, making clear his belief that the Festival wasn't separate from the town of Stratford, but rather its very livelihood. He said he'd do whatever it took to help both grow. Facing him, the company swayed with the same mix of feelings every new artistic director brought: anxiety, tedium, a smattering of indifference, and excitement both sycophantic and genuine. Mine was certainly genuine. I wanted nothing but to see my friend Richard succeed. "And just remember," Richard added, concluding his welcome, "You arrive in the snow, and you leave in the snow."

1995

I'll be fine. Just let this be it.

"... He worked here for seventeen seasons as administrative director," Richard told the company as they kept one sober eye on him, and the other on me. We were in tech week for *Amadeus*, so I had already taken my place at the stage management table in the Festival Theatre before Richard came in with the news. "He came to the Festival in its second season as a bookkeeper: 1954." Some of the younger members of the company clicked their teeth in awe and respect. "He saw Stratford grow from a Festival that presented two plays in one theatre over two months, to a Festival that presented ten plays in three theatres over six ..."

I'll be fine.

I knew the formality was needed, and I appreciated Richard's affectionate eulogy, but I didn't want a procession of condolences. I was still rent from it, but time was precious in tech rehearsals, and I only wanted to call the cues for this wonderful production, a production my father would have loved. It was only the day before that my dad, Victor Charles Polley, had died.

Sue and Neil picked me up in the middle of the night, and on the hour's ride to the cottage I asked every question I could think of. They didn't know much, only that he had died in his sleep, and that Mom called Dave first, and then Dave called Sue. The road crunched underneath the car, perforating the small silences that managed to slip between our disbelief.

At the cottage, the Killers and the Halls were already comforting Mom, but we each threw our arms around her anyway. She looked as if she had no more tears to shed. It was then, bathed in bright blue moonlight, that she told us exactly what had happened, occasionally glancing behind her, through the walls to her bedroom where she had found Dad's body.

He had shot a forty-four in nine holes of golf that morning, and had come within inches of a hole-in-one. He was telling this to Mom when he started feeling a pain in his chest. So they went to the hospital in Goderich. The doctor there told Dad he was fine, that he had probably sprained a muscle golfing, and that he should take some Tylenol and go to bed. He did as he was told and then didn't wake up. Then the ambulance came and took him back to the hospital in Goderich.

"We need to go there," Mom said.

"What do you mean?" I replied.

"The paramedics said if we wanted parts of him donated that I needed to be at the hospital to fill out the forms." I was shocked at the thought that they'd make her do this now, but Mom was somehow okay with it, so I told her I'd drive.

At the hospital, I sat Mom down in the waiting room and went to the reception area only a few feet away. The place was painted a sickening taupe and was nearly deserted.

"Excuse me?" I said to the nurse facing away from the counter.

"Yes?" she replied curtly, as if I'd interrupted her with my canvassing.

"I'm Nora Polley, Victor Polley's daughter. He arrived not too long ago. We were told we need to fill out some organ—" I choked up, but clenched my fist to get through it. "Organ donation forms, please."

The nurse turned and shouted to whoever was in the back, "There's somebody here about the guy that died!"

I wanted to leap over the counter and rip her fucking tongue out. Instead, I went back to Mom, who had heard the whole exchange but didn't seem to mind as much as I did, and stayed with her until a doctor came.

When the doctor finally arrived, I told him what we had been told. He looked compassionately at Mom and said, "Your mother didn't have to come. Anybody could have." I shook my head in quiet frustration.

When I had filled out the forms, we left the hospital. I swore I would rather die a thousand times than be hospitalized at that place even once. Mom didn't participate in my seething on the ride back to the cottage. She simply gazed out the window at the trees passing by under the red dawn sky, and from time to time released years of her life in deep sighs.

I had rehearsal the next day, so Sue offered to stay with Mom at the cottage until the funeral preparations were made. I told them I didn't want to miss a bunch of rehearsals and have to play catch-up. Their understanding didn't completely absolve my feelings of guilt. I just knew I couldn't sit there in it. It would consume me if I did.

I'll be fine. Just don't talk about it.

When Richard had finished honouring my father, the cast and crew made their way backstage so we could begin. Before we did, though, Brian Bedford ascended the aisle towards me.

I'll be fine. Just don't talk about it.

Brian put one hand on the table and leaned closer. "Thank you for being here, Nora," he said softly.

Okay. Just one person.

"Thank you, Brian." I replied, my eyes stinging.

Just one.

--

"As soon as I woke up and saw him, I knew," Mom whispered at the WG Young Funeral Home, just north of Madelyn's. She and I were looking down at Dad's body, his face pale and still. He was wearing a blue suit with a white shirt and blue tie. I felt uncomfortable at the sight of him. He looked like my dad, but slightly different. Eventually I looked away, but Mom didn't take her eyes off him, as if not even looking at him at all, but rather seeing through him to some memory only they shared. Then she asked me to get a comb.

"A comb?"

"Yeah. His hair's all wrong." She was wearing a black dress that made her look so very old, made her own hair look so much whiter, curled as it was in a small, loose perm. I knew it was weird, but whatever she wanted was just fine. Besides, Dad loved looking tidy and dignified. We were happy he had died in his sleep. It was a dignified way to go.

I approached Marg in the corner of the room where she was talking with David and Fred, and before I could say anything she threw her arms around me.

"I — I had a dream," she sniffled.

"Oh?"

"I didn't want to come because if I didn't then he wouldn't be gone," she went on, pointing to Fred, "but Fred said we were leaving tomorrow whether my bags were packed or not." Fred adjusted his glasses, watching intently. "That night I had a dream. I was looking for a black dress and then all of a sudden I was patted on the back. I turned and it was Daddy, and he said, 'No, don't be sad. I'm fine. You have that really nice blue skirt and blue top, and you know that blue is my favourite colour, as is yours. Wear that.' I said, 'Okay.'" She pulled away from me and looked down at her blue skirt and top. I didn't know what to say. Behind us, through family and friends, I could see that Mom hadn't moved. Marg continued, "He's with us, you know." It was then she told me about the storm up at the cottage last night. It tore up trees, and when Marg got there that blue tarpaulin on the Halls' property that Dad hated had been completely blown away. "It was Daddy letting us know he'd come and gone."

Though I wasn't a religious person, I smiled at the thought that Dad was somehow still around, checking up on us, telling me what he and Mom had bought at K-Mart and then returned the next day, telling me that he'd finally managed to get rid of that godforsaken tarp.

Marg took a tissue from her purse and wiped her nose.

"Do you have a comb?" I asked when the moment felt right.

She wiped her eyes. "I think so." The contents of her purse clacked around as she rifled through them. Eventually, she pulled out a small black comb. "Here you go."

"Thanks."

Mom looked as if she were whispering something when I returned. Her mouth was quivering slightly, but when I got close enough to hear, I realized that no sounds were coming out.

"Mom?" I said. She snapped towards me, knowing why I was worriedly looking at her. It was her Parkinson's. We didn't spend any time talking about it though because she took the comb, and thanked me. Then, as gently as she could, as if she were tending the last patch of grass on Earth, she combed his hair to the left, exactly as he would have wanted.

The funeral service was held late the next morning at St. James Anglican Church. People from nearly every decade of my father's life made their way through the vestibule to the pews. But as we gathered in the hall off one of the transepts with Dad's casket, Mom was kicking herself for not inviting the Perth Regiment, which Dad was a part of extensively before, during, and after the war. I would have told her not to worry about it, but I knew she'd rather be irritated than lonely. On any other day I also might have admired the stained glass that tinted his casket myriad colours, but everything was so muted to me then. I couldn't even cry.

SHAWN DESOUZA-COELHO

When we entered, the congregation stood to receive us. I was taken aback, never having seen anything like it before. We sat in the front pew, and the minister led us in singing "Onward, Christian Soldiers" for what seemed like fifteen verses. He then read the eulogy I had written. I knew myself enough to know I couldn't do it. I'd never finish it. Mom was sobbing by the end, though, having finally given up being irritated.

Victor Charles Polley, my father, died on July 12, 1995. He was cremated and his ashes were placed in Avondale Cemetery, where he now waited to play one more round of bridge with his wife Elizabeth and rest of the club.

1996 I'm sitting in Dad's seat in the Festival Theatre auditorium — house left, Aisle 3, Row D, #57 — and it's as if I've entered a long and winding tunnel where people are echoes and I'm the only certain thing in the world. I kind of like it here, for the moment, so I decide to stay. I click my stopwatch and watch the digital timer count up by the millisecond. I find its functions neat. I can stop it to record the time and then start it again without having to zero it out like I did on my old analogue one. I had to take it to Chris Wheeler to remove the beeping, though. I couldn't think of anything more annoying to an actor in the throes of a passionate scene than *BEEP*. I also bought my own headset. It's light and sleek, with a single earmuff. With my new gadgets, I sometimes joke that I'm technologically savvy.

For my twenty-fifth season the Guthrie Awards committee gave me a seat in the auditorium. I was flattered, since they never did it as a matter of course. Usually, people needed a thousand dollars to get one. I asked them to put Dad's name on it too because it didn't make sense that I had a seat and he didn't. He was more valuable to the Festival than I ever was.

A couple of years ago, Dad sat down for an interview about his life at the Festival. It was in Rehearsal Hall 2 at the Festival Theatre, which was a jewellery box compared to halls one and three, and he was sitting in a red chair in the corner. There was a camera on him the entire time. I rebuked him afterwards, and during. He was talking about how the student matinees began with the Loretto Academy nuns and schoolgirls, but he didn't take the credit. He never did. His was the Festival's work and never his own.

I think somebody is speaking to me now, asking me a question. He resembles Andrew. I answer him exactly, and I think he leaves in the direction he came. As I watch him go, the voices of the people nearby continue bouncing off the walls like pebbles down a big well, and I feel thankful for Andrew. Everything is still a bit blurry stage managing two productions, but with Andrew at least I'm free from my PSM duties.

Andrew's title this season is Assistant to the Production Stage Manager, but it's really his job, and will be officially next season. ARIEL continues to be a stunning success. There were a few bumps in the road, a few people opposed to its adoption, but it has completely changed the way we do things in stage management at the Festival. He and Chris are also now working on another program called EL DORADO. If ARIEL is about scheduling one day, then EL DORADO is designed to schedule an entire season, both programs making it impossible to be double-booked like I was four years ago with *Shirley Valentine* and *Romeo and Juliet*, a disappointment I carry with me like a tiny scar from childhood. So if anybody deserves to take over, it's Andrew. Besides, I'm done. I'm filled with more impatience and indifference towards being PSM than I know what to do with. Scheduling is little else than lines on the screen, just numbers and names sectioning time and space. I yelled at the PA the other day. I've never done that before. He didn't deserve it.

I laugh to myself then, so quietly that nobody can ask what the joke is. At the cottage earlier this year, Sue asked Mom if she had an egg slicer. Mom looked up from the sink and said, "I did, but he died." I think it's great that she's finding the levity in it.

To honour Dad, the Festival will give Mom two tickets to every production every season for the rest of her life. It's nice of them, especially considering he gave them seventeen years of his. Though, as I stare down at this armrest, tracing my finger over the recessed letters, I know I would give seventeen years and more of my own just to hear him call me "Ah" one more time.

I read the inscription aloud softly, just under my breath. "Nora Polley. Production Stage Manager, Stratford Festival. Daughter of Vic Polley, Administrator." I smile. I click the stopwatch and the numbers cease silently ticking upward. I zero it, and my smile slowly fades like steam in air. I head back to the office to start yet another day.

SHAWN DESOUZA-COELHO

1997

DOMENICO.   Filume', we have lived our lives . . . I have fifty-two
              years behind me, and you have forty-eight: two
              mature people who understand the meaning of their
              unifying gesture, and accept deeply their responsibili-
              ties. You know why you're marrying me: but I don't.
              I know only that I am marrying you because you told
              me that one of those three boys is my son . . .

FILUMENA.   Only for that?

There he was, Richard's Domenico, in his black tuxedo, speaking to his beloved Filumena. It was near the very end of the show, and I sat nearly onstage, just behind a grate, desperately lending him my care and attention. It was opening night of *Filumena*, Antoni's directing debut at the Festival, and this was Richard's return to acting after so long an absence. He needed me. That was what I kept reminding myself as I followed his every line, every one of which he'd run with his assistant before every performance, rebelling against his conviction that he wouldn't be able to remember them. He needed me. If he didn't, then I'd have to face the fact that my brother Fred was dead.

DOMENICO.   No. No, because I love you, we've been together for
            twenty-five years, and twenty-five years is a lifetime:
            memories, thoughts, a life together . . . I understood
            that I loved you because without you I found I was
            lost . . . and also because I believe it's a thing that one
            feels, and I feel it. I know you well and that is why I'm
            talking to you like this. At night I can't sleep. It's been
            ten months, since that evening, you remember? And
            I've had no peace. I don't sleep, I don't eat, I don't rest
            . . . I don't live! You don't know what I have here in
            my heart . . . something that stops me from breathing.
            I go like this — and the breath stops here.

"How are you doing?" Maloo asked as I gathered my effects for the start of the show. She had left stage management and found her home in the Avon wigs department. Her hair was blond now. And though I was sure others passed in and out of the Avon office door, it seemed to me that only Maloo and I occupied it. I had just told her the news.

"I'm fine. It was just so sudden. I mean, a heart attack at forty-six?" Before Maloo could reply, I added, "He was a smoker. Started right here at the Festival when he was nine. He played Mustardseed in *Dream* and some actor decided to give him a cigarette. And then last night—" I broke off, trying to catch my breath as it fled from me in small spurts. I glanced out the large windows to a lamplit Brunswick St. and then back to Maloo. "I'm sure it had something to do with that."

Maloo looked at me with such eyes then, as if she knew the worlds upon worlds of contradiction turning inside me. "When's the funeral?"

"Not sure exactly. But I'm not going."

"Oh? Because of the show?"

"No. Partly. Maybe. I don't know. My mom isn't going. She's too ill to make the trip. I figure I'll just stay here with her."

"You can just give your book to someone else," Maloo said, as if seeing through me.

I slid my fingers along the edges of the script on my desk.

It's opening. It will have just opened. They need me. And Fred was so far away. He lived out in Calgary for so long. Richard needs me. Ten years of stage fright. He needs me. I can't just give this book to somebody else.

"No, I can't," I replied, convincing myself it was true.

Nobody else can do this.

Maloo hugged me, and I yielded to her the full weight of my body, conscience and all. "Thank you for being here," she whispered. "Thank you."

Off to my right, in the darkness of backstage, I could see Maloo, taking me in with Domenico and Filumena. I smiled, thankful she was there because it meant somebody was actually seeing me. The cast and crew needed stoicism from their stage manager. They needed bedrock to stand on and invisibility to shine through. So I gave it to them, all the while thankful somebody was seeing the cracks beneath their feet and the flecks of my imperfect body and flawed reasoning. It made me feel appreciated.

I turned back to the stage and Richard, once again trying not to think of Fred as Filumena spoke.

FILUMENA.   Listen to me well, Dummi', and then we will never
             speak of this again. All my life I have loved you with
             all my heart! In my eyes you were a god . . . and I still
             love you, and maybe more than before.

--

Regret swelled within me when Mom left for Calgary and Fred's funeral. She had lost so much mobility by now we thought she wouldn't be able to handle the flight, but she downright refused to stay behind. I consoled myself with the thought that, by the time Mom had finally decided, it was too late for me to find a replacement anyway. I knew somewhere in my depths, though, that anybody could have replaced me. The only prerequisite was being able to read.

Later, when Sue told me what had happened at the funeral, my regret redoubled. In lieu of my presence, I wrote the eulogy for the service. But Fred and Janice's minister friend was away on holidays, so they got somebody else who didn't know Fred at all to read it. Prior to the service, they asked this new minister to read it through for them so they could tell him where to emphasize certain things. Apparently, he said, "Oh, I've done this a million times." Of course, he botched it entirely.

Before the service had begun, Dave said he was astounded by the number of people in attendance for a man of only forty-six. Fred had a whole life out there that none of us, save for Marg, seemed to know very much about. After one glance at the overfull pews, Dave joked, "It's lucky we know somebody here so we can get a seat."

When they entered, Fred's favourite song, "Desperado" by the Eagles, was playing. Mom shuffled down the aisle, cane in hand, with Sue beside her. Sue told me that as they made their way to the front somebody whispered, "Oh that must be his mother. Isn't she pretty?" Then Mom froze completely, and Sue wondered what she should do with her. We had been told that when this happens, we should sing to her, because in Parkinson's patients sometimes the signal from the brain doesn't reach the body, and music can somehow bridge that gap. Sue said she thought about singing to Mom there and then. She also thought about just pushing her or seating her beside some strangers halfway down the aisle. Luckily, Mom started moving again of her own accord, seating herself at the front where she belonged.

SHAWN DESOUZA-COELHO

Dave said that Mom was stoic throughout the service. In spite of the fact that Fred was her favourite, somehow that seemed right.

At the burial the next morning out in the country, it was teeming rain. Janice, now Fred's widow, put a flower on the coffin, mourning and damning him at the same time for leaving her alone to raise Christopher, who was a tough eleven-year-old. Christopher put a flower on the coffin as well, as did Lisa, who was in high school, and Matthew, who was now going off to study engineering. They lowered the coffin and everybody said their goodbyes.

I remembered all of this a few days later in the Avon stage management office, once more tracing the edges of my script with my finger. Out of the corner of my eye I spied Richard as he walked by towards the backstage area, a seemingly permanent look of concern on his face. He'd done beautifully, every night, but that didn't dissuade his dread. It therefore didn't dissuade my resolve either. He still needed a stage manager and so, every night, in spite of my regrets, I set to work being one.

 "Nora?" a voice called. Sitting at my desk, I turned to find Brian Tree standing in the Avon office door with his script in hand. He was a British actor with short hair and a stern look. He was funny without ever trying to be. "Sorry to bother you."

"Not at all." Truthfully, I wasn't doing much of anything. Rehearsal for Richard's *Much Ado About Nothing* was in half an hour, but I had come in much earlier on instinct. I had forgotten I wasn't PSM anymore. "What can I do for you?"

He held out his script. "Could you retype a page for me?"

"Sure. Just leave it with me and I'll have it to you in time for rehearsal."

"Thank you very much," he said, handing me the page and then rapping on the doorframe as he left.

As mundane as it sounded, I loved retyping the page for Brian. Having somewhat settled into my decision to never PSM again, I felt renewed. I was solely in service of the actors now, which was always what I cared most about. I'd grown enough to know that now.

With the retyped page in hand, I collected my book and Richard's script and rehearsal schedule, which I kept now because Richard constantly forgot things in the rehearsal hall, and I left the office.

When I arrived in Rehearsal Hall 1, Kim Hubbard and Corinne Richards were already setting up tables for the day's scene work. The room was large and rectangular, with mirrors along one side. It was nearly a full company call, so any moment now a swarm of actors would be arriving.

"Hey, Nora," Kim said. She had very kind eyes and was always smiling, it seemed, always impressed. She was wearing a green long-sleeve shirt. "Happy St. Patrick's Day."

I chuckled, seeing myself in the mirror and realizing I wasn't wearing any green at all. "I knew I forgot something."

Corinne laughed. She was older than Kim, and one of the best ASMs in the world as far as I was concerned. "Everything okay?"

"Just fine." I made my way to the stage management table. "Everything's great."

And it was. The actors soon filed in, chatting and bringing with them the pleasant odorous tinge of coffee and cigarettes, a few of them in green themselves. Rory Feore was smiling at something Eric Donkin was saying, the two of them quite far apart in age. Rory, Colm's brother, with short wavy hair and a constant vibration, was in his mid-twenties, while Eric was nearly seventy now, the blond of his hair only slightly faded. Beside them Bill Hutt sat, looking idly about the room. He perked up when Stephen Ouimette strolled in, and the two of them began conversing. Then Brian Bedford arrived, and the room buzzed a little louder.

I turned to Kim, who had just taken her seat between Corinne and myself, starry-eyed. The few years between her arrival at the Festival and now hadn't dulled her appreciation of the people and the work done here. I leaned over to her and said, "You know there are at least three people in here who have the Order of Canada?"

"I know!"

"Pretty overwhelming."

"Yeah. It's amazing."

"Don't ever lose that feeling." I told her this as a reminder to myself as well, a reminder to never stop loving their sounds and smells and the way they refreshed me as would water at the height of thirst.

When Brian arrived, I handed him his page and he thanked me again.

"Hello, hello, hello," Richard said to the three of us as he walked briskly into the room. He set his soft-sided briefcase down on the table, and I pointed to his rehearsal schedule. He swept over it and then called out to the actors. "Let's take a stab at Act 5, Scene 1." He then looked at me strangely, as if making sure he was correct. I nodded without moving my head.

Eric's Antonio and Bill's Leonato took their places for their entrances. James Blendick, a veteran of the Festival, and Tim MacDonald, who was relatively new by comparison, waited nearby, seated. They knew Richard would probably stop Bill to work on Leonato's lengthy speech about his grief at not knowing if his daughter Hero is chaste or not.

Sure enough, Richard did, and Eric waited patiently by, the way a scene partner should. Richard then decided to move on, so James's Don Pedro and Tim's Claudio entered. During the heated exchange, Antonio vehemently condemned Claudio for his treatment of Hero.

ANT.   He shall kill two of us, and men indeed:
         But that's no matter; let him kill one first;
         Win me and wear me; let him answer me.
         Come, follow me, boy; come, sir boy, come,
         follow me.

LEO.   Brother—

ANT.   Content yourself. God knows I loved my niece;
       And she is dead, slander'd to death by villains,
       That dare as well answer a man indeed
       As I dare take a serpent by the tongue:
       Boys, apes, braggarts, Jacks, milksops!

I glanced over at Kim again. Her mouth was half-open, goofily, and I knew I agreed with whatever it was she—

Bang!

So much happened in that fraction of a second. Bill and James and Brian Bedford turned away in shock, as if seeing themselves in Eric. Kim snatched up the phone and called the ambulance while Rory scrambled to the floor with Corinne, pumping Eric's chest, and Eric didn't move much at all. I could see him looking up at the ceiling, at Rory, as if all his life were now contained within the little movements of his eyes and neck. It was loud, so very loud, the sound of his body hitting the floor. It was as if gravity had slammed him into it, a sack of meat and bone it had bent to its whim. Then it was quiet, exactly as Robin had said it would be so many years ago when he tricked the women of *Parade*. Nobody got close, and nobody said a word. Stephen watched from the corner and Richard's hand was glued to his mouth as Rory tried to push a few more minutes into Eric. I was half-standing, entirely powerless and unprepared. There was no manual for this, none to tell me how to listen to a man taking what could be his final breaths.

Was this what Fred sounded like?

When the paramedics arrived, I broke rehearsal and overheard one of the actors say he needed a drink. I didn't fault him for it. I told them I'd call them with any news, but I sensed, like they did, that Eric's chances were very small.

The daze of the room latched on to me like a burr all the way down to the office where I sat by the phone, waiting for the hospital to call with an update. Kim was there, and Corinne, and I thanked them for their strength in light of my shortcomings. I had taken a first aid course at the start of my career, but could never stomach it. I thought I might faint, so I never took one again. Kim and Corinne both understood. And when the call finally came that Eric had died in the ambulance, neither of them questioned me when I started calling each company member one by one to relay the information. As I phoned, it wasn't lost on me that in my greenest years I'd once stood in the doorway of the Festival stage management office and watched in profound respect as Tom Hooker did the same. My sense of pride was merely atomic, though. Like him, it was just something I felt I had to do.

In rehearsal for the two weeks following, Richard imposed a moratorium on scenes involving Antonio, giving the company time to grieve. After two weeks, though, the memory of Eric's death still loomed large over the brightly lit room. Everything was the same except the sound, as if the hive were half-asleep. Richard stood up and addressed the cast.

"This is who will be playing Eric's part," he said, gesturing to the new face in the crowd. "Some of you might know him, but please welcome him. Joseph Shaw." The cast applauded as best they could, and Joe gave a little wave. Richard cleared his throat. "Let's take it from where we left off. Nora, what was the blocking for Antonio?"

I turned the pages of my book and told Joe where Eric had been standing.

 Lucy Peacock and I sat alone in the Festival Theatre stage management office after *Pride and Prejudice*, and I assured her it wasn't her fault. The door was closed, and, as she shook her head, the necessity of my timeless words met with their futility. I knew I'd never run out of moments to tell actors it wasn't their fault because actors who loved the work never stopped blaming themselves for the times when it didn't go as planned. Lucy was certainly one such actor.

"Where is she?" I asked her, leaning forward in my chair.

"In the parking lot with Brian, I think," Lucy muttered through a distant stare. "I could have cued her somehow," she added. I knew then that she was replaying the scene in her head, reciting the text line by line.

"Stop. There was nothing you could do about it."

"I froze too."

"I know." I wanted to tell her I did as well, but the truth was I didn't freeze at all. I still wasn't sure what that meant.

LIZZY.   I will make no promise of the kind.

LADY.   Miss Bennet I must warn you — I have not been in the habit of brooking disappointment.

LIZZY.   That will make your ladyship's situation at present more pitiable; but it will have no effect on me.

"Warning Lights 226 and 229, and Sound 176 to 178," I said over headset, as Lucy's Lizzy stood to leave before a large horse-drawn carriage, centre stage. In it sat Lady Catherine de Bourgh. I reached up and primed the switches for the right door and the left and right tunnels.

Let's bring it home.

LADY.   Not so hasty, if you please. To the other objections I have already urged, I have still another to add. I am no stranger to the particulars of your youngest sister's infamous elopement.

Silence enveloped the auditorium then, a powerful and distending silence. The floorboards creaked beneath the two actors playing horses as they shifted their weight and waited.

Has she . . . ?

LADY.

She's dried.

Even from the crow's nest of the booth, I could see each of their thoughts blink frantically: hers repeating the preceding lines and begging the next one to return, Lucy's questioning whether or not it was her turn to speak, and everybody else praying for the Lady's memory to return.

LADY.

Okay. This pause has gone on too long.
I leaned over to the God mic, switched it on, and prompted, "Is such a girl to be my nephew's sister?" The audience flinched at the intrusion of my booming voice into the vacuum that preceded it.

LADY.

She's not taking it.
"Is such a girl to be my nephew's sister?" I repeated, keeping my voice level to cut through the torrent of thoughts now drowning her.
Take the line.
I gritted my teeth slightly, almost mouthing the words.

LADY.

"Is such a girl to be my nephew's sister?" I repeated once more. For a moment I contemplated stopping the show entirely and clearing the stage for the next scene. Then, as if electrocuted, she spoke.

LADY.   Is such a girl to be my nephew's sister? Is her husband, the son of his late father's steward, to be his brother? Are the shades of Pemberley to be thus polluted?!?

LIZZY.   You have now insulted me in every possible method. I must beg to return to the house . . .

"The scene was hers," I reminded Lucy after we'd sat briefly in silence. "She was guiding it. Anything you said would have just drawn more attention to it."
"I know, I know. It's all just the adrenaline wearing off." I nodded.

"I just wish you didn't have to get on the God mic. But I know it's stupid to think like that. What's done is done. Still, though . . ." She trailed off, turning the events over again.

I wasn't sure why, but it was only then it finally registered with me: I'd used the God mic for the first time in my career. I felt indifferent, and that was maybe the most surprising thing. It certainly wasn't the first time an actor had dried on the Festival Theatre stage, but they usually found a way out of it, whether of their own accord or with the help of scene partners. Nobody could have helped tonight, though. Not in that scene, with two horses and a scene partner who did nothing but answer questions. Maybe it was the absolute necessity of what I'd done that gave me the strength to detach myself from its gravity. And when Lucy left the office, feeling better for having simply talked things out, I suddenly felt old.

SHAWN DESOUZA-COELHO

 "Ah!" a cheerful voice rang from the doorway of Mom's bright room at Cedarcroft Place, the retirement home we'd moved her to after it became clear she needed a level of care neither she nor we could provide. "The whole familia ees here!" It was Delma, Mom's nurse come to check up on her. She was a refugee from El Salvador in her late thirties, already a grandmother, with long black hair tied into a ponytail, pink scrubs, and a small gold crucifix around her neck.

"Desdemona!" Mom yelled, her body swaying to and fro as if she were constantly being prodded in a different direction. "I was just telling my girls they should write a play about this place."

"It's Delma," Sue reminded her, but Delma just waved it off. Today was one of the few days Sue's schedule lined up with my own. Usually, Sue would visit on Tuesday and Friday before three. Then from four to five I tried to be there. At five Mom had dinner, so if I couldn't come in the afternoon, I'd come at seven so we could watch *Wheel of Fortune* and *Jeopardy!* before she went to bed. We just didn't want her to feel like we'd abandoned her, which was the feeling I got, sad as it was, from a number of Mom's neighbours.

"I would come to watch your play," Delma said, smoothing out Mom's sleeves. We adored her because she always made sure Mom was well kempt. Her hair was always proper, and her room was always tidy, small though it was with a bed, TV, loveseat, washroom, and a wall filled with the graduation photos of her children and grandchildren. "How are you, Nora?"

"I'm good."

"She's well," Mom corrected, speaking to Delma.

Delma laughed, understanding the difference.

"I'm well," I amended.

"Gracias." Delma lived in Kitchener, and I didn't imagine it being easy for her. The city wasn't exactly known for its large Latin population. Maybe it was because of that, or because Mom just wanted to feel useful, or maybe both, but Mom had been steadily helping Delma with her English. "What would the play be about?" Delma asked, now straightening out Mom's bed sheets.

Mom smiled sinisterly. "Four old farts sitting around talking about their poop."

Delma gasped. "*Ay Dios!*"

--

"Remember, it's all about the legs," John Stead said, slapping his blue-jeaned thigh as afternoon light poured into Rehearsal Hall 1 at the Avon. Lucy nodded, hands on her hips. He tugged the loose end of the rope, and then handed it to her. "It's about the arms too, but the legs help conserve your strength." The other end of the rope was tied to a beam in the ceiling, put there at Jeannette's request.

SHAWN DESOUZA-COELHO

Jeannette's production of *As You Like It* had a lot to do with the passage of time, so the design used cogs and gears to symbolize clock-work. In the opening sequence of the play the entire cast marched like quartz across the stage. Rosalind, however, marched to her own beat. As did Lucy, the actress who played her.

Tuck the knees.

I practically mouthed the words as Lucy tightened her grip on the rope. Jeannette edged forward in her seat, her hands tensed too, but subtly so, as if the years she'd spent proving herself to this place had hardened into muscle memory. She, along with John and every other person in the room, was willing Lucy to succeed, as if thoughts could lift in place of arms and grit.

Strong foot pushing down, the other pushing up.

Lucy had been practising on a rope in her barn ever since Jeannette said ropes were going to drop from the ceiling to represent the Forest of Arden. She'd been practising ever since the dancers, cast as the Lords of the Forest, said the ropes were too tough and hurt too much. She'd been practising ever since she told Jeannette, simply, "Rosalind climbs the ropes." This season was filled with people doing extraordinary things.

At the annual pre-season company address in Rehearsal Hall 1 at the Festival Theatre, the mood was a bit strange. Standing with Antoni, his new executive director, by his side, Richard seemed as if he were building to something that only he and a handful of others knew about.

"This season," he began, gesturing to the group of young actors clumped together near the wall to my right, "we once again welcome a new cohort of the Birmingham Conservatory to our stage." Applause tittered throughout the audience. This was the program Richard had started two years ago to help nurture actors in classical theatre, providing them with mentorship and training from masters of the craft as well as giving them roles in the Festival's season. "All part of what I believe to be priority number one: cementing the Festival's future and, in doing so, cementing Stratford's future. It's something I've taken a lot of flak for in the media. I'm not going to name names, but we all know who has it out for me. But everything I've done has been to take care of the Festival and, in doing so, to take care of the town. Without the Festival there is no Stratford and without Stratford there is no Festival. It's as simple as that. But," and here Richard paused and took in the company, "there's something I'd like to do that's maybe just for me. By the time I'm done here, I vow to have programmed the entire Shakespearean canon."

I applauded loudly, the sounds of which couldn't but fill the space. I was the only one clapping.

"You try selling tickets to *Troilus and Cressida*!" Antoni lobbed, and a few company members chuckled. I wasn't deterred, though. I knew it would be difficult. We hadn't done some of Shakespeare's plays in many years. We'd done *Timon of Athens* once in all the time I'd been stage managing here, and we'd never done *The Two Noble Kinsmen* ever. Still, it was an admirable goal.

"Remember," Richard said, concluding his address with what had become a catchphrase, "you arrive in the snow . . ."

"*And you leave in the snow*," the company finished in unison.

Strong foot pushing down, the other pushing up. Like John said.

Lucy grunted, straightening her legs as she pulled herself a few inches off the ground.

"That's it," John encouraged. "Legs and arms. Legs and arms."

The Forest of Arden was suddenly alive, and we were all its Lords, or maybe just a crowd of cheering parents, of mothers and fathers proud to see success snatched from the jaws of sincere struggle.

Lucy grunted again, and raised herself a foot in the air. Her feet then slipped, and for a moment she dangled only by her arms.

You got it.

She rewrapped her feet in the rope, reclaiming stability, and then lunged upward another foot. I was in awe. Along the sidewalls, the men of the company were too, many of them knowing they couldn't muster the strength to reach even that height. It was ten years ago, in the same role, she'd first climbed down from the Festival balcony, and

SHAWN DESOUZA-COELHO

now, ten years later, Lucy climbed up, higher and higher, until she was a remarkable couple of metres off the ground.

By the time she'd settled, looking down on us from Arden's canopy, my cheeks hurt from smiling so widely. Our applause was instantaneous. Jeannette was on her feet.

"Okay!" Lucy heaved, looking at John. "How do I get down?"

John cackled and Lucy descended, clapping her hands together when she reached the ground. John squeezed her shoulder, and Lucy breathed a sigh of relief.

"Great. Now, let's do it with the scene," Jeannette then said.

So we did.

 "And in the event of an emer-gency," the coach attendant explained by rote, "break the glass and use the hammer to crack the four corners of the window." The seat beside me was empty, as I hoped it would be for the entire train ride to Chicago, so the attendant leaned over and tapped the air in the direction of the stated four corners. I was only half paying attention to her. It was nine in the morning, and the world outside seemed washed out. I kept sneaking glances at her breasts, contemplating the irony of her explaining life-saving procedures to a dying woman.

When the doctor had told me I had cancer, everything had gone very quiet. I was in my living room and the receiver in my hand almost vanished, reappearing only when I asked him what we should do next. He said he was going on vacation and that nothing need be done immediately. I told him I was going on vacation too, that I was leaving for Chicago tomorrow. He told me not to worry, and that it could wait until we both got back.

That night I stood in front of a mirror in my bedroom, naked with my arms to my side, noticing my body for the first time in what seemed like years. I was fat, and it showed, my skin lumping here and there like fifty-three-year-old dough, the sagging meat under my arms jiggling with every movement. I massaged my left breast, trying to feel what I was shown, that weird-looking spectre that haunted my mammogram, but I couldn't feel a thing, not even emptiness. I cupped my breast then, trying to imagine it halved. With the palm of my other hand, I pulled back the thin bangs of my very short hair, shielding it from view, and tried to imagine what the chemo would do to me. I winced at the sight of the old, bald pear in front of me. I closed my eyes and imagined dying.

As the train churned to life, it felt like there was nobody else on it. I wondered what Maloo would say when I told her the news. She had taken a contract job in the wig department at the Chicago Shakespeare Theater, and I was going down to see a production there of *The School for Scandal*, which had a bunch of Stratford actors in it. I hadn't told her yet because I didn't see a point in making her worry for the ten hours I wouldn't be able to speak to her on the train. Besides, there was nothing anybody could do for me right now.

Passing through a stretch of dense evergreen forest filled with trees much older than I, I caught my reflection in the window.

You've had a good life, Nora. You've met so many wonderful people over the years, and some not-so-wonderful ones too. You've made your parents proud, as an almost-shepherdess, as a student, as a stage manager. You've stepped behind the Iron Curtain and lived to tell the tale. You burned with Robin, brightly, until he and everybody else around him had burnt out. Your menstrual cycle lined up with five amazing women in Parade. *You are godmother to so many children, though it seems you'll never have your own. That ship's sailed twice now. The first departure was a choice you made, Nora, because you thought it would prevent breast cancer . . . Oh. I have cancer. What do I do with all of my stuff? I could give my furniture to the family and they could divide it up among themselves. I'll give my stage management stuff to Ann and she can decide what to do with it, even the new binder I got for Christmas last year. I was really excited to use it too. Maybe somebody else will get a kick out of it. It zips up, opens flat, has three-inch rings, and a place to put extra papers: everything a stage manager could want—*

I threw my hand into my bag on the seat beside me in a desperate attempt to find something to stop my mind from spinning. I pulled out a book and I had only just cracked the spine when I noticed a crushed cigarette pack in my bag. I took it out and shook it. The muffled rattle told me there were two or three left. I crushed the pack further, making certain to break each one, and threw it into the little garbage bag hanging behind the seat in front of me. I understood the mentality of smokers with cancer: "I'm going to die anyway." But, I didn't subscribe to it. The day I was diagnosed, I told myself I would never smoke again. Without skipping a beat, I opened my book and started reading.

When I met Maloo in Chicago, I waited until we were at her apartment to tell her. She was in shock when she heard, but eventually she said, "If you need any help with a wig or anything . . . anything you need, I will be there for you."

I steeled myself and said, "Well, Maloo, I just had a ten-hour train ride to think about it . . ."

"What is it?"

"When it comes time, can you shave my head?"

"Of course, Nora. Anything."

--

I was in my pyjamas and robe when my heart began leaping out of my chest. Ivy scrambled from me as I ran to the phone in my living room, trembling as I picked up the receiver and dialled.

SHAWN DESOUZA-COELHO

"Can I — Can I speak to Maloo?"

The man on the other end was confused. "Maloo? She's asleep."

"I know. I still need to talk to her."

I heard rustling then, and the distinct clicking of a receiver passed from one hand to another.

"Hello?" Maloo croaked.

"Maloo . . ."

"Nora?"

"I—"

"I'll come over."

"Thank you."

I waited in the middle of the street, the medication they'd given me for my nausea after chemo sessions hurling me into a delirium I'd never felt before. It was the dead of night, and no cars greeted me, no clouds, no moon, no light. There was no street, even, just the pressure of something strange beneath my bare feet. It felt like I was constantly falling on black ice, one moment up then suddenly down, and nothing made sense. I felt cold.

Then Maloo arrived. I met her with some kind of choking sound — my concerted thanks for her presence in the deserted road, my eternal thanks that she had finished her contract in Chicago and was once more doing wigs at the Festival — and she took me inside. I tried to talk and then eventually did and the walls turned their backs to us, covering their ears. The photos in my living room closed their eyes and knelt down, a congregation of my past selves reminding me of a persistence I seemed to have forgotten. The furniture shifted uncomfortably, and the whole house filled like a big balloon ready to leave the ground. The trees astride the road laughed at me, though no wind joked with their leaves, and the blank houses stared at me like I was made of stone, and the oceans took with them a little piece of the continent with every crashing wave, and inside me the Earth turned and turned, and I ambled around the hospital, ambled around the hospital, ambled around the hospital because the cure was worse than the disease, once with my mother who was hospitalized too when she fell and broke a bone in her back because she was sleepwalking, sleepwalked right off the end of her bed and I thought that was so bizarre because she couldn't get out of her bed even when she was awake and I crawled into the bed with her while she ate and we were just a couple of sick Polleys in pale blue gowns and Aunt Reta was there too dying in her own small way and Mom told me that everybody at Cedarcroft had taken to calling her "Dear" and she said they say, "Dear, can I help you with that? Dear, would like this?" and then she said, "So help me God, if they call me dear one more time—"

"Nora . . ."

—and then Andrew visited me the next time because there was always a next time and we watched television and he told me they missed me at work and I wanted to tell him I missed him and that we didn't see one another often enough anymore because he was in a relationship and that had nothing to do with me but instead we talked about movies and played cards and he left and I told myself that I would tell him next time because there was always a next time and I felt like I'd been wearing a hospital gown my whole life and that maybe I would vomit my organs out one by one and die there so the doctors gave me Haldol which is also an antipsychotic so now my whole body was a boat half-sunk and if I died now, on autopsy they'd open me up and find claw marks on the inside—

"Nora."

—but Marg told me I'd be fine because God would never take away two of Mom's children God wouldn't do that to her but God did that and more to my great-grandmother who had to watch six of her seven children enlist in the Great War and then had to hear that six of her seven children had died in the Great War and I didn't even know their names save for one the only one left and his name was Patrick and he was left so he could have Vic and Dad was left so he could have me and I was left so I could have the theatre but the theatre doesn't need me—

"Nora!"

"*What?*"

Maloo's hand was on mine and I stared at it for a moment, blankly. It felt like an old song, one I knew all the words to.

"It's going to be okay," she soothed. I breathed like I was asking for air, and my heart jogged. All around us the walls uncovered their ears, and faced us politely. "It's going to be okay." I felt like I could hear her say the words, quietly like a confession, all night. "It's going to be okay. It's going to be okay. It's going to be okay."

--

Our windows were down and the air was warm as it whipped by the burgundy pickup truck on the way to London and another round of radiation. The sun-baked manure of nearby farms sat with us like humidity. While I dreaded the exhaustion that was to come, I was quite calm.

"Smoke?" Pete asked from the driver's seat. I turned to him. He was holding a pack of cigarettes out to me. I opened my mouth to speak but then he blurted, "What are you? Crazy?" and snatched the pack away with a sly smile, putting it back in his door. I squinted at him and then laughed.

Peter Donaldson was always a bit rugged looking, a real salt-of-the-earth kind of guy. His hairline had receded quite a bit and he sported a stubbly salt-and-pepper beard. He was wearing a beige-green T-shirt and blue jeans. I was wearing something similar, with the addition of a red bandana on my head, which I used sometimes to cover what was left of my henna tattoos.

After Maloo had shaved my head the first time, I asked her to paint it. She sort of laughed, and then, game for anything, drew a bunch of Celtic swirls on my cold scalp in black marker. It looked great and gave people something to talk about because people rarely, if ever, knew what to say. Afterwards, we used henna, but it always ended up looking too pale. Next we'd try temporary tattoos.

I breathed deeply, always tired nowadays, always thankful for Pete, and Maloo, and Sue, and the Festival for giving me what little work they could so I wouldn't be defined by my sickness, and the others who had helped me and continued to do so. It still surprised me that people cared so much.

Last season, during contract negotiations with Antoni and his lawyer, it felt like nobody understood what stage management was asking for. It brought me to tears. Afterwards, Andrew told me to bring the issue to the actors and get their support. I thought they'd laugh in my face, thought they'd ask, "Nora *who*? *What* management?" In spite of this, we did take it to them, and Martha, along with Seana McKenna, a beautiful and talented veteran actress of the Festival, refused to sign their contracts until the matter with stage management was settled. I wasn't sure what we'd done to deserve that kind of solidarity.

"So, where are you moving to?" I asked, facing the window. Pete had been adamant that he take me to my very last round of radiation. I didn't have the heart to tell him I still had one more after this.

"That's a whole other story. Sheila wants to do the whole L.A. thing, but I don't know. I hate the place. It gets in my skin. It's all industry, no work, and what work there is . . . I mean there's no growth there. It's hard not to feel like a crab in a barrel. Where's the *work*? You know?"

I nodded. I had never been to L.A. before, but I understood him. I'd heard the same from countless actors coming through Stratford's doors who had gone across the border and plateaued there for a long time. "Where would *you* move?"

"Well, when Sheila and I were doing *Emily of New Moon*, I kind of loved living in P.E.I. while we were shooting. Have you ever been?"

"No. Closest I've been is Halifax, I would say."

"Beautiful there. Quiet. Great arts community. Everybody wants you to succeed. And the scenery—" He paused, as if seeing a gently rolling P.E.I. imprinted on the pale flatland around us. "Anyway, we haven't decided anything, but I'll let you know when we do."

"Please." After a beat, I changed the subject. "How's Mackenzie?"

"Good, good. She wants to be in show business. Surprise!"

I laughed. "And Drew?"

"Growing. Christ, is Drew ever growing. She's nine now."

"No!"

"Yeah. Time goes and goes. You know, we still use those school-houses your dad made for us to put the kids' photos in. Neat little things."

"Oh yeah? That's nice to hear." For a fond second, Dad flashed across my mind, sitting with red yarn, a needle, and a sheet of plastic canvas he'd cut into the shape of an old schoolhouse. Each had twelve windows, one for a photo of every year of school. Mackenzie and Drew each got one when they were born, as did many others.

The pickup whirred along, and my thoughts drifted in our shared silence. It wasn't often I got to spend time with people like Pete or Sheila, couples. They always had a way of retreating into their own worlds, and after that happened people like me with nobody to retreat with were left wondering why there was so much punch remaining in the bowl and so little conversation swirling around the room. I was grateful for the time we now spent together, more grateful than I could admit to him or anybody, really, even Ivy.

Holly never did come home.

"What's it like?" Pete asked, the road ahead winding to the left.

"What?"

"The radiation."

I placed my hand on my left breast, its bra cup now only half-full. Or half-empty. I hadn't figured out how to look at it yet. "Like a bad sunburn on a very sensitive part of your body."

"You're not going to throw up in the truck, are you?" Pete then asked, a mock look of dread in his eyes.

I chortled and shook my head. "No."

His eyes softened, and he smiled. "Good."

 **2002**

"All done, Nora?"

"Yes," I replied, holding the newspaper to one side as Krista cleared my nearly empty plate. I was sitting at the counter in Madelyn's, opposite the front door and beside the kitchen. All around, the room buzzed like a rehearsal hall, and I felt refreshed. This was my Sunday morning, every Sunday morning.

"More water?"

"Sure, thanks."

She carried herself deftly, Krista. As I watched her leave it struck me how much older she'd gotten. I counted her years on the upturned tips of my slowly wrinkling fingers. Twenty-eight. I imagined her taking over once Madelyn was done. When that would be exactly was anybody's guess. Madelyn was in her fifties and still spritely as ever. She was a fixture in town and in the diner. It was her home.

What else would she do?

I chuckled at the question and then looked through the window, as if beyond the vast expanse of bright grey clouds and glaucous trees. A few stools to my right, a gruff man in a red baseball cap sat down, dropping his keys and wallet on the counter. Jeff was his name. The employees had called out to him on his way in, as they did me and many others. It was like an episode of *Cheers* and I couldn't help but feel a little special.

I should thank Andrew.

Though he wasn't gone yet it was hard not to think of him, if only momentarily, in the past tense. He had decided, after being inexplicably moved to the Tom Patterson, that he would leave the Festival entirely after this season. I couldn't fault him. The job title was the same, but the duties simply didn't match up to his level of organizational expertise; the PSM at the Tom Patterson was in charge of a single theatre whereas the Festival PSM played caretaker to the daily schedules of the entire institution. Maloo had left already, having accepted a full-time position in wigs at the Chicago Shakespeare Theater. It was hard not to miss them, especially when immersed in the traditions we shared, like Madelyn's.

"Here you go," Krista said, pouring the ice water. "Jeff!" she then called. "You can't smoke that in here." Jeff huffed, yanking the cigarette from his mouth. He snapped up his keys and wallet, and left. We watched him long enough to see him light up just outside the door. "I was watching CBC the other night," she said to me, "and they were talking about this study on the harmful effects of cigarettes on unborn babies. They can get all these birth defects like weaker lungs or their births are premature. Really sobering stuff."

"I saw that too. It's terrible, isn't it?"

"Awful. You used to smoke, right?"

"Yes. I quit last year, though."

"Good for you."

"Yeah," I said dryly. "Now when I get pregnant I won't have to worry about quitting."

Krista laughed vaguely at my bizarre humour and then skirted past it by telling me she really liked my hair. It was full, cheek-length hair. Cancer-free hair. I thanked her, and then she left to wait on another customer.

In Krista's place, I noticed a young pigtailed girl near the far window, looking at me. She seemed curious and open, at least until we made eye contact, and then she darted guiltily back to her dad sitting across the table from her.

Huh.

I wasn't sure why, but I suddenly felt nostalgic, but for a place I'd maybe never been to. Brushing it off, I turned back to my paper, and the present, and continued reading.

When I had finished and paid my bill, I drove to the Giant Tiger just up the road from Madelyn's for want of anything else to do: yet another tradition Andrew and I had shared.

In the store, I strolled from aisle to aisle, looking at nothing in particular. I saw a turquoise shirt that might have gone with a deep purple set of earrings I owned. I checked the price tag on the sleeve and sighed.

If only it were on sale.

The prices weren't exactly high at Giant Tiger, but I was subsidizing Mom. We all were. She still had money, but it needed to be rationed out because nobody knew how long she would live. If Dad's death didn't kill her and Fred's didn't either, none of us knew what exactly she was waiting for. If she lived to ninety, she would have no money left.

If she lives to ninety, I'll be . . . sixty-two. Will I still be able to stage manage at sixty-two? If I can't, then how will I help keep Mom at Cedarcroft?

Feeling suddenly contrite, I let go of the sleeve and left the store.

--

SHAWN DESOUZA-COELHO

"Richard!" I called from the stage door. Across the parking lot, Richard looked up from the escape of his gold PT Cruiser. He was wearing a thin beige overcoat. "Richard," I repeated as I made my way down the stairs to him.

"Don't look at me like that," he said, coming around to meet me. The night was warm, and he was lit only faintly by the trace light of the stage door behind me and the distant moon above. "It's not what you think. I'm actually fucking relieved!" I cocked my head to one side, unable to believe what I'd just heard. "Truthfully, I don't know why I took the role in the first place. You should have talked me out of it."

"*Me?*"

"You should have said, '*My Fair Lady*? You don't do musicals! Professor Henry Higgins? You? You're too old.'"

"Well, you are."

"And you're no spring chicken either!" With that, Richard leaned back on the hood of his car and scrounged a pack of cigarettes from his pocket. He lit one, took a long drag, and exhaled slowly, the smoke drifting upward, eventually leaving behind only its smell. "I thought I could do it."

"I know," I replied, leaning beside him.

"I had all these plans for the season. The fiftieth!" He spoke to me, but stared into the far-off darkness hovering over the river. "We went through every production of *All's Well That Ends Well*, we talked about the cuts Guthrie made, we talked about my try at Parolles. We made notes. We talked. You know. You were there."

"I was." As was Dean Gabourie, Richard's broad-shouldered assistant director, the two of them throwing themselves into the work with a reckless abandon I hadn't seen since Richard's work on *Shrew* back in '88.

"I had a vision for what this season would be, for what it would mean. I wanted to celebrate the company. Gold neckties for the men. Gold shawls for the women." He smacked the hood beneath us. "Gold car for me. Sparse stages. Great fucking acting. But, nowhere in all of that had I planned to do a musical."

"Why *did* you agree to do it?"

Richard half-chuckled, as if replaying the events in his head, but didn't answer. Yesterday, he had performed the entire play without stopping, without flubbing a line, and without the need of a prompt. Tonight, everything went smoothly, but he left the theatre as if he'd never set foot onstage again.

A few actors passed by, waving to us on their way to the bar or home or both in whatever order. I heard a faint whistle in the distance.

"It's weird," Richard said, gesturing to the actors now heading up Queen.

"What is?"

"Reconciling the two sides of me: the side people see and who I actually am. You know, when I first joined the Festival company, I couldn't shower with the other actors? After the show, I'd wait for everyone to be done and only then could I shower comfortably."

"I didn't know that."

"I couldn't even cross the street sometimes for fear people might be watching. I still don't know why that was," he added, and then corrected himself. "*Is*, in a way. It's different now. I don't know what it is. It's just different."

In the silence that built up between us, I found myself thinking that everybody should read an actor's biography if for no other reason than to know the pressures solidifying in their heads: the pressure to make money, to break even, to perform, to take care of themselves and their family, to become something, to become somebody, to just remember their lines, their beats, and their blocking. In the solitude of the Festival Theatre parking lot, this was who Richard was.

"How's your mother doing?" he asked, lighting another cigarette, having already burned through the first.

"Fine. She hates applesauce now."

"Why?"

"She has to take her pills with it. I guess it makes them easier to swallow. So she just has that association, I guess."

"Oh."

SHAWN DESOUZA-COELHO

"Yeah."

Richard paused. "I almost made it, Nora."

I turned to him. "I know."

"Still, though. Fucking relieved."

The truth was, none of this conversation happened. Instead, the whole scene spiralled in my mind like a helicopter seed as I stood at the stage door and watched Richard slam his car door shut. I imagined stopping him, but the reality was he wanted to be left alone to address whatever mixture of exhaustion, relief, and self-condemnation now faced him, having made his decision never to return to the stage. After a moment, he started his car, pulled out of the parking lot, and drove off. I stared at the spot where I'd last seen him, and the seed kept spinning.

In rehearsal for *All's Well* a few weeks ago, Richard gave Sara Topham a direction. She was a talented young actress, with long dark hair and a slender frame. She was standing, facing David Snelgrove's Bertram.

"On the line 'Will you not, my lord?'" Richard said, "I want you to put your hand on his chest."

Sara did. "Like this?"

"Just like that."

"Okay."

Richard nodded to me.

"Whenever you're ready," I told the actors.

BERT. Change it, change it;
      Be not so holy-cruel: love is holy;
      And my integrity ne'er knew the crafts
      That you do charge men with. Stand no more off,
      But give thyself unto my sick desires,
      Who then recover: say thou art mine, and ever
      My love as it begins shall so persever.

Out of the corner of my eye, I saw Richard sit upright in his chair, as if suddenly strapped to a board.

DIANA.	I see that men make ropes in such a scarre That we'll forsake ourselves. Give me that ring.
BERT.	I'll lend it thee, my dear; but have no power To give it from me.
DIANA.	Will you not, my lord?

Diana placed her hand on Bertram's chest, and then Dean and I shared a knowing glance. At the same moment, Richard had very carefully, like the air in front of him was more fragile than new love, held out his hand too. It was as if it were his hand on Bertram's chest. It was as if he were Diana in that moment, and Bertram, for I could see the effect of Diana's hand imprinted in Richard's deeply held breath. It was as if he were acting out every role in his head.

When the scene ended, Sara nodded and the room was a resolute quiet.

"Yeah," Richard said. "Like that."

As I went back in through the stage door, the seed had finally landed. *Maybe it's for the best.*

2003

"Excuse me, Nora?"

At the stage management table in the Festival Theatre, I paused, my finger still on a switch. Nearby, Leon Rubin, the director of *Pericles*, had already turned to the stern and insistent voice behind me in the aisle.

This isn't going to be good.

My eyes met with hers, the technical director, towering above me.

"Could you come into the lobby with me, please?" she said before pointing to Leon. "You as well, please."

Leon threw me a furtive glance as we started up the aisle behind her, and though I attempted to reassure him everything was fine, I was confident it simply came across as excessive blinking.

It had to do with snow machines, of all things. In a previous production, Leon had used six of them to simulate snow onstage, and he wanted the same effect in *Pericles*. So I sent out an inquiry to the TD, who is responsible for the budgets, schedules, and all technical elements of productions in the particular theatre he or she is assigned, and she told me there weren't any snow machines. They didn't exist. But that didn't make sense to me. The Stratford Festival of Canada, as we called it now, didn't just throw away six snow machines. Sceptical, I went to the secretary of the production department to see if there was any record of them having been purchased or sold or lent out. That was my mistake. And, as soon as we hit the lobby and the house door shut, I made sure to emphasize that it was mine and not Leon's.

"This has nothing to do with him," I stated. "He never pushed me or anything like that. He doesn't need to be a part of this conversation."

Wide-eyed, Leon slunk back through the house door, vanishing from sight. The TD had her hands on her waist, livid and expectant. I felt like a cornered animal.

"Are you trying to do my job for me?" she fumed, more statement than question.

"Not at all."

"You went over my head."

"I know, and I should apologize for that."

"So go ahead, apologize for all the good that'll do. Why would you do something like that? I told you there were no snow boxes. There are no snow boxes. I checked. I checked again. Is that not enough?"

Is that not enough . . .

Looking at the woman standing before me, her word apparently meaningless to those around her, to me, I suddenly felt crushed by the full weight of my actions. I'd been exactly where she was, telling somebody just like me that Bobby Short was waiting and anxious for us to start and that person was telling me no. "Fuck no." My word was as meaningless to them then as hers apparently was to me now. She had to feel that way. How could she not? It had taken me some time to realize it, but like a riddle solved, I couldn't now see it any other way. The walls of these big institutions were somehow built to stratify without exemption along lines detected by feeling alone. That was what I now recognized in her, the feeling: the nagging judgments of her value, the need to be taken seriously, the need to prove herself. I felt ashamed.

Take the blame, Nora. Especially when it is your fault.

"It's enough," I admitted. "It's my fault entirely. I shouldn't have done it. I overstepped my bounds. You're absolutely right."

The TD exhaled, a deflated balloon. "Please, don't do it again."

I nodded, and watched her leave, her head hung halfway between high and low, maybe proud of her strength, but depressed she needed it at all. After a moment, I went back into the auditorium and let Leon know everything had been smoothed out and, taking the TD's word as sacrosanct, that there weren't any snow machines.

 The Cardinal and Lord Chamberlain spoke in hushed voices as Henry and Anne danced on the Festival Theatre stage in *Henry VIII*. Richard nodded approvingly a few seats over.

CARD.   Pray, tell 'em thus much from me:
There should be one amongst 'em, by his person,
More worthy this place than myself; to whom,
If I but knew him, with my love and duty
I would surrender it.

CHAM.   I will, my lord.

Lord Chamberlain approached the masked men, and whispered something inaudible. The men responded as one.

MEN.   Oui.

Lord Chamberlain then returned to the Cardinal.

CARD.   What say they?

CHAM.   Such a one, they all confess,
            There is indeed; which they would have your grace
            Find out, and he will take it.

CARD.   Let me see, then.
            By all your good leaves, gentlemen; here I'll make
            My royal choice.

HENRY.   Ye have found him, cardinal:

Henry unmasked and—

"*Tyranny by design!*" Richard cried to the auditorium. I turned, as did we all, but what I found there gave me pause. He was sweating profusely in the air-conditioned house. I tensed slightly, suddenly aware of the trash can beside me. "We have to cut the mask," he continued, standing and gesturing to the tall and talented Graham Abbey. "Look at him. Henry looks like he just frenched a leaf blower!" The actors onstage laughed, and Graham smiled infectiously, smoothing his hair. "We have to cut it."

"What if," I started before even realizing I was speaking aloud, "what if they fix it for him?"

"Who?"

"His friends. They're right there. If something happens to his hair, they'll just fix it for him like anybody would."

Richard tilted his head, as if letting the idea fall in. "Let's try it," he conceded. "But if it doesn't work, we're taking the fucking thing out!" He loosened his tie as he sat, and told them to run it again.

HENRY.   Ye have found him, cardinal:

Henry unmasked and sure enough his hair was mussed. This time, his friends went out of their way to fix it, making him look entirely more regal in the process. Suddenly, Henry was a ruler, one that people adored to serve. I thought it looked rather good, and Richard must have too because the scene carried on without interruption.

> You hold a fair assembly; you do well, lord:
> You are a churchman, or, I'll tell you, cardinal,
> I should judge now unhappily.

I snuck a glance at Richard as the scene progressed. He was wiping his forehead dry. It was at this point in the play, not too long ago in rehearsal, Richard had vomited without warning. One moment he was fine, and the next he was lurched over a trash can, which I then held as Henry and Anne became Graham and Sara again and all the actors worried in their own ways.

It was strange, though. Holding the bin into which Richard leaned and retched, I was reminded of Robin. Though Richard's lips were spittle-wet and his eyes glossy, and Robin had none of these symptoms, I recognized the exhaustion. On top of the poor diet, lack of exercise, and chain-smoking that were already killing Richard, this job was killing him too. Like the Canadian National Railway shops before it, the town had become unsustainable without the Festival. In the winters, Ontario St. was a muted stretch of road compared to its vibrancy during the Festival's season. And it was that pressure that spurred Richard to start the Conservatory, to reshape and redesign the Festival Theatre from the house to the lobby, to renovate the Avon Theatre, and to build and open the Studio Theatre to mark the Stratford Festival of Canada's fiftieth season. It was that pressure that sat with him every day like an ulcer. It was as if everything Robin

SHAWN DESOUZA-COELHO

wanted, Richard did, the two of them intertwined in their loves of Shakespeare, Stratford, and the Festival, and their death wish in taking on all three at one and the same time as artistic director.

CARD.   I am glad
         Your grace is grown so pleasant.

HENRY.   My lord chamberlain,
         Prithee, come hither: what fair lady's that?

I kept my eyes on the stage, on Henry and his scene partners. All the while, however, Richard and the trashcan circled me like binary stars. I was ready to run, if need be, to get one to the other, more as a friend than as a stage manager.

CHAM.   An't please your grace, Sir Thomas Bullen's daughter —
         The Viscount Rochford, — one of her highness'
         women.

HENRY.   By heaven, she is a dainty one. Sweetheart,
         I were unmannerly, to take you out,
         And not to kiss you. A health, gentlemen!
         Let it go round.

2005 Near the back of the sparsely filled Festival Theatre green room, I found myself sitting perfectly still. Seniority had equalized my effort to my workload, and I was calibrating myself for the day. I sipped coffee and spied Lucy on the patio chatting with another actor beneath an overcast morning sky. I tried to place him, the other actor, but couldn't. I didn't know what shows he was in, or even his name. I took a big gulp, as if the answers to either question were at the bottom of my cup. They weren't, and I felt indifferent about it. This was now the usual, the Festival having become so big that I sometimes went a whole season without even running into somebody.

Leaving the green room, I turned right and went through the hallway, past the stairs leading down to stage level and below. Seeing the newly minted corridor on my left, I decided to stop in to see the Festival's library. Another person passed me on my way in. He greeted me with a nod, and I did the same. I didn't recognize him either.

The library was a small, carpeted rectangle with one half bowed slightly to the left. It was lined with wooden shelves that had glass doors, and at the far end were two computers people could use to surf the Internet or check their email. Not long after Andrew had left to work at the Globe Theatre in Regina, ARIEL had been replaced with a system called Arden, so now everybody was getting his or her call times online, whenever, wherever. I took a moment from time to time to be thankful I didn't have to worry about that kind of stuff anymore. I was only a stage manager, called just like everybody else. I worked in pencil.

The library had been the work of a few Festival actors incessantly reminding the management at every company meeting that it would be nice if there were a place where anybody could go, on campus, to learn more about Stratford's history, the techniques of acting, to read some Shakespeare, etc. As I took in the room, winding around the tables in its centre, I saw that all this and more was available to anybody curious enough to go looking. There was a sign-out sheet on one table, and the topmost page was nearly full.

I wasn't sure why I decided to hunt for it then, but I followed the how-to acting manuals through to the directing books and the actor biographies, and well along before I ended up back by the entrance, empty-handed. There were no books on stage management. Not the Lawrence Stern book I had read back in the '70s when it was ostensibly the only one around. Not even the book Winston Morgan compiled and edited a couple of years ago, a collection of essays from different stage managers across Canada on a variety of topics. Ann even contributed one on stage managing a repertory theatre. Still, neither graced a single shelf.

I was staring off at the back wall, unsure what to make of our absence here, when my eyes suddenly focused and I felt so very warm. Just to the right of the far wall was a rug hooking of a black figure against a blue background and all around it yellow stars. I'd seen it hung elsewhere before. *Icarus*. Eleanor Nickless, who was once the wardrobe mistress here and Leo's dresser when he died, had finished it for him. Beside it was a framed colour photo with a caption that read: Leo Ciceri as Henry Bolingbroke in *Richard II*, 1964. I moved closer to the two mementos and smiled. Leo's eyes looked as kind as ever, the same eyes that greeted me so long ago in rehearsal on the day I was supposed to graduate from the University of Toronto, the same eyes that Tom had mourned and honoured through phone calls to company members when those same eyes had indelibly shut. I also saw that there was nothing explaining who Leo was or the origins of the rug.

What a shame.

--

After the closing of *Measure for Measure*, I found Richard upstairs at the Festival Theatre in his smoke room. It was a purpose-built, ventilated glass room beside his office that allowed him to smoke indoors without breaking any laws. The light from above reflected him in the window overlooking the parking lot. Outside, the late September night was thickly black. Dressed in a snappy beige dinner jacket and pink dress shirt, he waved me into his office. With my shoulder I nudged the door open. I had a package in my hands, wrapped in red and green: a gift for Richard to commemorate the occasion. Richard put out his cigarette and then joined me in his office.

"What's this?" Richard's lilting voice was gravelly as ever. "For me?"

"Actually, yeah," I replied, handing it to him. The wrapping crinkled as Richard shook the gift gently. I imagined him doing this beneath his Christmas tree, even at his current age of sixty-one. "Careful," I warned.

He set the box down on his mahogany desk, shifting papers aside and jostling some photos perched there, one of which was a photo of Antoni's children and him actually taken on Christmas morning. He somehow looked happier than the kids. Richard pulled the wrapping apart carefully and then stared at it for a moment or two.

It took me about a week to make, so I hope you like it.

Finally, he said, "We have to try it! Get the lights."

"Okay," I chortled, and then went to the switch by the door. Richard scrambled to find an outlet. "Whenever you're ready."

"Ready!"

TIK.

It was dark enough that I could barely see my own hands let alone Richard.

TIK.

Then, it was bright again as the room shone with the bluish-white light of the stained-glass lamp sitting atop his desk.

"Wow," Richard mouthed, taking in the walls where written in blurred letters were the names of every single one of Shakespeare's plays. My eyes fell on the last of these: *Measure for Measure.*

"Congratulations on doing the canon."

Richard looked down from the wall for a moment, and then up at me. "I'm retiring." My eyebrows rose and Richard didn't speak for another minute or so. Instead, we both lingered over and across the shadowy reminders of what he had accomplished until he said, at last, "I think it's time."

"I think it's long past time."

"*Well, why didn't you tell me?*"

"Would you have listened?"

"To you?" he smirked. "Of course not."

In the silence that followed, I switched the room's light on and he switched the lamp off. As he packed it up, he turned to me and asked, "Want to be artistic director?"

"No way."

"Come on! The pay isn't great, and you'll probably end up hated by more than a few people, unable to tell your friends from the parasites." He then gestured in a wide arc around the room. "But look at the perks! Cluttered desk. Parking-lot-adjacent office. Scenic, no? And, if you buy now, you can get your very own smoking room. I know, I know. You don't smoke. But neither do I, before and after every cigarette! I—" He dropped his hands, deflated, a boy who'd just realized Santa isn't real.

It was in that moment I saw how alone Richard was and how

long it had been since I'd seen him carousing with the company the way he used to. It had been so long since those nights at Down The Street, nights spent regaling actors with his stories and personality, they might never have happened at all. When was the moment, I then asked myself, when he stopped belonging to the company and started running it from on high? I couldn't imagine what that was like, to be surrounded by people but never know their true intentions. It wasn't something I ever had to deal with as a stage manager, where no amount of puckering made kissing my ass worthwhile. I also couldn't imagine the public scrutinizing my every decision, sometimes maliciously, or what it would be like for Richard to set foot outside this sphere of supposed power into the relative obscurity that would follow. Richard didn't even have a cat he could go home to complain it all away to. It was then I found myself more thankful for Ivy than ever, for staving off, in her small way, my own little loneliness.

I inched closer to Richard and squeezed his elbow. He bowed his head lower. Somehow it felt like enough.

--

PROS.   Go to: away!

Bill Hutt's Prospero stood centre stage near the end of *The Tempest* in an austere, cream-coloured gown. His white hair shone, and Alonso and Sebastian and the rest of his scene partners radiated energy towards him. He, in turn, fed it right back to them and the eager Festival Theatre crowd, Richard among them. Everybody knew they were witnessing history unfold.

ALON.   Hence, and bestow your luggage where you found it.

SEB.   Or stole it, rather.

Caliban, Stephano, and Trinculo left the stage, exiting up-centre. Even from the booth, I knew they were simply joining the throng of actors at the vom entrances who had asked me if they could be there to witness Bill's final performance and bow. I obliged because moments like these didn't come along very often.

PROS. Sir, I invite your highness and your train
       To my poor cell, where you shall take your rest
       For this one night; which, part of it, I'll waste
       With such discourse as, I not doubt, shall make it
       Go quick away; the story of my life
       And the particular accidents gone by
       Since I came to this isle . . .

From the booth, I couldn't help but marvel at Bill, knowing what it took to get him there.

Bill was eighty-five and taking on the role of Prospero, which was no small feat even for a much younger man. Richard took this into consideration from the very start, deciding the production would be a move-for-move remount of his 1999 production. The designer didn't even come to town, opting to send her assistant instead. Bill used his old costume. I was using Ann's script to call the show. None of this was a concern for Richard, though, who had one goal in mind: give Bill the final season he deserved. And nobody begrudged Bill for needing a minute or two in rehearsals, especially not the audience — his audience — rapt by the gravity of every pause he took onstage, some nearly a minute in purposeful length.

ALON. I long
       To hear the story of your life, which must
       Take the ear strangely.

PROS. I'll deliver all;
       And promise you calm seas, auspicious gales
       And sail so expeditious that shall catch
       Your royal fleet far off.
       Please you draw near.

All but Bill then left the stage, up-centre, and Prospero looked up at Ariel standing as he was on the balcony.

> My Ariel, chick,
> That is thy charge: then to the elements

"Lights 178," I said over headset.

> Be free, and fare thou well!

"Go."

I had held my tears back for the entire show, but couldn't any more as Ariel left. In his wake was a single spotlight and shimmering white hair and the sound of Bill's deep, lush voice. As Prospero spoke and his final speech came to a close, I felt so very lucky.

> PROS.   As you from crimes would pardon'd be,
>   Let your indulgence set me free.

"Lights 179, go."

With that, the spotlight faded to black as Bill left the stage. The applause was instantaneous and thunderous, from the audience, from Richard, from the actors underground, and from me up in the sky. Adrienne Gould, who was playing Miranda, handed Bill a bouquet of flowers during the curtain call and still the applause went on and on. Bill waved with his free arm, no doubt loving every last second of the crowd's adulation.

The celebration for Bill's retirement, as silly as the word 'retirement' sounds in a profession like theatre, was held in the Festival Theatre's new Marquee space just after the performance. The Marquee was located on the north side of the building, overlooking the Avon River, a new space that doubled as a venue for event rentals as well as rehearsals for shows on at the Tom Patterson since it was long enough to tape out the runway stage.

Entering from the doors near the backstage area, and having

     SHAWN DESOUZA-COELHO

already changed out of my blacks into jeans and a green sweater, I saw that Bill had already been seated at his throne at the far end of the room. It was a white and silver chair beside an ornate wooden pedestal with an arrangement of red, yellow, and white flowers. Holding a water bottle, Bill looked tired but, for the most part, enthused by the fanfare around him.

"Adrienne, dear," I overheard Bill say to her as they posed for a photo, her long dark hair tied into a ponytail, "you were the best Miranda I've ever had."

"No," she laughed, rapping Bill's chest.

"The best," he repeated emphatically. "And I had Martha Henry once. So that's saying a lot." He then squeezed her shoulder and whispered, "Don't tell Martha I said that."

Adrienne smiled. "It was a pleasure, Bill."

"All mine, my dear."

When Adrienne left Bill's side the party was in full swing. I drank from my wine glass as others chatted over theirs. Richard was out on the patio having a smoke, gesturing emphatically with his hands to some actors. I briefly wondered if they really cared what he was saying.

"Ruby, darling," Bill crooned to me, using the nickname he'd given me years earlier.

"How are you?" I asked, giving him a small hug.

Bill leaned in and in his usual deadpan way asked me, "Who *are* half of these people?"

"Fans."

"I like them. How's your mother?" Bill asked, his voice suddenly earnest.

"Recovering." I wasn't sure if I should continue, really. Bill was only two years younger than Mom, so I didn't know if he'd want to hear all the details of her heart attack. I didn't own a cell phone, so they called the stage management office and asked me if I wanted to take her to the hospital. I asked if she was resting, and they said yes, so I told them to just leave her. The conversation was frank, as if they were a cashier at the grocery store asking me if I wanted more bags. The truth was we had already signed a Do Not Resuscitate form, expecting the next catastrophe to be her last. She recovered though, cementing for us her resolve to continue on. For what, we still didn't know. I shifted the subject. "My mom and my sister Marg came to see the show earlier in the season."

"Did they now?" he smiled, waving to Sara Topham, who was talking to Peter Donaldson, far off across the room. Both of them waved back.

"They did."

"Where were they sitting?"

"Oh, in the wheelchair section. She hasn't got much mobility anymore."

Bill nodded and, after a moment, asked. "Well?"

"Well what?"

"Aren't you going to tell me how my performance was?"

I laughed. "I was speechless."

After another moment, Bill asked, sincerely as ever, "In a good way?"

--

It was a bright night as I pulled into my driveway, the late October snow crunching habitually under my tires. The day's rehearsal at the Grand was still thick in my tired mind so when I went inside, set my coat down, took my boots off, and turned on the kitchen light, I didn't even notice Ivy laying on the floor. I picked up her water bowl to refill it, squinting somewhat. I had the beginnings of cataracts, I was told, and would eventually need glasses if I wanted to continue making my living reading in the dark. My thoughts were immobile as the faucet ran.

We were in rehearsal for *The Blonde, the Brunette, and the Vengeful Redhead*, a one-woman show written by Robert Hewitt. It's a play where seven characters try, through their individual monologues, to make sense of the actions of the first character, Rhonda Russell, who killed a woman who supposedly seduced her husband, Graham. One actress plays all seven characters, including Graham. When Geordie

SHAWN DESOUZA-COELHO

Johnson pitched it to Lucy, she saw its potential instantly. I was the first person she called after she agreed, and I didn't hesitate for a moment to tell her I was all in. There were only three of us, trying to mount a production on a shoestring budget, and it was Geordie's first turn as director as well as Lucy's first one-woman show, so we were spent most days. But in spite of nights like these, when exhaustion transfixed me to the steady whishing of running water, I never once regretted my involvement. Here were two artists challenging themselves to burn brighter. How could I not support them?

Snapping to and turning the faucet off, I went to set Ivy's bowl on the floor. But, as I reached down, I saw her. She looked very strange to me then, with her eyes closed as they were, so devoid of tension, victims of gravity alone. I put my hand to my mouth and felt my lips soundlessly utter, "What do I do?"

I picked Ivy up, feeling the weight of her long life sink between my splayed fingers, and wrapped her in a lace pillowslip. I placed her in a shoebox, unable to believe how small the bundle had become. In black marker, I carefully wrote on the lid: Ivy, my friend. It wasn't until I had carried the shoebox into the backyard, and gotten a shovel, that I began to sob.

Sshk . . . Sshk . . . Sshk . . .

Was it something I did?

Sshk . . . Sshk . . . Sshk . . .

Was it just your time?

Sshk . . . Sshk . . . Sshk . . .

What?

Sshk . . . Sshk . . . Sshk . . .

If anybody saw me now, they would think me crazy: a wailing woman burying her cat in the frozen backyard in the middle of the night. To hell with them, though. This was something I felt I needed to do. It was what I felt was right. It was what I felt Ivy deserved.

Tup. Tup. Tup.

When I finished burying Ivy, I smoothed out the dirt and dropped the shovel to my side. I tried to think of something to say, but in the end could only apologize. For what, I didn't know.

As I ambled back around the house, I stopped in front of my driveway and wiped my eyes with my sleeve. I looked up at the half-moon. It looked exactly half, like it had been painstakingly measured, one side dark, and the other bright. My eyes softened their focus, without my consent, and I took in the whole image: the indifferent stars chiming, and the pale houses below them, and the deserted street in front of those, and my car in front of that, stoically reflecting blue from the moon's levelled half, and even the license plate in front of that, the one Jannine had given me as a gift. It read, AH KEV.

"Ah," I muttered, laughing painfully. "I can't do this again."

In the kitchen, I stood before the bowls on the floor, beside the counter. It was in the realization that no cat would ever use these bowls again that my tears rallied once more, following me even to my bed and a dreamless sleep.

--

On opening night for *The Blonde*, I took my place backstage at the Grand's McManus Studio, just off to the side. It was exactly where I needed to be, for Lucy and for myself. I needed to know my feet were on the same floor as hers. I needed her to feel that I was ready in case that floor, consisting of seven characters and pages upon pages of words and lines, ever fell out from underneath her. Lucy, too, was exactly where she needed to be. Though, as she took her beginners place, kneading her hands roughly, she looked more nervous than I'd ever seen her. Suddenly, with the muffled hum of the crowd through the walls and the white screen as her backdrop, she turned to me. Her red wig shook as she spoke.

"Why do we do this? Why am I doing this? Why would anyone put themselves through this fear and anxiety?" After a pause she confessed, "I'm absolutely terrified!"

I wanted to tell her that she belonged on the stage, that she could not be held from it. I wanted to tell her that she was Lucy Peacock, the very same actress who had been T-boned by a pickup truck just outside of Stratford and told the ambulance to drop her off at the Festival because she had a two-show day: *Hello, Dolly!* and *Fallen Angels*. I wanted to tell her why I knew she could do it, why I knew she could go on, but the truth was, I never understood how actors do it. I never understood what kept them going back to the rehearsal hall when the wounds of the previous day had yet to scab. I never understood what possessed them to spill their guts in front of tens, hundreds, and thousands of people. I never understood what skill it took to hit the same exact moment in that way, night after night, on a foundation of quicksand. No, I didn't tell her why she could do it. Rather, I asked her a question.

"What else would you do?"

Lucy laughed and nodded, seeing my point. It was a question all actors needed to understand because what it really asked was, "Is there anything in your life that you can do with the same passion you have for acting?" To this, the answer must be a resounding no because theatre will break your heart again and again, and it takes real strength to torment yourself like that, day in and day out, for the rest of your life.

Her anxiety allayed, at least for tonight, at least for the moment, Lucy steeled herself for her entrance. And with feet rooted to hers, I called the top of the show.

2006 It was like riding on honey, simultaneously effortless and fluid. We were remounting *The Blonde* in Stratford at the Studio Theatre as part of the Festival's season, the success of our modest production at the Grand last November unanimous and unequivocal. Lucy reprised her roles as Rhonda, Graham, and company, and so convincing had her Graham become that every night when he entered, programs would rustle, like stirring insects, as the audience checked to see who the male actor was in this supposed one-woman show. So convincing was her Mrs. Joan Carlisle — Rhonda and Graham's elderly neighbour who Lucy had modelled after my mother — that when Sue took Mom to see the show Sue thought she was seeing double. Yet, it was simpler than all that, much simpler.

Through the stage right tunnel where I'd found a place to call the show from floor level, unseen by the audience, I could see Lucy's Rhonda hit her mark downstage right, her red hair bobbed, dressed in khakis, a white shirt, and a beige coat. And I could feel it, her every footfall, radiate out to me in viscous waves, vibrating my soles and my bones and funnelling into my lungs the breath I needed to form that familiar two-letter word, a joy I begged the universe every show to let me have for just one more night.

"I don't know what I looked like," Rhonda said, "but hers was a big smile that suddenly vanished. 'Hi Rhonda. What are you doing here?' At that precise moment, the floodgates opened. I couldn't help myself and I couldn't stop the tears." Rhonda dropped her purse, and the momentum built. "They were streaming down my face. Well Lynette slams a whole lot of bras she's holding down on the counter, brushes aside a mother and daughter she's serving and wheels me into a change room. 'Be with you in a moment ma'am.' Don't know how many hours I was there. Lynette keeps ducking in and out. Kleenex, coffee, more Kleenex, more coffee, until I realized that I must have been in that little change room for over two and a half hours. Don't know how any of the women tried on bras. **With** Lynette's help I somehow pull myself together enough to get through the rest of the day. And the next one and then the following week and then month and then . . ."

2007

"Of Canada's three largest cities," Alex Trebek droned, "the one that's on an island."

"What is Montreal?" the contestant stated correctly before asking for another clue.

"About 67% of Canadians speak only this language."

"What is English?" the same contestant stated, once again correct.

Mom watched intently, eating bits of cut-up fruit at regular intervals from a special spoon with a large handle and a ninety-degree bend. It made the act of eating the work of the elbow as opposed to the wrist. Hers were arthritis-ridden, and a recent stroke had frozen her one hand into a closed fist. Beside me was the chart I'd made for her, saying things like "I'm hungry" and "I'm tired" and "I'm cold." The stroke also took away her voice.

It was evening when I got the call from Cedarcroft. From my living room, I then phoned stage management and told them I wouldn't be able to make it to rehearsal the next day because I had to go to the hospital. I did this with a somewhat heavy heart, as I had also been playing caregiver, in a way, for Richard.

Around the brightly lit tables we all sat in Rehearsal Hall 1 for the read-through of Oscar Wilde's *An Ideal Husband*, which was Richard's final show as artistic director. His extravagant *Comedy of Errors* had already opened, a production Richard threw everything he'd ever wanted at including dance breaks, bawdy slapstick jokes, and even a giant penguin with a hilariously caustic sign on its back that read "For the Critics." It was a celebration of Richard everybody clamoured to be a part of, including myself. Sara Topham chatted with David Snelgrove across the table from me, and beside them Brian Bedford smoothed out his shirtsleeves. To see Brian Bedford here, in his early seventies, playing the bit-part of a valet was a testament to Richard's influence. Even Bill had signed up to be a part of Richard's last season, to come out of retirement just to see Richard off, but sadly he'd been hospitalized for some time now. We were all just hoping for the best.

Tim Askew, the assistant director, checked his watch and then Richard's empty chair. I could have spent my days rehearsing with Lucy in the Studio on yet another remount of *The Blonde*, the production being that much of a hit, feeling more connected to a text and actor than I ever had in my entire career. Instead, I was here, for Richard, a tinge of anxiety coursing through me.

"Sorry, sorry," Richard yelled as he gusted into the room. He was sweating profusely, and when he finally sat he took a moment to gather himself. The actors didn't seem to mind, but my anxiety only grew. It wasn't that Richard was never going to make it, or that his absence was even a possibility. It just always hung in the air for the production team the question of what he was going to bring with him when he did come. Some days it was a grey cloud above his head, others it was a fog in front of his face, and others still it was sunshine shooting out of his hands and feet. Today, Richard seemed prepared. Then he began to talk about the play and I cringed inside.

"There's something to this text," he began, the actors alert, "and I think that, uh, our work here is really going to be about bringing that something to the light. When I wanted to do this play I, uh, thought, wow, what a great piece of work. There are all of these great moments in it, just some really great moments, and I thought, uh, well, let's do it, you know? Why not, you know? It's Wilde for Christ's sake!" The actors laughed, as if on cue. "It's Wilde! It's going to be a good show, because we've got a talented bunch o' people here. It's going to be a good show."

When Richard had finished, Brian Tree broke the silence that followed by asking, simply, "What time period is the play set in?"

"Time period?" Richard repeated, then looked to Tim.

"The play was written in 1895," Tim said. "So that's the 'present' the text refers to."

Richard gestured as if to say, "There you go."

"One of the Top 20," Alex Trebek hinted, "this 1946 film was based on a short story published as 'The Man Who Was Never Born.'"

"*It's a Wonderful Life!*" I blurted out. Mom turned her head to me and smiled. I was correct. She then made a sound, somewhere between a murmur and a gurgle. With speech therapy the hope was that her voice would someday recover. Whether or not she'd fully recover was still anybody's guess. I didn't know if anybody fully recovered from a stroke. For now, though, I pointed at the chart, starting from the top left corner and working my way across, the direction of reading, until Mom made another sound. I took my finger off the chart. She needed to use the bathroom.

--

Richard and I stood out in the hallway moments before we went inside, and with a crumpled look he tried to convince me he was keeping it all together. I rubbed his shoulder, feeling like I had to be strong enough

SHAWN DESOUZA-COELHO

for him. I looked through the rectangular window of the rehearsal hall door at the actors of *Husband* chatting away, unaware. I had to be strong for them too. Inside, though, the news was crumpling me as well.

When we entered, the rehearsal hall stopped like traffic at a red light, one person leading the other slowly to a standstill.

"I have to tell you all," Richard tried, standing near the stage management table, "that William Hutt has passed away." Sara put her hand to her mouth, tears suddenly welling in her eyes. "It was peaceful." Richard took a deep breath.

From the silence that fogged the room and seemed to last for days, an actor emerged, chuckling, "You know, Bill once did a show at the Grand, back when it was Theatre London. It was called *The Hollow Crown*. It was just a cabaret, a big Shakespearean cabaret, with pieces from various kings and queens of England, songs and speeches and whatnot. He put it on in the studio theatre. Nobody came."

"No!" Sara laughed.

I didn't know that.

"Closed in a week."

"You're joking," another actress said.

"The *studio*, no less." Everybody paused, as if picturing Bill standing in full costume in front of the studio's small but empty house. "Certainly took Bill down a peg."

"I bet," Richard agreed, wiping his eyes. "Some of you might know this, but on the first day of rehearsal in '65, I stood out on the Festival stage, part of the company's traditional meet-and-greet, and I must have had the goofiest-looking grin on because Bill comes up to me and says, 'Welcome home, Richard.' I don't know why he said it, why he said those exact words, but I'll never forget them."

"This was his home," another actor added. I followed his eyes around the room, trying to imagine where exactly in his home we were standing. The living room, maybe, since this was where he really lived.

And so it went, with the company bridging the chasms of their grief with little stories of Bill, filled with laughter and sorrow. I myself did the same, though I didn't speak mine aloud.

"Kikiki! Kikiki!"

I was walking through the institutional green hallways of the Vancouver Playhouse in 1985, on my way to Bill's dressing room to give him the half-hour call and make sure he wasn't overthinking his lines when I heard him warming up. I smiled. Prior to a show, it seemed as though I always heard Bill before I saw him.

"Eee! Eee!"

Tok̲! Tok̲!

"Ah, Ruby," Bill said, turning to me, pencil in hand. He was wearing a handsome brown three-piece suit with a red tie and a pocket watch. "Just in time. 22 Across, 'Disappointed.'"

"How many letters?" I asked, taking a seat beside him, somewhat relieved he wasn't thinking about his lines at all. His dressing room was little more than a mirror, a counter, and a few chairs.

Bill muttered as he counted the boxes. "Eleven."

"Oh, dear."

"Two 'L's near the end."

"Hm . . ."

"Crestfallen!"

"I was just going to say that," I said somewhat sarcastically.

Bill smirked, lobbing another one at me. "30 Across, 'B.C. Minister of Finance.'"

Huh.

"How many letters?" I asked.

"Six. Starts with—"

"Curtis."

Bill looked surprised. I too did a double take. I wasn't sure why I knew that.

After a few more back-and-forths, he looked up from his newspaper and asked, "What's the house like?"

"Seventy-two percent."

"Pretty good." He chuckled to himself, as if remembering something in the not too distant past.

Clarence Darrow is a one-man show about the American lawyer of the same name who worked some pretty high-profile cases like defending John Thomas Scopes for teaching evolution in a Tennessee school, and the thrill killers, Leopold and Loeb, who had murdered a fourteen-year-old boy just to see what it would feel like. The entire play is about the cases he had worked, so Bill was onstage the whole time, reciting page after page of text. I was there for him every step of the way.

When Bill brought up the issue of drying, we spent an afternoon brainstorming a system whereby he could call for a line and it wouldn't seem like I was prompting him. Eventually, we came up with a solution. It had dawned on Bill that Darrow mentions his wife in the play a few times. Her name is Ruby. So, I would sit backstage in the wings behind a scrim, and when the scrim fabric was lit, it would be opaque from the audience's perspective. From my perspective, though, it was still translucent. I would keep my light low, just bright enough to see my book, and if Bill needed a line he would simply say, "Ruby, what's next?" Then I would prompt him. It was perfect.

"Okay," I said, standing up. "It's the five."

"One more," Bill said as I reached the door. "15 Down, 'Best Canadian actor, first name William.'"

"Shatner." Bill let out a hearty laugh. "See you on the other side," I called back to him.

"Well," Richard said, realizing we'd lingered for maybe too long. "I think we should rehearse." The company agreed, and without any hesitation began their scene work, living the lives of other people in another world and another time where Bill never existed. What a sad world that was.

2008 Arriving at the Festival Theatre stage right door, I checked the backstage hallway behind me to make sure I was alone. Through the entrance, I spied the actors of *Hamlet* getting settled for the morning's work, the director, Adrian Noble, having just arrived. He was a dark-haired British man, not too tall, and nondescript. Very soon, he'd begin the day, a day regrettably filled with what seemed like teaching assignments for me. I breathed deeply, taking whatever little time I had to exhume and dispose of familiar feelings long buried inside: irritation, resentment, impotence, with the latter of the three making the very walls somehow prickly to touch.

It wasn't long ago I'd stood like this, before a rehearsal for *Much Ado*, with the announcement of Richard's replacement looming over me like a large, immovable stone. His replacement was actually four replacements: a triumvirate consisting of Des McAnuff, Don Shipley, and Marti Maraden as co-artistic directors, with Antoni as general director. That crippled me. Not the triumvirate — one look at a photo of the three of them, with Marti dressed in black, Don dressed in beige, and Des dressed in neon purple and lime green, told the viewer that Des's ascent to sole leadership was a foregone conclusion; his direction would assuredly eclipse theirs. What crippled me was the fact that, over and above them all, at the top of this artistic institution, we now had an administrator. For all of Antoni's artistic achievements, of which there were many, what choked me to tears as I walked into rehearsal the day it was announced was the fact that he was at the helm, steering as a businessman. Never before had I thought so earnestly of deserting this place.

I took a quick, steely breath, and walked into the auditorium. As I made my way to the stage management table in the house I caught Adrian's eye where he sat, front-row centre, and we exchanged greetings.

"Shall we?" he asked cheerfully.

"We shall."

We began with the party scene at the beginning of the play where Hamlet enters dressed in black and casts a pall on the celebration. While the rest of the company sat on the sides, Claudius entered with Gertrude, Hamlet, Polonius, Laertes, Voltimand, and Cornelius, along with some other lords and attendants.

> CLAU. Though yet of Hamlet our dear brother's death
>   The memory be green, and that it us befitted
>   To bear our hearts in grief and our whole kingdom
>   To be contracted in one brow of woe,
>   Yet so far hath discretion fought with nature
>   That we with wisest sorrow think on him,
>   Together with remembrance of ourselves . . .

As the scene played out I began to notice something odd, the oddest part being that I was the only one who seemed to notice it. I looked down at the markings on the page in my script as if they were written in ancient Greek. None of it made sense to me. Whether on purpose or by accident, Adrian had positioned the actors such that they were all impeding one another from the audience's view.

LAER.   My dread lord,
                   Your leave and favour to return to France.

CLAU.   Have you your father's leave? What says Polonius?

I glanced down at Adrian again, to see if he was seeing what I was. He seemed immersed in the scene, oblivious to the fact that an actor sitting house left was now craning his neck to see Polonius, which was something this stage was explicitly designed to prevent. The actors steadfastly worked the scene, not seeming to notice that they were masking one another. They only had to take a step one way or the other to rectify the problem. But, somehow, to everybody except me, the scene was going well. I wrestled, yet again, with the need to inform Adrian.

Earlier in the rehearsal process, in Rehearsal Hall 3, the actors set up for the scene where Hamlet, played by Ben Carlson, meets with Rosencrantz and Guildenstern and the Players. Ben looked pensive, always, as if the world were fine art he engaged with deeply, but forever from a slight distance. Every ounce an actor, in other words, and every ounce a Hamlet. I barely knew him, or most of them for that matter, and, in spite of my understanding that new management brought new faces, their novelty bothered me much more than I could admit, even to myself.

Off to one side, Tom Rooney waved and I waved back. He was from out west, a thin and fiercely talented actor with short sandy-blond hair. It was then I remembered that on the first day of rehearsal, at the table read, he had approached me and said, more question than statement, "Uh, just so you know, I didn't get a call about this rehearsal starting today." Never having called an actor about the start of rehearsal in my entire Stratford career, I looked at him like he was

     SHAWN DESOUZA-COELHO

a foreign currency. Then he added, cautiously, "So I just thought you might want to know that for next time." I crossed my arms and said, "Okay," simultaneously thinking that this must be something he's used to and trying to keep in mind that actors need routine to survive. Then, as now, I fought my growing sense of nostalgia for a time when everybody seemed to understand how this place worked.

When we started running the scene, something felt off, like a pebble in the heel of a shoe. I put myself in the audience's place, listening to Hamlet and Polonius speak while the Players stood near their truck.

HAM.	God's bodykins, man, much better: use every man after his desert, and who should 'scape whipping? Use them after your own honour and dignity: the less they deserve, the more merit is in your bounty. Take them in.
POL.	Come, sirs.
HAM.	Follow him, friends: we'll hear a play to-morrow.

Suddenly, the Players began to sweep the tables and chairs off the stage, and I again listened as any audience member would.

HAM.

Nope. Can't hear a word you're saying. I'm sure it's great, but I can't hear it over the sight of the furniture disappearing.

When Adrian stopped the scene to speak to some of the actors, I sidled over to Vikki Anderson, the assistant director. She perked her ear up towards me, both of us facing forward, watching the stage.

"You know what we need?" I said.

"What's that?"

"This scene is clearly in a street café. The Players are in a truck. We're outside. So what we need is a great big thunderclap, and three seconds of people pretending it's pouring rain and *then* they can pick up all the furniture and take it off. Then it'll make some kind of sense. Right now, they're taking it off apropos of nothing. It's very distracting."

We both looked at Adrian, standing onstage with Ben.

"You tell him," she said.

"No, you tell him."

She chuckled quietly. "No. It's your idea."

I sighed. She was right.

"Adrian?" I said, pulling him aside once we had called a break.

"Yes, Nora?" He already seemed uninterested.

"Would it be helpful if there was a big clap of thunder and *then* everybody took the furniture away?"

"What's wrong with the way it is now?"

"I think people will be wondering why the furniture is being taken away as opposed to listening to what the actors are saying."

Adrian contemplated this, and behind me I could feel Vikki willing the meeting to come to some kind of positive conclusion. I was as well. Finally, he said, as if it were a matter of course, "Let's take a look at it," and I felt my heart pump relief all the way down to my toes.

In the Festival auditorium, I called the first break of the day and then pulled Adrian into the aisle. "I think there's an issue with the blocking of the party scene," I said in a low voice, citing mentally my duty to the production.

"Oh?" he replied in his standoffish way.

"There were a few moments where the actors were masking one another."

He looked over to the stage, as if superimposing the positions of the actors onto its emptiness. After a moment he responded with, "I could see them just fine."

"Yes, but they can't." I pointed to the sides of the stage. I was losing my patience.

Adrian's eyes shrunk as he followed my finger, as if looking at some far off speck. "Are there going to be people sitting there?"

You're kidding me.

"Yes," I answered. "All of the people who can't afford to sit here."

"A lot of people?"

"Quite a few."

He nodded, ingesting this information.

Is this what it will be like for me with Richard retired? New faces who are great and talented but don't understand this place, that don't get Stratford?

Adrian was still ingesting.

Am I going to have to reinvent myself for every one of them just so I can fit in?

--

Richard died on September 9, 2008. I was in my living room poring over some knitting in the early morning when I found out. Lucy had called and then, after a few minutes, Peter Roberts did too. Phones were ringing beyond every horizon, in the homes of past and current company members near and fear, and if they were anything like me, they stood very still, smothered by the news. Yet, from my stillness came a kind of clarity.

Of course you're dead, Richard. Of course you're dead less than a year after leaving. You drank too much, you smoked too much, and you didn't eat right or exercise enough, but you also had nothing else to live for. The Festival was everything to you. It was your blood.

The next afternoon, Lucy delivered a speech after a performance of *Romeo and Juliet*, informing the audience of Richard's passing. She stood centre stage, and fought her way through it. I stood backstage as ASM, watching her on the monitor with the actors and crew huddled close, holding one another, the whole company like a big ball of yarn.

"It is with a sadness as deep as to the heart that we must share with you the grievous news that Richard Monette has passed away. Richard was the caretaker of this magnificent room and of the Stratford Festival for many, many years as an actor, director, and artistic director. His heart and his soul are woven into the boards and our lives. The entire acting company, crew, and the hundreds of people involved in all four theatres would like to dedicate the performance this afternoon and this evening to Richard Monette. The words spoken by Mercutio feel true: 'That gallant spirit hath aspir'd the clouds which too untimely here did scorn the earth.' As Richard's soul is but a little way above our heads, we ask that you might assist his flight. Give him your hands as we are all his friends."

A similar message was spoken at all of the performances that day. Pete spoke after *Love's Labour's Lost*, a production Richard had been interim director for, directing the show for two weeks when Michael Langham, the former artistic director of the Festival who Dad always managed to find money for, had to step out. I only learned later that Pete was sitting backstage with Brian Tree, the two of them waiting to go on for the curtain call, and he said, "I can't believe Richard's gone." Then, Pete cried quietly. Brian was at a loss for words. We all were.

A few days later, I explicitly told the Festival not to ask me to stage manage Richard's memorial. If they had asked, I would have, and I wouldn't have been able to do it. I would have botched it completely. It wasn't that I'd done one too many. It was that it was *his* and that alone was just too much. The Festival told me they understood, and I felt relieved that I would be able to sit in the audience, to watch and take the time to remember Richard. I'd never done this for anybody before. I worked through my father's death and my brother's, but for Richard I chose to sit with my grief. It just felt like the right thing to do.

I'd never seen so many people attend a company member's memorial before. The first level of the auditorium was packed, a testament to the number of lives one person can touch over the course of decades. Onstage was a photo of Richard, a younger version of him, looking directly into the camera and now out into the space that Bill once welcomed him home to. They played "Nessun Dorma," and afterwards Martha Henry took the stage. Referring to what had become a canonical moment in the Festival's history, she said, "He was our white knight, our knight in shining armour, he was the one who came to our defence." Everybody laughed tearfully. And as people followed, one by one, and shared their memories, steeped in the politics of this place, politics I never cared anything for but that demanded reservation and tact, that demanded we honour the dead while still maintaining that our future was with the new management, I had my own silly memories of him.

Richard, the generous man who added a fight scene to his *Henry VIII* where there wasn't one just so John Stead could say he had choreographed fights for all of Shakespeare's canon. Richard, the man of tradition who wore the horse pin I gave him every opening night and who once gave Goldie Semple his mother's necklace, a gift for her Katherina in his timeless *Taming of the Shrew*. Irene Poole had it now, passed down the line from Katherina to Katherina, from Goldie to Lucy to Seana, Richard's legacy enduring each time. Richard, the sometimes graceless man who once greeted Yo-Yo Ma, and then said to his wife, "You must be Mama Ma?" Richard, the actor who came off stage after opening night of *Filumena* looking as though he'd just shit himself. Richard, the director who sat upright in his chair and acted out entire scenes in his head. Richard, the friend who loved to laugh.

Several weeks before the memorial service, we gathered in Richard's backyard. Side by side in a small circle, we were grateful we could count ourselves among his closest friends. Coming through the screen door behind me, Richard's brother Mark thanked us all for being there. He looked very much like Richard. Nearby, a robin landed on Richard's birdhouse, a replica of his actual home. It hopped along, occasionally glancing our way, pecking feed from inside.

Antoni's son stepped forward into the circle, and a red balloon tied to a white string in his hand followed close by. As he spoke, the late summer air resonated with the raw sincerity of his eleven-year-old voice, and we, Richard's family as Mark put it, each cried in our own way.

"Uncle Richard told me to watch a movie once, called *The Red Balloon*. He said it was his favourite. I asked why and he told me to watch it and see for myself. We all watched it together, my dad, my sister, my mom, and me. I liked it a lot. The boy and the balloon became such good friends, but then the bullies stole the balloon away and threw rocks at it. It was really sad when the balloon burst. But then all of the other balloons in Paris came to the boy and gave him their strings. It was like they were all holding hands." He looked at the string in his hand. "And then all of the balloons tangled up around the boy and carried him up to the sky so he could be happy again." He let go of the balloon, and together we all watched as it glided this way and that, over the treetops and roofs, up to the clouds, where it was taken away and out of view by a wind too high to feel.

Afterwards, while everybody chatted, Mark asked if he could see me inside.

"What's up?" I asked, stepping into Richard's living room. There were a few boxes piled to one side where Mark had begun the process of packing away Richard's life. I was reminded of doing the same with Mom after Dad died and it finally came time for her to go to Cedarcroft. It was unenviable, that task.

"Richard would have wanted you to have this," Mark said, handing me the lamp I had made him for his retirement. In Mark's hands the blues and whites of the lampshade looked dull and sad, the words illegible.

"Okay." As I took it from him I asked, "How are you doing?"

"Fine, fine. Richard didn't take the best care of himself."

"I know."

"He loved you, you know. I'd be talkin' to him on the phone and I can't even remember how many times he'd said it, but Richard used to say all the time, 'Nora Polley saved my life again today.'" He laughed, and in my woeful confusion I laughed too, not knowing what I'd done to deserve those words.

--

"Morning," Ann said as we crossed paths, she coming from the washroom, me from the stairwell. We were both heading to Rehearsal Hall 3.

"Morning," I replied, looking like I'd just jogged here.

"Are you okay?"

I massaged my hip and pointed behind me. "Stairs."

"You should get that checked out."

"Indeed."

We made our way down the corridor and I pocketed my gloves as we turned the corner. "I'm not late, am I?" I asked over the shushing of my black winter jacket.

"No, no. Martha is still chatting with them. Besides," Ann winked, "it takes a while to introduce you."

"Oh, please."

As of last season, Martha Henry had taken over as director of the Birmingham Conservatory. With Ann taking on the role as her coordinator, the actors were assured not only an education in classical theatre, but also one in *Stratford's* classical theatre. Stratford might have been just another fish in the Canadian theatrical sea now, but it was still the biggest, possessing a production culture all its own. This year, Martha asked me to come in and speak about that culture, about stage management.

Ann and I entered the rehearsal hall, the blue doors swinging shut behind us. The afternoon light through the high windows crept in, but for the most part, as always, fluorescence did the heavy lifting. The six Conservatory actors were sitting on orange and blue chairs on the taped-out stage. They all looked eager, and I hoped it was because they recognized the privileged position they were all in. Martha sat opposite them. Her hair was slowly fading into grey, and she wore a thick red sweater. I hung my coat on the back of one of the two empty chairs beside her and took a seat.

"Thank you for coming, Nora," Martha said, her voice placid as ever. She could tame a lion with it, and I'd seen her do it many times before.

"It's my pleasure. Anything to help out."

"I was just speaking to them about the importance of stage management to the running of the whole production. I told them if they had any questions they should direct them to you." A few members of the group nodded as if to confirm. "I also figured that since you'll be working on the some of the shows they'll be part of next season, they should get to know you."

I cleared my throat. "Yes, I mean, stage management is such a complicated job on paper. Anybody who's ever read the Equity agreement knows there are like twenty-something pages devoted just to stage management, with many of those tackling our many varied responsibilities. I'm always at a loss as to where to begin so please, if there are any questions, I'd be delighted to answer them." A thin actress with short brunette hair held her hand up. "You can just shout them out, if you'd like."

"Sorry," she smiled. "What's the worst thing that's ever happened to you?"

I laughed. "Well, it didn't happen in a show, but . . ." I then told the story of the Russian border, adding some things here and removing other things there, the way a story naturally evolves with every telling. I was enthused that they found the tale somewhat spellbinding.

Another actor in a purple turtleneck then asked, "What was your favourite moment in your whole career?"

I chuckled, looking to Martha because she knew as well as I did that my favourite moment involved her. She glanced down at the floor, suddenly shy. I then told them about Robin's first year as artistic director, and being in the rehearsal hall for *Measure for Measure* when he put the water pitcher on the table in the scene between Martha's Isabella and Brian Bedford's Angelo. I described, in as much detail as I remembered, the moment where Martha made the choice to dunk her handkerchief into the water and wipe the dirt of Angelo's proposition off her. As I told the story, my words kept getting caught in my throat.

"I figured somebody was supposed to do something," Martha added, seeing the actors' expectant looks, "or why did he put the pitcher on the table? And Brian never touched it! So if anyone was going to do anything, it was me."

"Wow," said the actor who asked the question, as if he were trying to imagine himself making the same choice.

"Robin was enigmatic," I explained, having taken a breath and regained my composure.

"To say the least," Ann chortled, we three having nearly four decades of experience between us working with that enigma.

"You just did your best to keep up."

With that being the final word on that answer, another actor raised his hand. "Uh, so, I know this is a question directors and actors are often asked, but I was wondering," he said, gesturing to Ann and myself, "as stage managers, has anybody ever asked you what shows *you* want to work on?"

Ann shook her head.

"One person," I said, pointing to my left. Martha's eyes traced the floor once more. "It was at the Grand in London back in . . . Oh . . . What was it?"

"I can't recall," Martha replied.

"The late '80s, I think. Anyway, she asked me what play I wanted to do. And I thought she was asking me what show I would like to stage manage that she had already programmed. What she actually meant was what show would I like to *do*, if I could. She meant something that wasn't already in her season."

The actor smiled. "What was the show, if you don't mind me asking?"

"*Burn This*." And in light of their vacant expressions I then added, "It was a show on Broadway I really enjoyed, starring John Malkovich." At the sound of his name, the group perked up, as if suddenly addressed in a language they understood.

"Well, cool. Thanks."

As I rounded out my time with the actors, answering any questions they had about my job, as well as taking them through what an average day was like just so they knew where we were and how we supported their work, an actress asked when I started at the Festival and then, as a follow-up, "What was the Festival like in 1969?" I paused, almost overwhelmed by my wistfulness. The short answer was that everything was the same. The long answer was that everything was the same, only I had changed. I didn't tell them that, though. Rather, I made something up about working under Jean's artistic directorship, and my dad being in the building, and having to learn the names of every single company member, and there being no computers to help us, and who my mentors were, and what they taught me, and what happened to them. I was thankful for the question, more thankful than anybody in that room knew, because it had made my decision much easier.

--

The conversation between Antoni and myself was so brief it might not have even happened at all in the grand scheme of things. I had spoken first to the production manager, but I had to tell Antoni myself. We had worked together for so long, in so many different capacities, it only felt right.

When I stepped through the glass door of his office he had just finished taking a phone call and looked a bit flustered.

"Nora!" he said cheerfully. "Come in, sit down, please." I wasn't sure when I had realized it, whether at that moment or long before, but through countless years of dealing with personnel, the public, and the press, he had cultivated a politician's tone: smooth, knowledgeable, and superficial. In that moment, though, I was a little surprised he was using it with me.

"Hi," I replied, sitting. "I just wanted to tell you that next season is going to be my last."

Antoni raised his eyebrows. His voice warmed instantly, and I felt appreciated. "I hope everything's okay."

Where to start, Antoni?

I could have told him it was my newly acquired diabetes, or the fact that I had duplexed my house and had started working winters at the Festival Archives so that I could actually afford retirement. I could have told him I was so tired in the night that I couldn't see myself waking up in the morning, even though I knew I was the senior stage manager on staff, expected to be here to set a good example and to hold my director's hand and help him along. I could have told him it was that expectation that worried me because I was growing more and more intolerant of these people who didn't know anything about this place and didn't do anything to learn. I could have told him I remembered a theatre that made me feel I was part of a family, like somebody was looking out for me, watching over me, where everybody knew that if Jack Hutt was on the scene, then everything was going to be okay. I remembered a theatre bonded to the town so strongly that Dad could call the bank manager in the dead of night and have him open up

SHAWN DESOUZA-COELHO

the doors so a down-on-his-luck actor could get some money to leave town. I remembered a town that surprised the country and itself when it erected the tent and billeted strangers and kept attending this place long after the Festival seemed like it had forgotten the town entirely. I remembered the Festival standing for something. I remembered when it wasn't just a job to be taken, but an honour to be cherished, being part of the Festival company. I remembered that to touch the balcony pillars was to enjoin myself through the oil of my skin with the long and lasting lineage of actors and directors and family that came before, artists that toiled and toiled until midnight and even into the early morning because the play was all. I remembered wanting to spend my days and nights and eternity here with them, to see them work and play and hurt and heal and then do it all again next rehearsal. But mostly, I remembered being happy, stage managing truly brilliant work. Now, this place seemed like a play factory, and everybody was laughing at a joke I just didn't get.

"Everything's fine," I told Antoni, after a brief silence. "I just wanted to tell you, so you know."

Antoni considered this for a moment and then said, simply, "Thank you, Nora."

2 0 0 9

Part 1

"Michael took his first steps on Sunday," Sue said, sitting beside me.

"Oh, yeah?"

"Yeah. Right over there." She pointed behind her. Neither of us looked, but I imagined Jannine's little boy stumbling and could almost hear his brave footsteps punctuating the silence in tandem with Mom's weak breathing. "Jannine brought him over on a whim."

I looked over at Mom's nightstand and the photos of a very young Sue. They were taken back when Dad was overseas during the war. Sue, too, had brought them over on a whim. In the glass that framed them I could see the windows of Mom's room at Cedarcroft frosted over in parts, a cloudy January afternoon washing everything out with grey light. I thought I saw Sue's reflection too, but it could have been any old Polley. We were all starting to fit the bill.

"How many steps?" I asked.

"Just one or two."

"Jannine must have been so proud."

"Mom too." After a beat, Sue then said, "So Obama's president."

"Mom and I watched his inauguration last night. Very exciting."

When the nurse phoned me that morning, I was at the Festival Archives. She told me Mom was on her deathbed, and if I wanted to see her, I should come. So I did. When I got here she was in the state she was in now, so I called Sue and told her Mom wasn't dead, but she was going to be soon so Sue should come too. Before Sue arrived, she called Dave in Sudbury, where he had made his home, to tell him.

Still neither of us faced the other, Sue's eyes and mine fixed on our mother as she lay in bed before us, slowly letting go of what was left of her lingering life. Two weeks ago, she decided to stop eating and taking her medications. I asked Cedarcroft to respect her decision because I knew that Mom knew she was finally dying. Really, it looked to me now like she was sleeping, her eyelids occasionally fluttering, her blue nightgown gently rising and falling — and then not. My eyebrows raised as her breath suddenly faded to nothing. I at last looked at Sue, who then looked at me.

Is this . . . is she?

Mom then gasped back to life, and both Sue and I sank back in our chairs, feeling as though somebody were playing a horrible practical joke on us. Mom had been doing this for quite some time, petering out and then stomping back in.

Delma came in and greeted us with honest sadness, which was a bit surprising considering she'd been around death day in and day out for almost a decade. Maybe it wasn't something a person ever really got used to. Or maybe it was just that she cared for Mom.

Seeing the look on our faces, Delma asked, "Again?" We nodded and she chuckled softly, looking at Mom. "She's strong." Delma pulled Mom's blankets down a bit, as if to lighten the load on her chest. She then fluffed up the sides of Mom's pillow and caressed her cheek. Even now, at ninety, Mom still looked spry, with not very many wrinkles to say otherwise. Sue and I could only hope to be so lucky. Delma touched Mom's hair with the back of her hand, like it was tall grass, and she whispered something I didn't hear. She then took out a comb and lightly teased Mom's fraying ends back into place. From wherever Mom was, she didn't give any sign that she felt it. Instead, she began to stertor, letting out these long, raspy breaths, and Delma drew a cross on her chest.

"What's wrong?" Sue asked.

"That's the beginning of the end," Delma said sombrely. The three of us then spent a moment or two watching Mom, listening to the sounds of the beginning of the end. "I'll come back to check on her later." She said it in a way that I understood to mean there wasn't going to be a later, and really she just wanted to give us our privacy.

"Thank you, Delma," I said.

"Yes, thank you," Sue added.

Delma smiled, lingering at the door to take one last look at Mom before leaving.

A few minutes passed with nothing but Mom's breathing filling the space between her and us. Then, in the hallway, a man in a wheelchair rolled by and I thought I heard him say, "I like that."

"Okay," the nurse soothed, as if he was a toddler, and the two of them went out of sight. I was thankful Mom would never suffer people speaking to her in that tone.

"Do you think it hurts?" Sue ventured.

"Not sure." After a pause, I said in jest, "Let's ask her."

But then Mom stopped breathing again entirely. This time it was like somebody hit the mute button on a remote. Our chairs creaked but we didn't lean closer. We didn't listen for a twitch, a breath, a pulse, or any sign of life at all. We expected Mom to spring back. Then days and weeks and months passed in those few seconds, and I fought the urge to prompt her because her pause was going on for far too long.

Breathe. You have to breathe. That's how the scene continues, Mom. Mom?

SHAWN DESOUZA-COELHO

Sue went out to get the onsite doctor, leaving me with Mom for a minute or so. I didn't take my eyes off her for fear I'd miss something important, but all she did was lie perfectly still.

When the doctor arrived, he ambled to her bedside, as if there were no rush, and pressed two fingers to her neck. He bowed his head slightly and said, "She's gone." I sighed in relief, the kind that walks hand-in-hand with closure. The doctor continued, "You must never think you didn't do everything you could. You girls were really good to your mother."

"Thank you," I replied. Why it felt nice to hear it from somebody outside of our own family, I didn't know.

Shortly after the doctor left, I used the phone in Mom's room to call Marg.

"Hello?" Marg said.

"Marg, this is the telephone call you didn't want to get. Mom's died. Could you call Janice?"

"S-Sure."

"Goodbye."

"Bye."

When the people from the funeral home arrived, Sue and I stepped into the hallway. Neither of us had any interest in seeing Mom's body dealt with in that way. She was a person who lived and raised five children, who played bridge and drank rye, who quit smoking just to see her granddaughter Sonja's wedding and did just that some years ago. We wanted to remember her that way, and not as a heap of tired organs that now needed to be dealt with.

As we waited, Sue phoned Dave. I glanced around the hallway at the elderly residents, a few of them stopping on their way by to see what was happening. Their nonchalance startled me somewhat. It was as if they were reading a street sign on a road they'd travelled many times before. When Sue hung up, she told me Dave was just about to drive down.

"How is he?" I asked.

"Fine. He'll be here as soon as he can."

The people from the funeral home then rolled a gurney out of

Mom's room with a long black bag on it. The bag shook slightly as they pulled the gurney down the hall, around a corner, and out of sight.

Bye, Mom.

Over the next couple of days, the whole family arrived. Marg and David stayed in my upstairs apartment, the first tenants to occupy my retirement plan. Janice stayed with her parents. Dave and Susanne stayed with Sue. When it finally came time to clear all of Mom's stuff out of Cedarcroft, there was very little any of us wanted. Sue took the photos hanging on the wall, and said she'd recreate their arrangement in her home. Most of Mom's clothes went straight to the Salvation Army. Everything else was taken to the onsite chapel and we made an announcement saying, "If anybody is interested, have a look. If you like it, take it, enjoy it." Within minutes, a few seniors came. Off in the corner I heard a familiar voice, that old man who had said, "I like that." He was more or less toothless, and seemed agitated, his gaze darting from one item to the next, as though he was having trouble finding whatever it was he had liked.

Mom's funeral was very much like Dad's: very Anglican and very straightforward. St. James Church was full of people, some that we remembered very well and others that none of us could recall. They stood as we entered, and near the end of the service Dave and Jannine read the eulogy, which I had written but knew I wouldn't for the life of me be able to say. There was just no way I was going to be able to get through it all. Both Sue and Marg were of the same mind.

"My parents," Dave read, addressing the congregation, his hair lightly greying at the sides, "had been married for fifty-four years. When my dad died we expected that she would be gone shortly after. But that didn't happen. Then her favourite son, Fred, died." Dave gripped the paper tightly, fighting the memory of Fred's death or maybe a more distant one of the two of them, the boys, at the dinner table talking, one with a calculator in his hand, the other with a chip on his shoulder.

Two strokes and a heart attack.

Dave took another moment.

The line is, "Two strokes and a heart attack."

SHAWN DESOUZA-COELHO

Jannine put her hand on Dave's shoulder.

Okay, now this *pause is going on for too long.*

"Two strokes and a heart attack," I prompted. The audience tittered at the intrusion, all the while assured I wouldn't have done it if I didn't have to.

Dave smiled, and then cleared his throat. "She had two strokes and a heart attack and still she hung around. She had grandchildren and then great-grandchildren. So, what on earth was she waiting for? Turns out she was waiting for the American people to elect a black president." The congregation erupted in a fit of laughter, and when they had finally settled, Dave began talking about me, and my role in Mom's final ten years. He called me her daughter, her friend, her bookkeeper, her chauffeur, her server, her confidante, her chief advocate, her—

"That's enough," Jannine interrupted, playfully.

I smiled and the sides of my eyes grew hot and wet. I hadn't yet cried my share, and Dave was seeing to it that I did. The truth was, I never begrudged my mother any of the last decade, neither the time nor the money nor the energy I spent with, on, and for her. I wasn't a saint. Lyb was my mother and I owed her everything. It really was that simple.

Dave stopped abruptly, once again choking up amidst another long pause.

"Sorry," I called out to him. "I can't help you. I didn't write this part."

He took a deep breath and composed himself, concluding the eulogy with, "We are such stuff as dreams are made on; and our little life is rounded with a sleep."

Gertrude Elizabeth Polley, my mother, died on January 21, 2009. She was cremated and her ashes were placed beside my father's in Avondale Cemetery, joining him at the bridge table for another hand.

2009

Part 2

I was in the booth, but I wasn't. I was calling the show, but I could see myself do it. I was where I needed to be, and also where I wanted, which wasn't a bad way to spend Halloween and the last night of my career.

I turned the page, and with each scene and line that passed, it wasn't lost on me that that would be the last time I would hear these words, in this way, in this place.

"**Warning Lights 211 to 216, Sound 39, Video 10, Fly Cue 10,**" I intoned over the headset.

That's the last time I'll ever call those cues.

I didn't linger on the thought as there was still so much else to think about and still so much to come. Through whatever headaches this production had brought, it had one

ANT.   So is my horse, Octavius; and for that
    I do appoint him store of provender:
    It is a creature that I teach to fight,
    And, in some taste, is Lepidus but so;
    He must be taught, and trained, and bid go forth;
    A barren-spirited fellow.
    Do not talk of him,
    But as a property. **X** And now, Octavius,
    Listen great things. Brutus and Cassius
    Are levying powers. We must straight make head.
    Therefore let our alliance be combined,
    And open perils surest answered.

OCT.   Let us do so: for we are are at the stake

saving grace. "**Lights 211, Sound 39, Video 10,**" I warned once more. Ben and Tom, Brutus and Cassius: my reminders of a career well spent, and why this job was worth my years, stacked as they were in fortunate seasons, one after another after another. Just this one scene between two actors, intelligent and talented. "*Go.*" With that magical word, the stage shifted from one camp to the next, Antony's to Brutus's. "**Fly Cue 10** *Go,*" I called, and banners rose at the back of the stage. "**Lights 214,** *Go.*" Brutus hit the deck and his first position. "**Lights 215,** *Go.*" He moved to meet the incoming army. "**Lights 216,** *Go.*" I watched and breathed in rhythm with his love, and nothing more.

And bayed about with many enemies, X

Antony exits.

And some that smile have in their hearts, I fear
Millions of mischiefs. X

Octavius *exits.*
Brutus, Lucilius and their army *enter.*
Pindarus meets *them.*

BRUT.   What now, Lucilius, is Cassius near?
LUC.   He is at hand, and Pindarus is come
To do you salutation from his master.
BRUT.   He greets me well. Your master, Pindarus,
In his own change, or by ill officers,
Hath given me some worthy cause to wish
Things done, undone: but if he be at hand,
I shall be satisfied.
PIN.   I do not doubt
But that my noble master will appear
Such as he is, full of regard and honour.

BRUT. He is not doubted. A word, Lucilius;
How he received you, let me be resolved.

LUC. With courtesy and with respect enough;
But not with such familiar instances,
As he hath used of old.

BRUT. Thou has described

A hot friend cooling: ever note, Lucilius,
When love begins to sicken and decay,
It useth an enforced ceremony.
Comes his army on?

LUC. They mean this night in Sardis to be quarter'd;
The greater part, the horse in general,
Are come with Cassius.

BRUT. Hark! he is arrived.

Enter Cassius and his soldiers.

CASS. Most noble brother, you have done me wrong.

BRUT. Judge me, you gods! wrong I mine enemies?
And, if not so, how should I wrong a brother?

CASS. Brutus, this sober form of yours hides wrongs;
And when you do them—

I **flicked** Tom's cue light up, smiling brightly from on high in this dim hovel that never felt bigger than when occupied, and then I **flicked** it down. With that, I was audience again, to another world and the two world-class actors ferrying me there.

BRUT. Cassius, be content.
Speak your griefs softly: I do know you well.
Before the eyes of both our armies here,
Which should perceive nothing but love from us,
Let us not wrangle: bid them move away;
And I will give you audience.

CASS. Pindarus,
Bid our commanders lead their charges off
A little from this ground.

BRUT. Lucilius, do you the like; and let no man
Come to our tent till we have done our conference.
Lucilius and Titinius guard our door.

Their armies fall asleep.

This is what I'll miss most.

2009

Part 3

"This is lovely," Sue exhaled as we entered the Marquee. The white linen of the dinner tables shone brightly, and at the centre of each there was a tall clear vase of small yellow-orange lilies. Around the room, well-dressed company members smiled at us from behind and above water glasses.

"Which table is ours?" Jannine asked, standing beside Sue. She looked every bit as impressed as her mother.

"I'm not sure," I said. I caught one of the caterers on her way up the stairs, a skinny woman with long blond hair. "Hi, I'm Nora Polley. Do you have any idea which table is mine?"

"Nora . . . Um . . ." she began, before pointing to a table with a green balloon tied to the back of one chair. "Guest of honour."

This was the Festival's Loyal Service Dinner, an annual celebration to honour the employees who had served it for twenty-five, thirty, thirty-five, etc. seasons. For my thirtieth season, I was honoured with a pin. For my thirty-fifth, a bust of Shakespeare. At this, my forty-fifth season as an employee, which counted the teenage years I'd worked at the box office, I had no idea what to expect.

We took our seats, and Jannine poured Sue and myself a glass of water. It was a table of eight, and perhaps it was hubris to think all eight seats would be filled. I invited Sue, Jannine, and the four directors I had grown with over the years, the ones with whom I shared a special connection.

Jeannette arrived first, giving me a hug. As the four of us chatted, I felt a hand on my shoulder. It was an old hand, but sturdily built. He had been working with it his entire career, building wigs for the Festival.

"Mr. Shields," I said jovially, turning to the hand's owner.

"Cookie," Clayton smiled. "They really rolled out the red carpet for us, didn't they?"

"Ha! Yeah right."

From across the room, somebody I didn't recognize called for Clayton. He waved and said, "We'll talk soon."

When he was out of earshot, Jannine turned to me and asked, "Who was that?"

"Clayton Shields," I said simply. "He's retiring this season too. He was in the wig department around when I first started here. I stayed with him in a hotel in Ottawa when we went on tour with . . . I can't remember what show. But I remember the fire alarm went off in the morning, so I ended up having to go out on the balcony and leap over the partition separating ours and Kenneth Welsh's because Ken was still in his room. I looked through his balcony door and he was still asleep. So I banged on it a few times and screamed his name, and even with all that *and* the fire alarm, it still took him a little while to wake up."

Jeannette set her water glass down as she chuckled. "I've never heard that one before."

"It's a good one."

John Wood came second, his gait much more laboured than usual.

He could be a firecracker sometimes, but looking at him now in his grey tweed jacket, he was anything but.

I stood to greet him. "How are you?"

"Fine, fine," he replied, knowing exactly what I meant. "It happened. Bound to happen eventually." No more was said about John's recent heart attack as he took a seat between Jeannette and Sue. "Who else are you expecting?"

"Oh, well—"

Just then David William walked in, the first artistic director to name a stage manager as an associate director at the Stratford Shakespeare Festival, as we were to call it now. He was still lively for over eighty, though his grey hair had receded quite a bit more since last I saw him. In the moment, I couldn't remember exactly when that was. He was wearing a black sweater, and it was only then I realized everybody else at the table was wearing the same colour. I felt like I was at a funeral. I greeted David as he sat beside me.

David and Jeannette got on like old friends then. He was artistic director when she first began directing at the Festival, so there was a familiar trust between the two. I'd felt that trust, that patient camaraderie that only developed in tandem with time, with many people, a few of whom were now here at this table eyeing the décor. I was silent for the most part, mentally tallying the days of my career and the only two performances I'd ever missed: *Romeo and Juliet* back in '92, due to a scheduling conflict, and *Dream* this season, due to gallstones. I smirked proudly. Both were completely out of my control.

After a few minutes passed, I found myself somewhat nervously surveying the two remaining empty chairs. I didn't know if they would be filled. It was always a toss-up whether or not he would come. I knew that when I invited him. All the same, though, I wanted him to be here. Next to Richard, it was he I cherished most as a direc—

I'll be damned.

I smiled widely and stood with open arms to greet Robin and, behind him, his partner Joe. Robin's hair had greyed, and he had filled out a bit, but his eyes were still as fierce as ever. With his black suit and blue tie, he was still impeccably dressed.

Shortly after our re-introductions, I noticed a small wooden box Robin had set on the table. He pushed it closer to me. I tilted my head, trying to make sense of the size and shape of it. It looked about right for a jewellery box, but the lid lifted off like a dome and inside was a small pewter bell.

Thank you?

Robin smiled gallantly, and then proceeded to read the menu. I didn't know what to say. It was just so typically Robin. Covering the bell and thanking him sincerely, it was clear to me that time hadn't eroded his sense of mystery. He still loved challenging the intellect.

Near the end of the night, Des took the stage and introduced both Clayton and myself.

At the Guthrie Awards ceremony earlier this season, Des had decided to honour both Clayton and myself with the Derek F. Mitchell Artistic Director's Award. It was my second, the first given to me by Richard back in '94. But, shortly after Des had referred to me as both "strict" and "fiercely loyal," neither of which I took as a compliment, I already knew who he was talking about, so I stood up and began walking to the stage. Des shouted, "Oh, would you sit down and let me finish!" The audience laughed, and he did too, but I knew he was fiercely aggravated by it.

But, here, in the Marquee for this Loyal Service Dinner, having waited until the end of his speech, and having already arrived onstage, I felt breathless. In my hand was an open envelope and a piece of paper.

"Read it out loud," Des urged mildly.

"I can't," I replied, already feeling my throat tighten. "You'll have to."

It was an understatement to say that I was surprised. Des didn't have to do it. He could have given me another pin. Instead, to honour my forty-fifth season with the Festival, he named the Festival Theatre stage management booth after me. Standing before the company, braced by their applause, I felt truly honoured. I also couldn't help but find it a bit ironic considering I had always preferred to call the show from the deck.

**2010**

8:06 a.m.

The bed creaks as I roll to the side and sit up. The morning sun slips through the slits in my curtain and I'm shocked suddenly into alertness. 8:06 a.m.

No, Nora. Six minutes isn't sleeping in.

I shake my head at the years of conditioning stage management has cast onto the clay of my body. The old habits seem amaranthine, even a year after retirement. I'm still having the same nightmare, the one where I'm late for a performance and arrive at the wrong theatre, only now it doesn't make sense anymore. I stand and slowly change out of my pyjamas before heading to the kitchen for breakfast.

Now that my house is a duplex, the kitchen is just to the right of my bedroom on the first floor. It's been an easy adjustment having somebody live above me, an adjustment made easier by the fact that she's an actor so she isn't home very much at all, especially during the day. In the kitchen, the noise is my own as I shuffle to and from the cupboards, pouring myself a bowl of cereal.

I take it to the living room, and as I eat I can hear the drips of melting snow through the window. A car sloshes by, spraying the fresh white ground with salty mud. I turn my attention to the package on the coffee table, a cardboard box about a foot cubed.

Shoot.

The box is open, so I set my bowl down and from the dining room retrieve some Scotch tape. While I'm there, I see my Prompt Book open on the dining room table with its various parchment papers, cards, and photographs in disarray. I had been looking through it the night before. Even a year later, it still brings a smile to my face.

The Prompt Book was given to me shortly after I retired by an ASM committee who had solicited past and current company members to write thank yous and well wishes to me to honour the occasion. These memories sat now like the cut text of a lifelong production script in this mahogany box shaped like a stage manager's binder. On its front there is a small gold nameplate that reads: Nora's Memory Prompt Book. I take a moment to tidy the box's contents, remembering briefly my retirement, how the company surprised me after the closing of *Julius Caesar* with a champagne toast backstage at the Avon, how Andrew flew in from Regina and Maloo from Chicago just to be there for it. I was speechless.

Closing the box entirely, I survey the tape in my hand. Letting go is harder than I thought it'd be.

In the living room, I tape the cardboard box shut and a sense of anxious finality punctures the air and me.

I could tell her it got lost in the mail. I could say I might go back, and if I did, then I'd need this headset and this stopwatch and . . . I'm not ready to leave.

I set the roll of tape down and pick up my cereal as I stare at the still lingering bequest to my niece Jennifer out west, who has decided to take up stage management.

It's her turn now. Your time has passed. Send it today.

I'll send it tomorrow.

I finish eating and set my bowl in the sink. I put on my coat, my boots, and my gloves, grab my wallet and cell phone, and head out the door.

8:57 a.m.

The Stratford Festival Archives, where I now work part-time, is just down the road from my house on Douro, so I arrive with a few minutes to spare. The building itself resembles an aircraft hangar. Its parking lot is a massive construction, but it's rarely ever populated by more than a few cars. Right now, it's just mine and two others.

Beside the entrance, a set of bright red doors, I put in my security code. The doors click and I head in.

"Good morning, Nora!" a voice rings in a thick Italian accent as I brush the snow from my boots on the mat inside. I look up to find Francesca Marini, the archives director, walking away from me towards the kitchen. She's a tall woman with hair that's greying despite her relative youth. She's always beautifully dressed and some-times rather provocatively so. She arrived in the summer, replacing Jane Edmonds, the previous archives director, who had unfortunately died of cancer a year earlier.

"Morning," I say to her while she's still in earshot. I notice for a moment how small my voice sounds in the warehouse where I now stand, a pebble rippling in the large pond of rows and rows of full cos-tume racks reaching to the far back of the building. To my right is another door, requiring another code. I enter it and step into the archives proper.

I hang my coat up in the foyer with its green walls and visitor sign-in sheet before heading into the carpeted corridor leading to the Jane Edmonds Reading Room, named so to honour her years of

SHAWN DESOUZA-COELHO

service in the archives. There was, after all, a time when the archives were the work of her alone. The room itself is large and green, with a large-screen television on the wall near the entranceway. To my right reside shelf upon shelf of red tomes containing thousands of newspaper clippings from past Festival seasons. I skirt around the few circular tables dotting the room and wave to Christine.

"Morning, Nora," she says, waving from behind her desk. Christine Schindler is a thin woman with wavy, shoulder-length black hair. She works at the archives full time, working on special collections such as large donations of photos from whomever. She also has three children at home, two of whom were born only a short while ago. I don't know how she does it.

"The weather is biting this morning, isn't it?"

Christine shivers. "Too cold."

I step into the workroom, just beside Francesca's office. Surrounded by light-blue walls, I set my wallet on my desk on the far side of the room and get to work.

9:05 a.m.

On the long table beside my desk, I push aside two cardboard boxes that read "Richard" on the side. Another two of these are below the table, and another four are just over by the entrance underneath a white shelf containing binders filled with souvenir and house programs from past seasons. In total there are eighty-three boxes distributed throughout the archives like Easter eggs, all containing Richard's personal papers, bills, letters, and whatever else Mark could find lying around. They are to be sorted, but without a volunteer to do so, they remain as they are.

It was a bit weird at first when they came in, seeing Richard's life summed up as little more than a pile of receipts he had accumulated and probably forgotten about. Now, they're just another thing to be dealt with.

Aren't we all in death, I guess.

Francesca passes by the doorway on the way to her office as I unwind the string tying the manila envelope I had been working through just yesterday. Putting on a set of white cotton gloves, I remove a single photo from the stack of photographs inside. As I set the photo down, Christine goes through the room, leaving out the back, taking the stairs to the prop storage room. The black and white photo belongs to a set of production photos for the Festival's 1979 production of *Richard II*. It's a thirty-person group shot of the jousting scene, taken from front-row centre, and since there are only two names listed on the back, it's my job to identify everybody else in the photo. The problem is, except for these two people, everybody is facing away from the camera. Deducing who exactly these people are is my current task. I love it. It makes me feel like all my years at this place are still worth something. It makes me feel valuable.

I reach back to my desk and retrieve the manifest I'd begun yesterday. The names Jim McQueen, Frank Maraden, Geordie Johnson, and Christopher Blake are written on it. I knew one of the faces shown was Bolingbroke, which Jim had played, and that there were in fact three Bolingbrokes and three Richards in that production since the show was triple-cast. The person standing in the middle of the photo attracting everybody's gaze must therefore be Frank Maraden, Richard to Jim's Bolingbroke. Then, I used a program for the show to look up who the Heralds were, just off to either side of Frank. Turned out they were Geordie and Chris.

I take a second and look over the photo, referring to the sheet of paper to see who is left. There are quite a few.

Okay, she has a crown so that's easy.

I write down Marti Maraden.

Whose hair is that?

I tap the pencil on the table while staring at the 'do, as if knocking on the person's door.

Whose hair is that . . . ?

I snap my fingers.

Lorne Kennedy!

I write his name down as well.

Alright, now that's the Lord Marshal. I can tell by his position on the stage.

I take out another series of photos from the envelope and sift through them until I find an identical costume and an identification: Joel Kenyon. I write down his name.

"Sorry to bother you, Nora," Christine says. I give a start, not having heard her come back in. "Sorry. I think we missed this on our last pass through the prop shelves."

In her hands is a little black booklet with white pages. I know it instantly as Paul Gross's notebook from *Hamlet* back in 2000. I was an ASM on that production.

"Oh, we have to keep this," I say, taking the booklet from her and flipping through it. The words "To be or not to be . . ." have been hastily scrawled across many pages. I show it to Christine and she smiles, studying it like it was new, like I'd removed the tarnish from fine silver. "This kind of stuff we should keep because it's priceless in a way. It's all the stuff that was purchased that should be deaccessioned; I think, anyway." I hand the booklet back to her.

"Great," she says. "Just wanted to check."

Christine leaves, continuing a task we'd begun a few months prior. We had gone through the prop shelves, day after day, sticking little red dots on props in order to designate which ones were to be removed. The archives are only so big, and there's enough clutter as it is. As with the photograph in front of me now, I was put to use there because a fair number of props weren't labelled at all, and it was my job to identify them.

I turn my attention back to the production shot and continue putting names to faces. There are two actors dressed in identical tabards.

Those must be the pages, since the Heralds are spoken for. Hm. They're about the same height, kneeling.

I check the program again.

Only one person is listed. Jeffrey Guyton.

I log him.

But then who's the other person?

I sift through the production photos to find an image of the two pages, but only one page is facing the camera, and it isn't Jeffrey. It's actually Donna Goodhand. I log her too. I inspect the group photo again.

In the group photo, which is which? Is Jeffrey on the right or left? Wait a minute . . .

As I'm staring at the image, I see clearly both of their feet behind them as they kneel. One pair is far bigger than the other.

That must be Jeffrey!

I write down both names in their proper positions, taking the time to give myself a pat on the back. I feel a vague sense of guilt but then remind myself I'm not a stage manager anymore. It's allowed.

11:00 a.m.

We gather in the break room for tea and cookies, a tradition Jane had started many years ago. I close the door behind me and sit with Christine, who is drinking what smells like green tea from a pale blue mug. Francesca doesn't join us, and I've never thought to ask why.

The break room itself is small, with green walls, a microwave by the entrance atop a shelf where tea is stored, and a massive concrete table at its centre that took six burly men an afternoon to lug in here and is now absolutely immovable. The far wall has a large window overlooking a factory and SINvention, our local sex shop.

"Peppermint?" Christine asks, perking up slightly. Between us, in the middle of the table, is a small Christmas tree, about the size of an upright box of cookies, complete with red and green ornaments.

I take a sip from my mug. "Mm-hmm."

"How is it?"

"Have you never had it?"

"I've been meaning to."

"It's pretty good."

There's a lull as we both drink at the same time. Then I speak first.

"Looking forward to any shows next season?"

"*Richard III* mostly."

"Should be a good one."

"Seana as Richard will really be something."

"That's for sure."

"So you really held her hand before the final casket scene in *Merchant*?"

I chuckled, nodding. "Every night. That part I know I didn't embellish." The thought that Christine had bought my book delighted me more than I let on.

Shortly after retiring, I finally got around to writing a book of sorts. It was a little thing called *A Birthday Book with Theatre Stories*, and, just as the title indicated, it really was just a bunch of stories from my years as a stage manager at the Stratford Festival. In it, I wrote briefly about my time with Seana backstage during *The Merchant of Venice* in '89, where every night I'd hold her hand before the final casket scene. Then when it was time to go on, she would give my hand a little squeeze and out she went.

I found it hard to remember some of those stories, so I put a little disclaimer on the copyright page of the book that read, "All these stories have some basis in truth. Over time they may have acquired embellishments in the telling. If you are mentioned in one, please accept the compliment in the spirit in which it is offered." I told myself that if I ever wrote another book, I'd put the same disclaimer in. It is, after all, other people's lives too.

11:42 a.m.

BRRING! BRRING!

What the hell?

BRRING! BRRING!

Oh right, my cell phone.

At my desk, I reach into my wallet and retrieve my cell. I'm still getting used to having it, and God only knows what possessed me to get it in the first place. It seems like everybody is calling now just because they can, regardless of the time of day. It's enough to make me wistful.

"Hello?"

"Nora, it's Dave," is the reply I get. In the background a car horn blares.

"Oh, hi. What's up?"

"I'm here with Sue. We're going to be a bit early. Is that okay?"

"That's just fine."

"Great. See you soon."

"See you."

I hang up and put the phone back into my wallet. I spend a moment taking in the room, as if seeing it through Dave's and Sue's eyes, anew. They're coming to see where I work now, which is sweet of them. I told them I was done at two, but I guess the winter weather was kind enough to let them into town sooner than they'd anticipated.

I continue identifying photos until I hear the doorbell ring.

12:37 p.m.

"I'll get it," I say to Francesca, who is already stepping out of her office.

"Are you expecting someone?"

"I am indeed. My brother and sister are coming. I wanted to show them around."

"Oh, how lovely! I wish to meet them."

DING!

"I'll introduce you."

I arrive at the door, and Dave ushers Sue into the warehouse.

"Thanks," Dave says, sniffling. "It's not great out there. That's for sure." Sue agrees and the two of them brush the snow off their jackets and out of their hair. I've been inside all day, so I hardly even noticed that it had begun to snow. "So this is where you work," Dave adds, taking in the warehouse and the vast expanse of costumes.

"Almost."

"Do these just stay here, or what?"

"Most of them can be rented by other theatre companies or television productions. That kind of thing."

"Rad."

"You can't rent a Halloween costume, though."

Over at the door leading to the foyer I enter my code and the door clicks. As I open it for them I say, "*This* is where I work."

After they hang up their coats, I give them the five-cent tour of the place, showing them the reading room and explaining who Jane was. I introduce them to Christine and Francesca, the latter of the two being absolutely over the moon to meet them. They spend a couple of minutes chatting about myself and Dad and the history of the Festival, and I can tell she's impressed with their experiences growing up around the place.

"So this is where the magic happens?" Dave asks, seeing my work station. He looks as if he's seen water in a lake, his expectations met exactly.

"Yes it is."

"Great, great. Good."

"What's in there?" Sue asks, pointing to the room behind her.

"That's the viewing room. Anybody can go in there and watch movies or archival footage or listen to original cast recordings of shows."

"That's neat."

"And what's that?" Dave inquires, pointing to a large stack of papers on another table.

"This is a project I've inherited from Jane," I answer, pulling the stack closer. "It's actually the script for *Richard III*, but on each page you can see there are different-coloured lines through different passages. Each coloured line corresponds to a cut made by a director, and each colour represents a given production of *Richard III* dating all the way back to 1953."

"When the Festival began?" Sue asks almost incredulously.

"Exactly." Dave whistles, and I continue. "So the script is actually a composite script, containing information about choices made by every director. The idea is that we'll have one of these for every production."

"And you're in charge of that."

I nod.

Dave looks up from the page in his hand. "Doesn't the Festival put on something like four Shakespeare plays every year?"

"They do indeed."

"Well *there's* some job security."

I laugh. "Indeed. I do a little bit each day, if I can."

"How long does it take you to do one?"

"A couple of weeks."

"How many plays did Shakespeare write?"

"Thirty-seven."

Dave mentally tabulates my timeframe based on the two numbers. "This is going to take years."

"I know."

"You're probably the only person in the world," Sue said, "for whom this would be interesting."

It's then I realize I'm smiling at the thought of toiling over those hundreds of production scripts, of poring over the photographs and sitting with the newspaper clippings and footage. I realize it's memories we're storing here, for anyone who wishes to remember, and I suddenly feel immensely proud to be a part of that process.

When my day is just about finished, we all decide to grab a late lunch. I pack up the composite scripts and grab my coat and wallet, saying goodbye to Christine and Francesca on our way to the foyer. Francesca tells Dave and Sue to come back anytime. They say they will, and I hope they do.

Before we leave, I tell them I'll meet them at the restaurant, and that I have to run home first and get something. Outside, the wind picks up, side-swiping us with snow all the way to our cars.

2:13 p.m.

When I arrive at home, I carefully plod to the front door. I open it and scoop up the package on the coffee table in the living room. I take it to my car, get in, and drive, liberated and hopeful, to the post office.

**2011** Backstage at the Festival The-
atre, I was filled with yearning
and celebration at the sound of
Sheila's strained and spritely
voice. She'd just received a
sonorous round of applause as
she hit the deck and took her place behind the lectern to welcome the
company. She said Pete would have said that was a really cheap way to
get a standing ovation.

"Thank you all for coming today," Sheila went on to say. "On
some weird joke of Pete's, the weather is doing what it's doing today.
Thank you to Nora Polley, first of all, who came out of the vaults of
the archives to put this together for us with such grace and ease . . ."

When Peter Donaldson was diagnosed with lung cancer a few years
ago, he kept it private for as long as he could, continuing to work,

staunchly refusing to be defined by it. He did shows at the Festival, and in Toronto at Soulpepper, the Factory Theatre, and Canadian Stage. He worked and worked until he just couldn't anymore, the consummate professional.

"...Pete loved this stage. He was as at home here as he was at home. He belonged up here. It was no big deal. He loved everything about this stage. He owns every square inch of it. While he was working he could do it all. He even liked all the natural wood."

The audience roared, knowing the Festival Theatre stage was anything but natural anymore. I instinctively turned in the direction of the balcony pillars, seeing their original form through the backstage walls and buttressed years, and my sense of loss rallied. They were thick with ancestry once.

When Sheila phoned me to ask if I would speak at Pete's memorial in Toronto at Soulpepper, I declined.

"I can do some programs for it, if you'd like," I offered instead.

Sheila considered this for a moment, disappointed in my response. Finally, she said, "No, I don't think I want any programs. Or, no, I do want programs, but I don't want one of those order of events things in there. I can't stand those. They're like church bulletins. People just end up flipping through the pages and thinking, 'Oh, it's only half over.'" We were silent for a moment. Then Sheila sighed. "You know, I don't even know if we should do one in Stratford. It's just ... going through it all twice, you know?"

"I do."

"You don't sound convinced."

"No."

"Why?"

"Pete's been here for what ... twenty, twenty-five years? He grew up here. I think you owe it to the town and the Festival to let them mourn him. It's for them, really. It's always for them."

"You're right," Sheila conceded. "You're right. Will you stage manage it?"

"Of course."

SHAWN DESOUZA-COELHO

All Sheila had to do was ask. I owed Pete that much, not just because of how he helped me, but also because, on top of being a devoted father, committed husband, and concerned friend, he was a great actor and he deserved every ounce of adulation he received. But, as Sheila spoke fondly and sometimes in spurts upon this most unnatural stage, in the back of my mind crawled a tiny selfishness I could hardly admit was there. It had been over a year and a half since I'd stage managed anything, and being backstage now at Pete's memorial was a tender joy for me all-conflicting.

"My mom and dad loved coming here to see us onstage," Sheila continued. "They loved voices. And they could always hear Pete, even with his back to them. I could always hear Pete. I think a lot of people in this room could always hear Pete. A few years ago, the girls and I bought a seat for Pete up in the balcony: Row A, Seat #123, and the quote says, 'Every man has his faults, and honesty is his,' and that was Pete."

As Sheila continued her introduction, and the memorial got underway, with Des, Antoni, Chris, and a host of others sharing their thoughts and memories of Pete, I wondered briefly what he would say about all this. Then I laughed softly. He'd probably say, "I really don't know what all the fuss is about."

2012

"The usual, Nora," Lacey said brightly, setting a plate of wet scrambled eggs and very crisp bacon sans home fries in front of me. Her straight hair was long and dark, and she had sincere eyes. "The toast will be right up."

"Thanks," I said, folding my newspaper and setting it on the counter beside the plate, an act of muscle memory more than a conscious thought. Every Sunday it had been this way for as long as I could remember, the lilting sounds of Madelyn's supporting my tinkling knife and fork. Krista was a bit older now. Her husband Peter now ran the kitchen. And Lacey, her teenage daughter, now served tables. Madelyn herself wasn't here today. "How's your mother doing?" I asked Krista as she walked by.

"Oh, fine. A bit tired. You know how it is."

"How long has she been running this place?"

"God, well, since 1985. So, I guess that's . . . twenty-six, no, twenty-seven years." She said the last part as if realizing it for the first time. "I've been here just as long."

"That's a long time, for sure."

Krista waved to a customer on his way out and then turned back to me. "You're working at the archives now, right?"

"Yes I am."

"How's that?"

"How much time do you have?"

Krista laughed, and then noticed my nearly empty glass. "More water?"

"Sure."

"Coming right up."

Lacey returned with the ice water, and once I had finished my brunch, I paid and left. Krista saw me off with a wave.

Almost ritualistically, I drove to KW Surplus in the next plaza, just up Huron. They always had such great deals on things and every week there was something different, but because it was all surplus, once the stuff was gone, it was gone. It was great for people like Ann, who needed things in bulk.

Every Christmas, Ann filled shoeboxes for young children. Little boys and girls, who would otherwise have to do without for the holidays, instead got these shoeboxes stuffed with things that little boys and girls would like: toy cars, crayons, colouring books, etc. A month ago I bought her a couple dozen Hot Wheels cars because they were selling for twenty cents each. Last week I bought myself a huge bag of hundreds of beads of all different shapes and colours and sizes. It cost five dollars. I didn't need them then, nor did I need them now. But I had them. That seemed important to me.

 As I plodded over the little bridge in my car at four thirty in the afternoon, I breathed in deeply the crisp, fresh air and the scent of sun-soaked leaves. I turned right at the stop sign because that's where Richard was buried, and I wanted to say hello to him first.

Avondale Cemetery opened in the late 1800s, very near to when my grandparents were born. It started, like all cemeteries did, when some townspeople decided to bury their loved ones relatively close to one another. Over the years it had become quite large, filled with lush green grass, and lots of trees, accommodating the ever-growing town with space to spare. It was very Stratford in that sense, at least the Stratford I knew growing up. This was where Dad was buried, and Mom, and with them the Killers, the Halls, and the Carrs. This was where Dorothy and Reta were buried. This was where Bill was buried, and right near the corner of the fourth intersection where I now parked my car was where Richard was buried.

Richard's gravestone was large and black, with cherubs on either side of it: exactly the kind of over-the-top thing Richard would have loved. Beside it, on the corner of the intersection, was a wooden bench dedicated to him. I chuckled at the sight of it now, remembering that Lucy had called me once to say the bench had been stolen, and to ask if I knew where it could be. I couldn't for the life of me understand why her first instinct was to call me.

Hi, Richard.

I pulled my thin black jacket tighter around my neck.

Things aren't shaping up well right now at the archives. Their exhibits aren't selling well, and thanks to the financial sinkhole Des left they cut my hours. I ran into Antoni in the parking lot and he said he was sorry they had to do that. He said he told them they had to give me something.

I paused on the thought that, after so long a career, I was inches from being let go entirely. A feeling of terrible weightlessness mantled my heart.

I don't know what I'd do without this job. Would people still hire me? There was a time I was confident I'd never be out of work. Now, I just don't know. Would you still hire me?

A gust of wind blew. I smiled, taking it as a yes.

Thanks, Richard.

On my way to my parents, left at the intersection nearest Richard's plot, I spied Sara Topham far down the road. She was wearing a long, thin, beige coat, standing with one hand on Bill's monolithic white gravestone. I didn't call to her or wave because I knew she came here to be alone. Avondale was a kind of sanctum to actors, a place they knew nobody would dare bother them to talk about shows.

Compared to Richard's, my parents' and Dorothy's gravestones were demure, pink thumbs sticking out of the ground. They didn't need much space though since they were all cremated. There were some weeds growing around the stones, so I plucked them and tossed them aside. I stared aimlessly for a while at the empty space in the bottom right corner of the small square plot, my future grave.

Mom, Dad, sorry I haven't been to see you in a while.

Sara walked past up the road, away from Bill's gravestone towards Richard's, watching the ground with her hands in her coat pockets.

When you died, Mom, I sent a letter to the family telling them I was very proud of them. I told them to give me a call at four o'clock some day because now I would have nothing to do. Nobody called today, so I took that as a sign I should come see you. And Dad, of course. Hi, Dad. I'm going through your stuff at the archives right now. All the newspaper articles about you back in the sixties. Letters to the editor of the Beacon Herald when you were let go from the Festival . . . The letter Guthrie sent you. Only I understand all of it.

I took off my glasses and rubbed my eyes because everything had become blurry.

I miss you.

Bill's gravestone, just up the road, was tall and slender. At its base and on a little ledge some ways up sat small stones of all kinds: black, grey, greyish white. I wasn't sure when the tradition started, but every now and again people would leave them there, a gesture of their remembrance.

I heard you, Bill. Did I ever tell you that? Maloo and I went to Vegas for my sixtieth birthday, and we went to see Kà, that Cirque show with the "Wheel of Death," and the lights dimmed and there you were. Your voice. The Voice, as Mom would say, introducing the show.

I chuckled at the memory, thinking it so bizarre to hear him while at the same time missing every second of it.

I don't have a stone, Bill. I had a couple of them, but the surgeon removed them with my gall bladder a while ago. They removed my appendix at the same time. It was called a Lefebvre procedure, named after the doctor there who had done one. I presented a Lefebvre Procedure Trophy to my surgeon because I was his first. Then, when I was lying in bed recovering, a doctor comes in and says, "I'd just like to introduce myself. I'm Dr. Lefebvre." It was funny. It was something you'd do. "*I'd just like to introduce myself. I'm Dr. Hutt. Yes. Dr. Bill Hutt. That's right. The Dr. William Ian DeWitt Hutt.*"

On the way back to my car, I spotted Sara sitting on Richard's bench. She was mumbling something to herself, words I recognized as Juliet's lines. We exchanged smiles, and then I got in my car and went home.

 I wasn't pretending to be
Cordelia's understudy when
I broke down. I didn't slip
through the house doors, or
creep to an aisle seat on the
right, one row down next to a
boy with buzzed hair. In his place sat my friend Maggie Woodley, an
immensely intelligent woman, slender with white hair. We'd met at
the archives where she once volunteered, our friendship solidified by
our love of Richard's famous *Shrew*. We were sitting house left, a few
rows up, and on the Festival Theatre stage, Edmund was lying on the
floor. Around him were Albany, Edgar, and the Second Officer. The
play was taking all the right time, and I found myself leaning forward
ever so slightly because my favourite part was coming. Edmund began
to speak and still it sounded as if he were talking to me and only me.

EDM.	Your speech hath moved me.
	My writ
	Is on the life of Lear and on Cordelia
	Quickly send — to the prison.

As the Second Officer left to save Cordelia and Lear, I glanced around the theatre. Where once I saw a sea of youth, I was now met with a reflection of my aging self and the thought that some of these people might have been swimming with me five decades ago. I grinned plaintively at the actors, knowing there was a stage manager watching over them and that at one point, it was a Polley.

ALB.	The gods defend her.

I then watched as Edmund was carried off stage, my elbows finding solace in the wooden armrests. Here it was, the big moment. From offstage, Colm's Lear came on with Sara Farb's Cordelia in his arms, her head resting against his chest, a little withered bird.

LEAR.	Howl, howl, howl, howl! O, you are men of stones!
	Had I your tongues and eyes I'd use them so
	That heaven's vault should crack. She's gone for ever.
	I know when one is dead and when one lives;
	She's dead as earth. Lend me a looking-glass;
	If that her breath will mist or stain the stone;
	Why then she lives.

The strained words from his mouth as he laid her down, the tender way he reached and recognized and really truly saw Cordelia alive there on the stage standing over her imposter . . . That look of longing . . .

When the house lights finally rose, I was sobbing, a quiet shaking I'd never known before. It was as if something in me had suddenly risen too, a penumbral feeling giving form to the last few years. And if there was ever a doubt in my mind, it was dispelled then and there with the slow wracking of my body.

"It was very beautiful," Maggie said in response to my unabashed weeping.

"No," I cried softly. "It's not that."

She turned to me. "What's wrong?"

"I think I've just realized how much I miss it."

"Stage managing?"

I nodded like a hurt child. "I would have loved to have sat and watched that night after night."

Maggie put her hand on mine, and waited with me until the theatre emptied and I had cried my longing away.

--

"Any idea why we started so late the other night?"

"I think there was a problem with someone in the audience."

"Yeah, somebody collapsed or something in the front row."

"Were they alright?"

"I think so."

It was forty-five minutes before the start of *King Lear* and three of its actors had come into the green room. They lined up for coffee and began chatting about some incident that had happened in a previous performance. The early evening sky was half blotted with clouds, and waning sunlight draped the patio in yellow and red. I was sitting near the middle of the room, alone, my eyes fixed at a point in space around the centre of my coffee cup, not really looking at all, but listening.

"Where were you that you didn't hear?" the first actress said, turning back to her cast mates.

In the corner of the room, two staff women on break talked quietly.

"I'm in my own world before the show," the second actress replied, her voice much higher than the first. Of the three, she was the only one empty-handed. "There could be an earthquake and I wouldn't notice it."

The third spoke then, a relatively older actor. "I'm the same. I only heard about it because I was talking to the ASM at the time. It was

SHAWN DESOUZA-COELHO

dealt with relatively quickly." He got a coffee as well, and having paid with the other two, they crossed my table without a word and sat near the back of the room.

None of them knew me, so it only made sense that none would stop to say anything. Even after all this time, I was still getting used to this new normal. I couldn't be in the rehearsal hall, so on days like today, when all I wanted was just to be around the actors, I'd sit and listen and hope. The hope was the smallest part of the equation, but, as was usual with hope, somehow the biggest too. I hoped that somebody would walk in whom I recognized and who recognized me.

It was long hours, Nora.

I drank some of my coffee.

"Is something going on with that lighting cue?" the third actor said to the first and second.

"I don't think so," the second replied.

"Yeah," the first confirmed. "It felt late."

It was stressful mornings, afternoons, and evenings.

"Well, we'll see how it goes tonight," the third stated. "If the same thing happens again, I'll ask somebody to have a look at it."

It was sleepless nights.

Suddenly the second actress lowered her voice, as if in reverence. "Have you seen *Mother Courage*?" The other two said they hadn't, but were planning on it. "See it! Seana is just . . . amazing. There's this one part near the end where she takes a blanket and—"

"Ah, don't tell me!" the first actress shouted. The two ladies in the back turned to look at the three of them. The actors laughed, and apologized. She went on, much quieter than before, "I'm going to see it. No spoilers."

It was a joy.

I took another drink of coffee, finishing what was left of my little cup.

It was a privilege.

Having thrown it out, I approached the three actors.

"Hi," I said, extending my hand to the third actor. "Nora Polley. Nice to meet you." The two actresses watched patiently, as if I was a bus just pulling into the stop. Any second now I'd get to whatever it was I came here for.

"Hi, Nora," the third replied, shaking my hand.

"I just wanted to say you were great in *Lear*. A really great production all around. I've seen it a couple of times and always end up bawling."

"Oh," he laughed graciously. "Thank you very much." He said it as if I'd just given him a penny and now he was wondering just what he'd do with it. "Yeah, it's pretty solid." He turned to the other two for input and they agreed.

"Good evening, ladies and gentlemen," a woman's voice came in over the speaker by the entrance, "for this evening's performance of *King Lear*, this is your half-hour call. One half-hour." I perked up at the sound of her, a budding branch on the cusp of spring. It was Corinne. "If you have not signed in, please do so now at the callboard."

"Well," I said. "I'll let you all to it."

Just as I turned to leave the third actor reached out with, "Sorry, do you work here? You look familiar."

"I work in the archives."

He contemplated this for a moment, and then agreed with himself. "Maybe that's it."

"Maybe. Anyway, good show."

"Thanks. You too." It was an impulsive response, awkward and amusing to everybody there. "I mean, have a nice evening."

"You too."

On my way out, and in the distant wake of the three actors, Stephen Ouimette burst around the corner. He was sweating a bit, probably having just arrived to the theatre.

"Well, hello!" I said.

"Nora, lovely to see you," he replied, rubbing my arm. "How are you?"

"Can't complain."

"I hear that." He spoke to me as he poured and paid for a coffee. "I was thinking about you the other day. I was thinking how great it is that

SHAWN DESOUZA-COELHO

you're over at the archives now. It just makes sense, in a way. Doesn't it? I think so. You get to pass on all of that knowledge of yours."

"That's true," I replied, suddenly more aware of the distance between us.

"That's valuable, I think. Anyway, it was great seeing you. We'll talk soon."

"Good show."

"Trying, just trying," he called back to me before turning the corner and rushing out of sight.

The two women at the back passed me by on their way out. I stood unmoved for a time, in the quiet of this room well used, and enjoyed the many ghosts that still haunted it. I decided then to stay for just a little while longer, and listen.

"Do you think this room is big enough?" Liza asked in her Scottish brogue, checking her watch. She was a short, driven woman with long red hair and glasses.

Roy Brown chuckled as he tidied and organized folder after folder of photographs on the break room table. "I'm sure it will be fine," he said in a low voice, his slightly trembling hands betraying his nonchalance.

"You know he's a perfectionist!" Liza justified. Christine laughed quietly as she walked through the reading room to her desk. "How did he sound over the phone?" Liza asked me. "Excited?"

"Well, I only spoke to his partner." I picked up one of the photographs. It was of Maggie Smith's Hippolyta, dressed in gossamer and entirely dreamlike. "Isn't it remarkable?"

"Absolutely *fantastic*."

"It's the eyes. Robin always had a way of capturing their eyes, of making them seem alive. He would put on music to get them in the mood, fan smoke through the air with a cafeteria tray, anything to get them to live in that moment."

We spent a few moments of our own, the two of us, staring at Maggie, drawn into whatever vast and vibrant world swirled behind her eyes.

It wasn't long ago that Liza Giffen had taken over as the archives director, shortly after Francesca left to take a professorship in the States. I instantly took a shine to her. One look at her and I knew she was in this for the long haul, that Stratford wasn't just a job. It was a home she was eager to make her own. Part of that process meant curating exhibits, and her first was no small order.

She had decided she wanted to showcase Stratford's golden years through the eyes of the one person whom she thought had the biggest impact on the Festival, Guthrie notwithstanding: Robin Phillips. I told her Robin was all-controlling and that if she was going to properly represent him, then she needed his input.

DING!

Liza and I both jumped at the sound of the bell. Roy laughed, and both Liza and I steeled ourselves. To say I wasn't nervous would be to lie. But it wasn't the regular tension that accompanied an invitation to Robin, the regular question of whether or not he'd show. It was something else altogether. I'd heard stories here and there for a few years now about Robin being a bit out of it. I never knew what to make of these stories, whether or not to believe them. He seemed fine in what little correspondences we kept. But when we opened the door to the archives, I was entirely unprepared for the man standing before me. All of us were.

Robin's partner, Joe, greeted us first, with Robin close behind. I tried then and there, in that fractional moment, to remember a time when Robin wasn't impeccably dressed and impeccably groomed. I couldn't. So then who was this completely unshaven man wearing a pair of old slacks with a sporran from his kilt, jowly in his old age, hair grey and frizzy, eyes . . . his eyes . . . They looked as if they didn't recognize me.

Does he know where he is?

"Thank you so much for coming," Liza said, shaking Joe's hand. "Mr. Phillips, it's my pleasure and honour to meet you." Robin shook her hand firmly, tempting us with the image of his former commanding self. Liza, however, knew he simply wasn't that man anymore. I could tell that whatever monument to Robin she had built up inside of her had suddenly blown over like cardboard.

"Thank you for inviting us," Joe said. There were deep-set bags under his eyes.

Liza pointed to the foyer before which Roy held the door open. "You can set your coats down in here and then Nora and Roy will assist you." And with that, Liza was gone.

After Joe helped Robin with his coat, the pair sat in the break room on either side of the table, Robin beside me, Joe beside Roy. I began taking them through each set of production photographs, starting with 1975. Robin said nothing. Instead, he stared down through the table and maybe even the Earth itself. Every so often I heard Roy shift his weight in his seat. I heard Liza in her office, behind her closed door, typing. So it went for three envelopes' worth of photographs. Still, Robin said nothing.

He doesn't know why he's here.

Halfway through the fifth envelope, Robin's gaze suddenly focused, but only enough to let him say, "Nice picture," before falling back to where it was, which was nowhere at all really. I set the photograph aside and for the next thirty-two productions, each containing ten to twelve photos, whenever Robin commented on any photograph in any way I set it aside as a possibility for inclusion in his exhibit. These were few and far between.

When Robin and Joe left, I spent I didn't know how long trying to make sense of the man I'd just seen. Liza came out of her office, and I didn't know why but we whispered.

"Why did you leave?" I asked her.

"I didn't want to make him uncomfortable. I've seen people in that situation before. Strangers frighten them."

I shook my head, almost frightened myself. It was like Robin hadn't come at all.

--

In June, we were ready to open the Robin Phillips exhibit. We tried to capture all of Robin's productions in their many forms. Some were shots of the whole cast, others were smaller groups, and others still were just one or two people looking as if they were in a different world altogether.

As we hung the photographs I found myself trying to remember exactly where I'd been at the time each photo was taken. Even if I wasn't stage managing the production, I was probably in the building somewhere. That was how I chose to remember my years with Robin, as if we were permanent structures, outgrowths from the bedrock of the place. We were load-bearing and immovable. And, when we'd finished hanging, it was delightful to see all of Robin's work united, laid out for others to admire, especially those who weren't old enough to have experienced him first-hand. His really were the Festival's golden years. We told Joe he and Robin could see it anytime they were ready. Eventually, that day came.

We had no illusions about Robin's second visit. We were both still nervous, of course, Roy and myself. Liza knew better than to participate. And when Robin arrived, clothes more wrinkled than before, how hard it was to reconcile this image of him with my memory. The man I knew wasn't there anymore. He was gone. Robin was completely gone. He and I sat at the one of the tables in the reading room as Roy took Joe through the exhibit, and all the while Robin asked "Where's Joe?" between brief interludes of vacantly acknowledging the pictures on the wall.

We spent the next twenty minutes in this routine until Joe thanked us, and, in turn, we thanked him and Robin for coming. As he left I felt relieved that he got to see the exhibit, no matter how little he actually got out of it.

As I returned to my desk, my mind flashed on a photograph of Robin I'd seen recently. It was of him and Marti Maraden sitting on the steps of a rehearsal hall stage. He was half-turned towards her and away from the camera, but still I could see his smile as he colluded with Marti. He was probably telling her some secret about herself that even she didn't know. That was the power of Robin's insight. He was brilliant.

One month after Robin's second visit to the archives, he died. The Festival flew its crown flag at half-mast that day.

--

I arrived early to Robin's funeral, shortly before four in the afternoon, in order to make sure everybody knew exactly what they were doing; to run a brief rehearsal, in other words. It was the only thing I knew how to do. Behind me the performers, Laura Burton among them, waited as I walked through the nave, up to the altar where the choir of men and women of all ages was still rehearsing in spite of the fact that I'd already booked the space for four.

"Excuse me," I said to the minister who was near the house left transept. "We were hoping we could rehearse a bit, just to make sure everybody is on the same page about things." I pointed to the back of the church, catching Laura's eye in the process. I wasn't sure what I saw there, but then I wasn't sure what I felt about any of this either.

The minister glanced at the choir and then back at me. "Actually, this won't be too long. You can come back in half an hour."

"*Actually*, we can do what we need to do in five minutes."

My tone was enough to force the minister to stop the choir right then. A tinge of pride washed over me at the thought that I still had that in me. We ran through the order of events as it was outlined in the program Ann and I had made. Once we had finished, with a little over thirty seconds to spare, the choir resumed their rehearsal and Laura sat at the piano and waited for the service to begin. I took a seat at the

SHAWN DESOUZA-COELHO

very back. I didn't really think about it. It just felt right. Maybe I was just used to the view.

Some time later, as people trickled in, Laura began playing music written by Bert Carriere, music Robin had used in his productions of *As You Like It* and *Twelfth Night*. I waved to those who passed by on their way to a seat further up. It was like a high school reunion, and I found myself flooded with fond memories of people I hadn't seen or heard from in a very long time. Heather Kitchen was one such person. She waved on her way to the front pew. Joe had asked her to read Robin's eulogy, as she had worked with him in the '70s and '80s, and out west at the Citadel Theatre, growing with him as a colleague and a friend for so many years. When Ann arrived, she took a seat beside me.

"Still strange," she said, as if asking my opinion. She waved to Joe Totaro, who had just entered. I did as well, and together we watched as he took his seat at the front beside Heather. He was reading a transcript of the video that had preceded Robin's Governor General's Award acceptance speech.

"I never knew Robin to be a particularly religious person," I said. "Did you?"

Ann shook her head. "*Spiritual* is the word I'd use."

I let the word simmer for a moment and then agreed. Still, it didn't dispel the fact that Robin's funeral was strangely Anglican. We gathered at St. James Church, which by now must have witnessed the mourning of thousands of lives little and large, and it was a straightforward church funeral service, an evensong complete with hymns Joe had selected. It even had a recitation from the priest straight from the Book of Common Prayer.

Laura continued to play, and more and more people flooded into the pews. Once everybody had entered, and the service had gotten underway, it struck me, as it had at Richard's memorial, just how many people Robin had touched with his single life. A sea of hundreds of heads shifted, tilted, and swayed, each one with a mind Robin somehow knew and understood.

When it came time, the minister asked Joe Totaro to come up and say a few words. Behind him the choir sat and waited patiently, listening. Laura remained where she was, where I always pictured her if her name was mentioned in passing or in earnest, at the piano.

"Thank you," Joe said simply, taking his place behind the lectern and adjusting the microphone. Joe, who chanced upon the Festival after a whim took him to Stratford months before he was supposed to arrive. I wondered then how many seats in this church were filled with stories like that, of serendipity and opportunity. That was certainly how I felt having worked with Robin: like I was stupidly lucky.

"I think the most important thing about being a director," Joe recited, echoing the words Robin himself had spoken in his video, "is that you're awake so that when something wonderful happens you don't miss it. Because in all honesty, you have to say, 'I don't know.' When something terrific happens, 'I know.' I think it's wonderful to not know what the result could possibly be.

"I've dealt most of my life with Shakespeare. I always say, you know, 'For God's sake, read carefully,' because somewhere there will be a clue to something."

Behind Joe the choir had begun to rustle and so had some of the audience at the sight of it.

Um . . .

"It's like a map. It's taking us right to the very essence of what we are. I admire, beyond imagining, the texts of Shakespeare. But the thing that grabs you is beneath it, is this huge and overwhelming love. He has such a compassion for human beings.

"I think we get awfully fey about being artists, because we're dealing with paint, or because we're dealing with classical language, or because we're dealing with orchestras, and you want to say, 'Well, my dad was an artist.' He was a gardener, very little education, but what he could do in a garden: just truly amazing, amazing."

One of the choristers was standing, and on his cell phone. How I knew to whom his call was directed, I couldn't say. I just did.

He's calling 911 . . .

"I think every walk of life has artists. Every walk of life is capable of beauty. If it's music that drives you, or if it's painting, or if it's

SHAWN DESOUZA-COELHO

literature, or if it's the theatre, or if it's . . . It doesn't matter. But the world of the imagination is . . . is hugely important."

The chorister kept glancing down from his cell phone to the odd gap beside him in the line of bodies where it seemed as if somebody was missing.

"Whatever I do I must not diminish the imagination, but I must allow it to expand. I try to come up with a design, a space in which anything could happen, and I throw in the components that I think the text has suggested and therefore might be usable at some point. The text is important because it's the roadmap, because it leads us there, but it's leading us to a truth. I can't imagine that it isn't the same for painters. The painting is leading us to a truth."

Is nobody going to say something?

I looked at Ann, but by her attentiveness to the remainder of Joe's speech I gauged that she didn't seem to think the disturbance warranted intervention either. It was gnawing at me, though, so when Joe finished and was about to take his seat I stood up.

"Ladies and gentlemen," I intoned, the sea of heads swivelling to see where the voice had come from. "We appear to have a crisis in the choir. Let's take a small pause while we deal with this and then we'll get back to you."

And so we did. Shortly after, an ambulance arrived. Apparently one of the choristers, an elderly woman, had fainted. As she was lifted onto a gurney, I made my way up to Joe and Heather.

"I didn't want to interrupt you," I told Joe, standing in the pew behind them. "But I didn't want Heather to start her eulogy either."

"I was just glad you said something."

"Somebody had to say *something*." I turned to Heather. "We're just going to let this clear and then we can start again."

She looked up at me, smiled, and said, "As soon as I heard your voice, I thought, 'We're okay.'"

Joe laughed in agreement, and I stayed with them as the minister led the congregation in hymns.

What the hell?

Everybody was startled after a few verses because suddenly the organ had gone haywire, belting out notes the organist wasn't even playing. Then, as if on a switch, everything went back to normal. Both the minister and organist were dumbfounded. After a few test keys, they continued on, their hymns riding atop ripples of quiet amusement from the crowd. Then the lights began to flicker and I had to laugh. Here and there a head turned to me for a response, but before I could say or do anything the lights righted themselves of their own accord. Heather and I shared the same thought.

Robin's playing his games again.

As the paramedics carted the elderly woman out I thought of my father, and the storm that swept through the cottage the day after he died. He was just making his presence felt too.

Once the final verse of the final hymn had been sung, the minister took the floor once more. "Well," he said stoically. "I think that it's time for Heather to speak."

The moment before Heather stood up, I put my hand on her shoulder as if to signal her to wait a moment. I looked around to make sure everybody was settled. I then turned back to Heather, who was still waiting for her cue, and gave her a little nod. As she took her place at the altar, I took mine at the back of the room.

"There were often two props," Heather began after introducing Robin as a member of the Order of Canada, a Governor General's Award winner, and the recipient of a whole host of other accolades he had earned throughout his long career, "that Robin wanted in the rehearsal hall. One was a drum . . . "

THUMP! THUMP! THUMP!

To everybody's delight, Laura hammered on a drum, and those who were part of his rehearsals remembered, maybe with a crippling twinge of anxiety, his infernal drumming to keep pace and mark beats.

"The other," Heather continued, "was a bell. He called it the Perfection Bell. If a moment was performed perfectly, Robin would ring it. It was a rare thing to have it rung for you . . . "

By the time Heather finished her eulogy, I was in tears. Then those tears turned to laughter as the ceremony concluded with just the right

SHAWN DESOUZA-COELHO

amount of upbeat country western twang in Lynn Anderson's "Rose Garden." It was Robin again, telling us he absolutely didn't want us to take this whole thing too seriously.

I arrived at home some time later and set my wallet and coat down in the foyer. I wasn't sure why it took me so long, but as I stepped through the threshold of my living room, I found my gaze fixed on my side table and the small wooden box resting on it, the one Robin had given me for my retirement. It seemed strangely new to me then. I moved to it slowly, and lifted its dome with a nervous hand. Inside of it was a pewter bell. He had never used a bell in my rehearsals with him. That was why I didn't understand. And it was only now, in the wake of Heather's eulogy and forty years as a stage manager, that it suddenly made sense. Robin gave it to me. He gave me the Perfection Bell. I found the card that had accompanied his gift and read it as if for the first time with enlightened, grateful eyes.

Dearest Nora. So many thank yous for so many things. A perfect career! Fondest love, always. Robin.

Afterword

There are undoubtedly a few questions left in the reader's mind, chief among them the book's authorship, especially in light of the first-person perspective adopted throughout. While it is certainly Nora Polley's life documented in these pages, and she vetted every word contained herein, her life has been written through the lens of my, Shawn DeSouza-Coelho's, authorial voice. I chose to ground the narrative in the first person because I wanted to remove as much distance as possible between the reader and Nora so that I might strengthen the reader's immersion in Nora's world. So, while the book is written in the first person, that perspective bears no relationship to the question of credit. Indeed, when it came down to the book's authorship, Nora and I agreed that because the bulk of the labour fell to me — a labour spread across two and a half years of interviews, research, and drafting — that I should receive sole credit for the book.

All of the play text quoted in this book was taken, where available, from the archived prompt books of those specific productions. This means that what the reader has read is not the play as it was published, but rather as it was performed, complete with the changes each director made to the script.

A couple of events in this book have been deliberately altered from their true accounts in order to protect people's privacy: either the event was shifted in Nora's chronology, or names were obscured or left out.

On a more personal note, Nora's life as it has been depicted here is the amalgamation of her many stories, but also the stories of over fifty past and current members of the Stratford Festival in addition to those of her family and friends. It was an honour interviewing them all, and it is my sincerest hope that, as Nora's preface says, they each take the spirit in which this book has been offered as complimentary.

Lastly, thank you Nora for all you've told me, and for the lessons your life has taught me. It is a privilege to be your friend.

SHAWN DESOUZA-COELHO

Acknowledgements

Without the help of these individuals and institutions, listed as they are in no specific order, I would not have been able to write this book in as much detail as I have. If I have forgotten somebody it is entirely unintentional. Do know I thank you sincerely for your contributions.

Nora Polley, Sue Coburn, David Polley, Margaret Shaw, Jennifer Shaw, Antoni Cimolino, Stephen Gartner, John Stead, David Collins, James Blendick, Chick Reid, Sara Topham, Jeannette Lambermont-Morey, Steven Sutcliffe, Seana McKenna, Dean Gabourie, Brian Tree, John Wood, Andrew North, Skye Brandon, Barry MacGregor, Ann Skinner, Kim Lott, Julie Miles, Angela Marshall, Stephen Russell, Laura Burton, Liza Giffen, Janine Pearson, Pat Quigley, Colleen Blake, Christopher Blake, Roy Brown, Juan Chioran, Stephanie Vaillant, Christine Schindler, Peter Roberts, Joseph Totaro, Stephen Ouimette, Martha Henry, Michael Benoit, Simon Marsden, Tom McCamus, Lucy

Peacock, Melissa Veal, Tom Rooney, Sheila McCarthy, Rory Feore, Heather Kitchen, Ann Stuart, Maggie Palmer, Maggie Woodley, Dr. Francesca Marini, Barbara Budd, Anita Gaffney, David Campbell, Andy Mark, Madelyn Carty, Krista Moore, Peter Moore, Dr. Mathias Schulze, Jeannie Lee, Reid Vanier, The Debling Family, Dr. Jennifer Roberts-Smith, Dr. Paul Stoesser, the 2016 Tyrone Guthrie Awards Committee, Canadian Actors' Equity Association, Military Services Canada, Stratford Festival Archives, Stratford Perth Community Foundation, LW Conolly Theatre Archives, National Arts Centre Archives, City of Toronto Archives, University of Toronto Archives and Records Management Services, Dalhousie University Archives, Theatre Ontario, Jack David, David Caron, Jennifer Hale, and the rest of the stunning cast and crew at ECW Press.

Bibliography

Anouilh, Jean. *Dear Antoine: Or, the Love that Failed.*

Avrich, Barry, dir. *The Madness of King Richard.* 2003; Melbar Entertainment Group, TV Movie.

Burns, Martha and Susan Coyne, dir. *Robin and Mark and Richard III.* 2016; Independent, TV Movie.

Calvit, Christina. *Pride and Prejudice.* Adapted from the novel by Jane Austen.

Davies, Hubert, dir. *Move Your Mind.* 2010; National Film Board, online release. https://www.nfb.ca/film/move_your_mind/

De Filippo, Eduardo. *Filumena Marturano.*

Garebian, Keith. *William Hutt: Masks and Faces.* Oakville, ON: Mosaic Press, 1995.

Good, Maurice. *Every Inch a Lear.* Victoria, B.C.: Sono Nis Press, 1982.

Harwood, Ronald. *The Dresser.*

Havel, Václav. *The Memorandum.*

Hewett, Robert. *The Blonde, The Brunette, and the Vengeful Redhead.*

Ibsen, Henrik. *Hedda Gabler.*

Johnston, Sheila M. F. *Let's Go to the Grand! 100 Years of Entertainment at London's Grand Theatre.* Toronto: Dundurn, 2001.

Jonson, Ben. *The Alchemist.*

Knelman, Martin. *A Stratford Tempest.* Toronto: McClelland and Stewart, 1982.

Malone, Toby. "'Distract Parcels in Combined Sums': The Stratford Festival Archives' Prompt-Book Collections." *Canadian Theatre Review* 156 (Fall 2013): 66-71.

Molnár, Ferenc. *The Guardsman.*

Monette, Richard and David Prosser. *This Rough Magic: The Making of an Artistic Director.* Stratford, ON: Stratford Festival of Canada, 2007.

Morgan, Winston. *Stage Managing the Arts in Canada.* Toronto: S.M.Arts, 2000.

Murrell, John. *Waiting for the Parade.*

Patterson, Tom and Allan Gould. *First Stage: The Making of the Stratford Festival.* Willowdale, ON: Firefly Books, 1999.

Pettigrew, John and Jamie Portman. *Stratford: The First Thirty Years.* Toronto: Macmillan of Canada, 1985.

Plummer, Christopher. *In Spite of Myself: A Memoir.* Toronto: Alfred A. Knopf Canada, 2008.

Polley, Nora. *A Birthday Book with Theatre Stories.* Self-published, 2010.

Reid, Barbara and Thelma Morrison. *A Star Danced: The Story of How Stratford Started the Stratford Festival.* Toronto: Self-published, 1994.

Rintels, David W. *Clarence Darrow.*

Rodgers, Richard and Lorenz Hart. *The Boys from Syracuse.*

Shakespeare, William. *All's Well That Ends Well.*

Shakespeare, William. *Antony and Cleopatra.*

Shakespeare, William. *As You Like It.*

Shakespeare, William. *Cymbeline.*

Shakespeare, William. *Hamlet.*

Shakespeare, William. *Henry VIII.*

Shakespeare, William. *King Lear.*

Shakespeare, William. *Macbeth.*

Shakespeare, William. *Measure for Measure.*

Shakespeare, William. *Merchant of Venice, The.*

Shakespeare, William. *Much Ado About Nothing.*

Shakespeare, William. *Othello.*

Shakespeare, William. *Richard II.*

Shakespeare, William. *Richard III.*

Shakespeare, William. *Romeo and Juliet.*

Shakespeare, William. *Taming of the Shrew, The.*

Shakespeare, William. *Tempest, The.*

Shakespeare, William. *Troilus and Cressida.*

Shakespeare, William. *Twelfth Night.*

Shakespeare, William. *Winter's Tale, The.*

Sheridan, Richard Brinsley. *The School for Scandal.*

Smith, John N., dir. *Offstage, Onstage: Inside the Stratford Festival.* 2002; National Film Board, VHS.

Stern, Lawrence. *Stage Management.* New York: Routledge, 2016.

Wilde, Oscar. *An Ideal Husband.*

Wilde, Oscar. *The Importance of Being Earnest.*

index

Names of characters appear in uninverted form. Locators preceeded by "PS" indicate photographs in the Photo Section found at the middle of the book.

SHAWN DESOUZA-COELHO

SHAWN DESOUZA-COELHO

Shawn DeSouza-Coelho is a writer based in Toronto, telling stories in whatever form they demand. He's also a theater theorist/practitioner, professional magician, scholar, and sometimes poet. Shawn spent two seasons in the Stratford Festival acting company.